NEW YORK, NEW YORK!

As part of our celebrations marking the centenary year of Leonard Bernstein's birth, John Wilson conducts the composer's two most popular Broadway musicals – *West Side Story* and *On the Town* – which both see the Big Apple itself play a lead role.

PROMS 38 & 39 • 11 AUGUST
PROM 57 • 25 AUGUST

See also pages 30–41

LUNCHTIME DAZZLE

The astonishing American JACK Quartet makes its Proms debut with a bold programme in the 'Proms at … Cadogan Hall' chamber music series, pairing two scintillating classics by Iannis Xenakis with two world premieres.

PROMS AT … CADOGAN HALL 5 • 13 AUGUST

See also pages 96–101

BALLET DOUBLE

One hundred this year, the Orchestre de la Suisse Romande makes its Proms debut with a concert featuring two colourful Ballets Russes works: Debussy's *Jeux*, in which a game of tennis takes an erotic turn, and Stravinsky's tale of the lovelorn Russian puppet Petrushka.

PROM 45 • 16 AUGUST

See also pages 8–15 and 18–21

DiDONATO SINGS BERLIOZ

Lustrous American mezzo-soprano Joyce DiDonato takes the dramatic solo role in Berlioz's *La mort de Cléopâtre* ('The Death of Cleopatra'), in an all-Berlioz programme conducted by today's foremost interpreter of the composer, Sir John Eliot Gardiner.

PROM 71 • 5 SEPTEMBER

See also pages 8–15

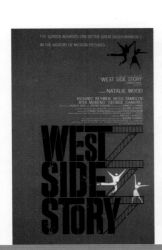

WEST SIDE STORY   IANNIS XENAKIS   VASLAV NIJINSKY AS PETRUSHKA   JOYCE DiDONATO

Contents

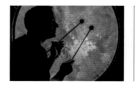

BBC MUSIC

RESTORATION DRAMA

70

As the Victorian Theatre at Alexandra Palace hosts Gilbert and Sullivan's *Trial by Jury*, KATE ROMANO traces the venue's troubled history

CONTEMPORARY COLLABORATIONS

74

Conductor JULES BUCKLEY talks about the variety of musicians he has collaborated with at the Proms since 2010, from Quincy Jones to Jacob Collier

MAGICAL MOMENTS

78

From the Ten Pieces Prom to Sunday matinees to family workshops, there's something at the Proms for all the family, as ANDREW McCALDON explains

ALL TYPES OF BEETHOVEN

88

TOM SERVICE looks at Beethoven symphony interpretations, savouring the range on offer this year

BRANDENBURGS OLD AND NEW

92

PAUL GRIFFITHS reports on a project to give Bach's Brandenburg Concertos new life by pairing them with fresh responses from six living composers

NEW MUSIC

96

DAVID KETTLE previews innovative and varied new works by eight female composers who have each been given their first-ever BBC commission

LOVE, FAITH AND HONOUR

102

RICHARD WIGMORE introduces Handel's *Theodora*, whose noble Christian heroine, the lover of a Roman convert, dies for her beliefs

THE PROMS ON RADIO, ON TV, ONLINE

104

Follow the Proms on TV, radio, online and on social media

CONCERT LISTINGS

121

Full listings and details of pre-Prom events

BOOKING AND VENUES

161

INDEXES

180

The BBC Proms 2018 Festival Guide is also available as an audio book, in Braille and as a text-only large-print version. See page 168 for further information.

Welcome to the 2018 BBC Proms

As you browse through this festival guide, I hope you will be struck by the astonishing range of this great festival – embracing not just the best classical music of the past, but also the work of some of today's most exciting composers. I cannot think of any other festival in the world that celebrates classical music in such depth: this year we have more than 90 concerts over 57 days, ranging from solo recitals to Mahler's 'Symphony of a Thousand' (with the help of five choirs), and featuring an unrivalled line-up of soloists, conductors and orchestras from the UK and around the world.

You will also find a number of threads running through the season with connections to the remarkable year of 1918. We start with the First Night of the Proms which, alongside that Proms favourite, Gustav Holst's *The Planets* (first performed in September 1918, towards the end of the war) also features a contemporary response to that conflict in a new piece by one of today's most eclectic young composers, Anna Meredith. A joint BBC commission with 14–18 NOW and the Edinburgh International Festival, *Five Telegrams* features spectacular visual projections created by 59 Productions, and draws on the talents of the Proms Youth Ensemble and the National Youth Choir of Great Britain.

The First World War influenced a whole generation of composers in the first half of the 20th century and, in particular, we explore the way British composers responded to its aftermath. Marking the centenary of the death of Hubert Parry, we pay tribute to his extraordinary qualities as a teacher of distinguished pupils such as Vaughan Williams, Holst, Ireland and Frank Bridge – all of whom were profoundly influenced by the war. In two special projects taking place beyond the Royal Albert Hall we also look at other countries involved in the Great War. Marking the 50th anniversary of the London Sinfonietta, we return to the Roundhouse in Camden for a matinee concert in which Messiaen's *Et exspecto resurrectionem mortuorum* – his great commemoration of the fallen from both world wars – is placed alongside a suite of new pieces from composers representing a cross-section of the countries caught up in the conflict. And, for the first time, the Proms visits the city of Lincoln, where Stravinsky's *The Soldier's Tale* is performed – aptly – in the converted Drill Hall.

As the Great War was ending, one of the 20th century's greatest musicians was born. Leonard Bernstein would have been 100 this year and it is hard to overestimate his influence as conductor, composer, pianist and educator. We reflect all these aspects this summer, with highlights including concert performances of two of his Broadway musicals, *On the Town* and *West Side Story* (both conducted by John Wilson). We also recreate the first of the two concerts Bernstein conducted at the Proms (appropriately led by Thomas Dausgaard, a former pupil), celebrate some of the other American composers Bernstein championed, and showcase two key 20th-century works that he helped to bring into the world: Berio's *Sinfonia* (dedicated to Bernstein) and Messiaen's *Turangalîla Symphony*, which he premiered in Boston in 1949.

Perhaps Bernstein's most lasting contribution to musical life was his commitment to broadening the appeal of classical music,

Claude Debussy (1862–1918) – the 'godfather' of modern music – at the beach in north-west France, 1911

particularly through the famous TV broadcasts for both adult and younger audiences that he presented with unique flair. His 100th birthday would have been on 25 August and, as part of a bank holiday-weekend Bernstein celebration, we present our own exploration for audiences of all ages of what makes up the sound of an orchestra. In a similar vein, and following on from the success of last year's exploration of Beethoven's 'Eroica' Symphony, the Aurora Orchestra presents a special Late Night Prom which dissects Shostakovich's Symphony No. 9, culminating in a complete performance from memory.

Elsewhere, the Proms features a number of events aimed at reaching ever-wider audiences, including two Ten Pieces Proms, based around the latest selection of music that has been explored by schools up and down the country, and a Relaxed Prom given by the Bournemouth Symphony Orchestra, which spotlights its groundbreaking, disabled-led ensemble, BSO Resound.

In 1918 women over the age of 30 were given the right to vote – a significant step forwards for women's suffrage. To celebrate this anniversary, each of our Proms at … Cadogan Hall chamber-music concerts features a world premiere from a woman composer who has never previously been commissioned by the BBC. This series sits alongside a huge range of contemporary works that feature at the Proms this year, continuing the tradition of 'novelties' beloved of Proms founder-conductor Henry Wood. Most intriguing of all is the creation of six new 'Brandenburg Concertos' to sit alongside Bach's originals – with all 12 works being played over two concerts on the same day. And, 100 years after his death, we also celebrate the composer some consider the 'godfather' of modern music, Claude Debussy, as well as another brilliant French composer, Lili Boulanger, who died tragically young in 1918. Together, they provide the perfect starting point for a broader exploration of 20th-century French music throughout the festival.

These are just some of the interlinking threads across the summer, but I hope you will find many other individual highlights of your own – whether it is Gilbert and Sullivan's *Trial by Jury* at Alexandra Palace, as the restoration of its Victorian Theatre nears its completion; a range of imaginative

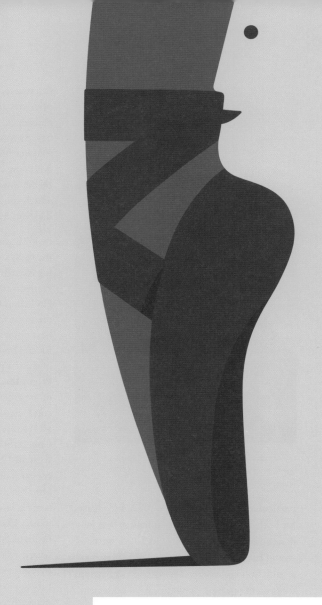

Proud to make ballet and opera part of more people's lives with BP Big Screens.

We believe arts and culture should be accessible to all. That's why, since 2000, we've helped bring live outdoor screenings from the Royal Opera House to over half a million people across the UK and beyond. bp.com/arts

Join us at a variety of outdoor venues across the UK to experience Swan Lake on 12th June, La bohème on 26th June and Don Giovanni on 12th July.

programmes from our own BBC orchestras; the chance to hear two of the world's youngest orchestras (MusicAeterna and the Estonian Festival Orchestra) alongside the 100-year-old Rotterdam Philharmonic Orchestra and Orchestre de la Suisse Romande; or the first appearance in the UK of the Berlin Philharmonic under its new Chief Conductor Designate, Kirill Petrenko. And, just as in Henry Wood's day, when classical repertoire was mixed with popular fare, you can enjoy a celebration of British folk music with the BBC Concert Orchestra, a return to the Proms for the National Youth Jazz Orchestra, two projects with Proms favourite Jules Buckley (including one devoted to the extraordinarily talented Jacob Collier) and a celebration of Argentine tango, along with its thriving variant as it has taken hold in Finland.

Encouraging and supporting new talent remains a key part of what we do and we are proud to celebrate it each year at the Proms, whether it is an exciting young international artist appearing for the first time, or a chance to showcase one of the outstanding BBC Radio 3 New Generation Artists. This year we mark the 40th anniversary of BBC Young Musician, which has done so much to bring outstanding young performers to the attention of a wider public. The roll call of winners and finalists is hugely impressive, and a number of them will take part in our celebratory concert over the opening weekend.

Last year, many of our concerts played to full houses and the first day of booking always sees the box office dealing with the enormous demand. But it's important to remember that no concert is ever sold out in advance. Promming, at £6.00 per ticket, remains one of the great bargains of concert-going, and season ticket-holders can hear all 75 concerts at the Royal Albert Hall for less than £3.40 per concert. For those who can't attend in person there is the opportunity to hear every concert live on BBC Radio 3, with 24 Proms broadcast

Kirill Petrenko, who becomes Chief Conductor of the Berlin Philharmonic next year, makes his Proms debut

on BBC TV – all available for catch up for 30 days on BBC iPlayer too.

So, whether you join us in person, by radio, TV or online, I hope you will find much to enjoy in this summer of outstanding music-making. •

David Pickard Director, BBC Proms

A warm welcome to the BBC Proms 2018.

This year's programme is as gripping and wide-ranging as ever, spanning a new commission by Anna Meredith that will light up the Royal Albert Hall on the First Night; a whole range of French music inspired by the centenary year of Debussy's death; centenary honours, too, for Hubert Parry (died 1918) and Leonard Bernstein (born 1918); lunchtime Xenakis; a ballet double bill of Debussy and Stravinsky; and a concert celebrating the folk music of Britain, Ireland, Scotland and Wales. There

really is something for everyone. At BBC Radio 3, where you can hear every Prom live and on demand in superb sound, the Proms *is* summer to us and, if you like what you hear in this year's programme, rest assured the same wide range and intelligent ambition is available to you on air the whole year round.

Leonard Bernstein played a wonderful role in inspiring children to find out about music through his Young People's Concerts, and we are proud of our focus on youth this year – including a celebration of BBC Young Musician in a special concert to mark the competition's 40th anniversary and, of course, Ten Pieces, which continues to introduce young people to the lasting experience of classical music, as well as an appearance by the BBC Proms Youth Ensemble on the First Night. New commissions abound and we continue to welcome artists new to the Proms. Let the Proms 2018 be the sound of your summer – whether you listen in person, on BBC Radio or TV, or online. •

Alan Davey Controller, BBC Radio 3

Impressions in Colour

As this year's Proms marks the centenary of Debussy's death with a mini festival of French music, CAROLINE POTTER considers the range of influences – from nature to art and literature – that inspired Debussy and his Parisian contemporaries to evoke myriad moods in shifting hues of luminous sound

Does the concept of a national musical style have any meaning? The classical music of every European nation has always been marked by influences and trends beyond its frontiers, as throughout history composers have travelled and exchanged ideas with their international peers. At the same time, educational institutions and concert-giving organisations based in Paris predominantly served composers of the same background who spoke the same language. These composers also shared a literary, artistic, social and political environment. But music is an art form that respects no geopolitical borders and, beyond whatever common ground that might be shared by French composers, they exist in an international marketplace, with Paris as one of its key musical centres.

It was only when Hector Berlioz moved to Paris as a student in 1821 that he heard an orchestra for the very first time; there were no opportunities at all to hear orchestras in La Côte Saint-André, the small town outside Lyon where he grew up. However, his childhood years marked him in other ways: hearing a religious procession – with a marching band approaching and then receding into the distance – was something he never forgot, and the evocation of a passing procession, increasing and decreasing in volume to suggest changing proximity to the listener, is present in many of his orchestral works, including the *Symphonie fantastique* (1830). When he moved to Paris, he enrolled as a medical student but spent much of his time enjoying one of the leading musical centres of Europe. The conductor François-Antoine Habeneck's performances of Beethoven with the orchestra of the Société des Concerts du Conservatoire had a huge impact on him, as did performances of Shakespeare by an English troupe. There was opera too, where much orchestral innovation took place, and in which arena success was at the time considered essential for a French composer.

In the first half of the 19th century, chamber music was comparatively less prominent in Paris, although a small number of composers bucked this trend. Louise Farrenc (1804–75) was one significant exception, a pianist and professor at the Paris Conservatoire whose extensive body of chamber music is only now becoming better known. Later, Camille Saint-Saëns was active in every musical genre, including chamber music, and in February 1871 he was one of the founders of the Société Nationale de Musique. The Society's motto, 'Ars gallica', reveals its intention to promote French music, and

CLAUDE DEBUSSY
PRÉLUDE À L'APRÈS-MIDI D'UN FAUNE (1891–4)

For Pierre Boulez, this 10-minute-long work marked the dawn of modern music, and its sound-world is indeed revolutionary. Rather than using the full, Romantic orchestra, Debussy focuses on a narrow range of instruments that respond to his imaginative prolongation of Stéphane Mallarmé's poem. A solo flute represents a faun dreamily pursuing nymphs. The solo flute's theme, tonally ambiguous and unaccompanied at the start of the piece, is harmonised differently each time it appears, perhaps suggesting the different ancient landscapes of the faun's wanderings. Were these nymphs real, or a dream? Mallarmé leaves this question open, and the concluding fade-out of the piece suggests that Debussy does too.

Design by Léon Bakst for the original production of *Prélude à l'après-midi d'un faune* (music by Claude Debussy, choreography by Vaslav Nijinsky), premiered by the Ballets Russes at the Théâtre du Châtelet, Paris, on 29 May 1912

9

indeed the year of France's abject defeat in the Franco-Prussian War was also the starting point of the extraordinary French artistic flowering of the Third Republic. However, composers associated with this avowedly patriotic organisation did not exclude foreign influence: far from it. Saint-Saëns's symphonic poems draw on those of his Hungarian friend Franz Liszt, and the group of composers who gathered at the Schola Cantorum around the Paris-based Belgian César Franck added late-19th-century twists to Austro-German symphonic structures. Works such as Franck's Symphony in D minor focus on the development of a single theme that appears in different guises across its three movements. (Franck also followed Beethoven's lead by having the symphony end in the triumphant parallel major key.) The Schola Cantorum group also brought chamber music to new heights in France.

But the greatest orchestral innovators of them all were Debussy and Ravel, who are often mentioned in the same breath, even if their approaches to the orchestra were very different. Debussy's early *La damoiselle élue* (1887–8) and *Prélude à l'après-midi d'un faune* (1891–4) demonstrate his quietly revolutionary orchestral writing: rather than composing for the full, late-Romantic orchestra, Debussy uses only those instruments whose timbres create the atmosphere he wants. The string-and-harp-dominated orchestra and subdivided female chorus of *La damoiselle* immediately evoke the world of Dante Gabriel Rossetti's poem, and similarly the solo wind lines of *Prélude à l'après-midi* represent Mallarmé's dreamily wandering faun. In both works, Debussy omits the timpani and uses the brass sparingly, and he almost never brings the orchestra together in loud climactic passages; these sounds and effects simply didn't represent what he wanted to say.

These two early works also exemplify Debussy's attraction to literary sources, far more prevalent in his work than links to the visual arts. His other primary source of inspiration was the natural world; he captures something that is timeless in a musical snapshot that could continue well beyond the bounds of the concert hall. The first movement of his *Nocturnes* (1897–9), 'Nuages', depicts clouds gently drifting, and the introduction of a flute and harp in the central section of this movement comes as a moment of relief, like a brief glimmer of sun that is soon hidden again. Similarly, the orchestral seascape *La mer* (1903–5) portrays the sea in different moods and at different times of day, using intricate rhythmic interplay and layered orchestral colours to

evoke the play of light on the water. Rather than painting a picture, Debussy captures the feel of the sea: there is no suggestion that this is an example of the Romantic pathetic fallacy whereby the sea somehow stands for personal feelings.

Ravel's approach to the orchestra was that of the brilliant showman. His orchestral invention owes something to Nikolay Rimsky-Korsakov, with whom he shares a taste for fairy-tale evocation. There are two works titled *Shéhérazade* in his catalogue: an early overture (1898) and the more frequently heard set of three orchestral

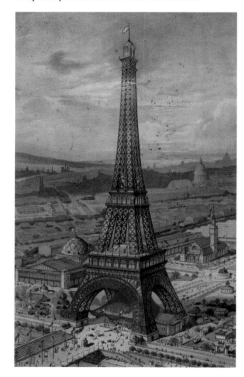

The Eiffel Tower, built to mark the entrance of the 1889 Paris Exposition Universelle, at which Debussy heard the intoxicating sounds of Javanese gamelan music

Three's company: a sketch based on one of Bakst's stage designs for the 1913 Ballets Russes production of *Jeux* (music by Debussy): the scenario concerns a boy and two girls who go in search of a tennis ball but discover more amorous 'games'

songs (1903), and Ravel could be seen as something of a musical Scheherazade, captivating the listener with stories in sound. Many of his orchestral pieces started life as piano works that he later reclothed in orchestral colouring: *Ma mère l'Oye* ('Mother Goose'), was first composed for piano duet. Much of Ravel's music has an identifiable model, such as French keyboard suites of the 18th century, which informed his *Le tombeau de Couperin*. His Piano Concerto for the Left Hand is a telling example of Ravel being motivated by a restriction: writing to a commission from the one-armed pianist Paul Wittgenstein, he created a work whose piano part has all the grandeur and power of a concerto for two-handed pianists.

Incidentally, Debussy and Ravel's relationship was cordial at first, although it soured around

1904, almost certainly for personal rather than aesthetic reasons. Debussy separated from his first wife in that year; Ravel and other friends supported Lilly Debussy financially for a time after the split, which Debussy viewed as a betrayal. One thing Debussy and Ravel have in common is that they were both freethinkers. Some of their contemporaries associated with the Schola Cantorum had positions as organists and wrote liturgical music, although in the early 20th century there was a new French wave of religious music written for the concert hall, spearheaded by Lili Boulanger and Florent Schmitt. Boulanger was a devout Catholic and composed three Psalm settings in her short life, all of which show her striking ear for orchestral colour and original flair for choral writing (for instance, she often exploits

the crossover in range between the lowest female and highest male voices).

Musical innovation in France often happened when composers collaborated with artists working in another genre. In particular, ballet was a locus of experiment in the early 20th century. Dance had been a favourite entertainment of Parisian audiences in the 19th century – it was expected that operas would include a ballet sequence in the second act – and, beyond the stage of the Paris Opéra, music halls such as the Folies Bergère staged lighter dance performances, often by collaborators who also worked in highbrow genres.

The Ballets Russes created a buzz when they arrived in Paris in 1909, combining the lightweight *divertissement* ballets that were already popular with the Paris public with more exotic story ballets to new music. Léon Bakst's costumes played a large part

MAURICE RAVEL
DAPHNIS AND CHLOE (1909–12)

Boy meets girl; boy dances with girl; girl is abducted by pirates; the legend of Pan and Syrinx is mimed; the lovers are joyfully reunited. Ravel vividly underlines the gestures of this flimsily plotted ballet, which is now a rarity on the stage. *Daphnis and Chloe* had a long and sometimes difficult gestation, not least because the choreographer Mikhail Fokine's vision of an ancient Greek setting did not accord with Ravel's: the Greece of the composer's dreams was one mediated by 18th-century French painters such as Fragonard and Watteau. The finished ballet is Ravel's longest work, a masterpiece of orchestration that is one of the lushest of all Ballets Russes scores.

MAURICE RAVEL
L'ENFANT ET LES SORTILÈGES
(1920–25)

A naughty child in a fit of temper breaks his toys, throws his schoolwork away, rips the wallpaper and attacks furniture and animals in his home and garden – and they take revenge on him. Ravel delights in creating short pastiche numbers for Colette's characters, moving through a dizzying array of styles from pseudo-medieval to popular song of his time. Yet it always sounds like Ravel, not least in its brilliantly imagined orchestration including, in the percussion department, a Swanee whistle and cheesegrater. The child comes to see the error of his ways and, at the end, seeks comfort from his mother – the opera's last word is 'Maman'.

Nikolai Tsiskaridze (*left*) and Ilze Liepa, in a scene from *Prélude à l'après-midi d'un faune*, whose alluring opening flute solo has been credited with signalling the dawn of a new musical era

in the success of the new Russian ballets, and with *The Firebird* (premiered in 1910) the 28-year-old Igor Stravinsky became the new fashionable composer of Paris. The following three years witnessed the premieres in Paris of Stravinsky's *Petrushka* and *The Rite of Spring*, Debussy's *Jeux*, Ravel's sumptuous *Daphnis and Chloe* and – to its composer's chagrin – a choreographed version of *Prélude à l'après-midi d'un faune*. These works show not only the huge impact of the Ballets Russes on the contemporary Parisian musical scene, but also that the company swiftly moved away from its original focus on Russian fairy tale towards a much more eclectic and international house style. The director of the company, Serge Diaghilev, was perennially short of money but never skimped on his productions: Stravinsky's and Ravel's ballets are written for huge orchestras, though Diaghilev encouraged Ravel, against his better judgement, to substitute instruments for the

wordless chorus in *Daphnis and Chloe* so that the ballet could be performed in an alternative version in smaller theatres.

In the 1920s the Ballets Suédois took up the baton of innovative dance companies based in Paris. The Swedish troupe's commissioning policy heavily favoured French composers, particularly members of the short-lived group Les Six (Germaine Tailleferre's *Le marchand d'oiseaux* was one of its hits), although Sergey Prokofiev and Cole Porter (orchestrated by Charles Koechlin) also appeared on their bills. Perhaps the most notorious Ballets Suédois production was Erik Satie's final work, *Relâche* (1924), a collaboration with the artist Francis Picabia, which has a film by René Clair (with music by Satie) as its entr'acte. The use of film as part of a mixed-media

production was standard practice in the music hall: French composers have never been afraid of mixing so-called lowbrow and highbrow forms, nor of experimenting with novel media collaborations.

In French music from the 19th to 20th centuries, a curiosity about other cultures is a continuing thread. At the same time, composers' interpretations of non-Western cultures reflect broader social and political shifts. The first decades of the 19th century saw the publication of the multi-volume *Description de l'Égypte*, the outcome of a vast study under Napoleon's auspices that aimed to catalogue ancient and modern Egypt. This colonial outlook was later reflected in music in a less scholarly manner; in the 19th century, exoticism was all the rage. Works such as Saint-Saëns's 'Egyptian' Piano Concerto (No. 5), Édouard Lalo's *Symphonie espagnole* and Léo Delibes's *Lakmé* show the extent to which audiences were attracted to exotic display. (They also show that there was little real musical distinction between depictions of Egypt, Spain and India.)

Paris had the opportunity to move beyond this type of Orientalist fantasy at the 1889 and 1900 universal exhibitions, when traditional music from all over the world came to the city. The Javanese gamelan (percussion orchestra) and dancers, and the Annamite theatre performers from French Indochina at the 1889 exhibition, had a huge impact on Debussy, both directly on piano pieces such as 'Pagodes' ('Pagodas', from the piano triptych *Estampes*, 'Prints') and more distantly: the opening of *La mer* is based on a pentatonic mode of a type used in some gamelan music that is foreign to the Western tonal system. For his part, Messiaen's omnivorous appetite for rhythmic invention saw him taking an early interest in ancient Greek and Hindu rhythms, which in his work are completely recontextualised, making no reference to their musics of origin. By the time of the 1931 Paris Exposition Coloniale Internationale, recordings of music from outside the Western classical tradition were part of the display, reflecting a more ethnomusicological approach that is fully absorbed in the music of André Jolivet and Pierre Boulez. It is also noteworthy that the colonialist slant of the exhibition prompted protests from authors including André Gide, the Surrealists and journalists writing for the Communist daily *L'Humanité*. And it is interesting to note that later 20th-century and contemporary composers, including the Japanese Yoshihisa Taïra (1938–2005), the Moroccan Ahmed

DEBUSSY, RAVEL AND IMPRESSIONISM

'Impressionism' is a word often used to describe the music of Debussy, Ravel and other French composers of the late 19th and early 20th centuries, but it was not a term of which Debussy approved. Debussy wrote to his publisher in March 1908, 'I am trying to do "something different" – in a way *realities* – what the imbeciles call "impressionism".'

The term was first used in an artistic context by Claude Monet for his painting *Impression: Sunrise* (1872, *left*), and critics seized on the word as an insult to Monet, whose innovative approach was rejected by the conservative establishment. Fifteen years later, the same insult was hurled at Debussy by the same establishment types when his piano-and-orchestra work *Printemps* (1887) was attacked for its 'vague impressionism'.

No composer likes being summed up in one word, but why did Debussy so dislike the label? The word had negative connotations of vagueness and blurriness, even though precision was a central concern of Monet's, for instance. The tiny brushstrokes on his canvases blend colours in a new way when viewed from a distance. The innovation of the Impressionist painters was to leave the studio to capture ephemeral effects of light outdoors, and this is where we can draw parallels with Debussy. The composer's love of nature was a central preoccupation he shared with Impressionist painters: themes of water, wind and other natural phenomena are commonplace in his works, *La mer* being the most celebrated example. Just as the Impressionists were open-air painters, so Debussy can be considered an open-air composer. He wrote: 'I prefer those few notes an Egyptian shepherd plays on his flute: he is part of the landscape around him, and he knows harmonies that aren't in books. The musicians among us hear only music written by trained composers, never the music of Nature.' Debussy always cherished freedom from academic musical constraints.

Where does that leave Ravel? Debussy and Ravel shared many interests in art and poetry. Both had a strong feel for orchestral colour, and they had common musical ancestors in Chabrier and Russians such as Mussorgsky and Rimsky-Korsakov. They were both patriotic Frenchmen but not narrowly nationalist and certainly not xenophobic: in 1916 both refused to join the anti-foreign Ligue Nationale pour la Défense de la Musique Française. But Ravel, who once (only half-jokingly) said he might be 'artificial by nature', is at his furthest from Debussy if we try to label him an Impressionist. Ravel is very much an indoor composer, whose fondness for pastiche and love of everything mechanical has no parallel in Impressionist art.

Debussy and Ravel were the towering figures of French music of their time but, while they are both often labelled 'Impressionist' composers, the term is a poor fit for at least one of them. The term might also imply that the visual arts – perhaps even particular paintings – were centrally important to the composers, whereas in fact literary influences were far more significant for both of them.

2018 SEASON

REGENT'S PARK OPEN AIR THEATRE

PETER PAN
by J.M. BARRIE
by arrangement with Great Ormond Street Hospital Children's Charity

THE TURN OF THE SCREW
music by **BENJAMIN BRITTEN** libretto by **MYFANWY PIPER**
after a story by **HENRY JAMES**
a co-production with English National Opera

AS YOU LIKE IT
by WILLIAM SHAKESPEARE

LITTLE SHOP OF HORRORS
book and lyrics by **HOWARD ASHMAN** music by **ALAN MENKEN**
based on the film by **ROGER CORMAN** screenplay by **CHARLES GRIFFITH**

THE ROYAL PARKS

0844 826 4242*
openairtheatre.com
*9am – 9pm; calls cost 7ppm plus your telephone company's access charge.

Peter Pan Photo: David Jensen | Feast Creative

OLIVIER MESSIAEN
TURANGALÎLA SYMPHONY (1946–8)

'It's a love song,' said Messiaen of his gargantuan symphonic work for orchestra with solo piano and ondes Martenot. This simple description belies the multilayered complexity and extreme moods of the *Turangalîla Symphony*, which ramps up the typically French love of orchestral colour to the maximum. Its invented title, based on two Sanskrit words with meanings encompassing speed, life, love and the play of time, shows Messiaen's main compositional preoccupations of this period – though his use of 'symphony', unique in his *oeuvre*, is more surprising. It is a symphony in the word's original sense of 'sounding together': a work of supreme rhythmic and timbral invention that is powerful, captivating and occasionally downright bonkers.

Essyad (born 1939) and the Chinese Qigang Chen (born 1951), have been drawn to Paris and strongly marked by French music, as if they were reappropriating the exoticisms beloved of previous generations.

Paris has been a source of inspiration for so many composers, some of whom, through long-term residence or formative visits, might be considered honorary French nationals. Chopin's career was focused on Paris, Copland was one of Nadia Boulanger's first American students and George Benjamin was one of Messiaen's last pupils. An earlier George, Gershwin, was an American tourist in Paris who was inspired by the energy of the city in the late 1920s. The title of Delius's *Paris: The Song of a Great City* sums up these composers' feelings about Paris; Philip Heseltine wrote, 'For Delius, Paris is not merely a city of France … it is a corner of his own soul.' Paris is not

only a pre-eminent musical centre but also an idea that continues to capture the imagination of composers worldwide. ●

Caroline Potter is Visiting Fellow at the Institute of Modern Languages Research (School of Advanced Study, University of London). She has published widely on French music and her book Erik Satie A Parisian Composer and His World *(Boydell Press) was named the* Sunday Times *Classical Music Book of the Year.*

Fauré Pavane; Daphnis and Chloe
PROM 2 • 14 JULY

Saint-Saëns The Carnival of the Animals – excerpts; **Ravel** Tzigane
PROM 3 • 15 JULY

Debussy Pelléas and Mélisande
PROM 5 • 17 JULY

Messiaen Turangalîla Symphony
PROM 6 • 18 JULY

Messiaen Et exspecto resurrectionem mortuorum
PROMS AT … ROUNDHOUSE, CAMDEN • 21 JULY

French organ works
PROM 10 • 22 JULY

Works by Couperin, Rameau, *etc.*
PROMS AT … CADOGAN HALL 2 23 JULY

Debussy La damoiselle élue
PROM 16 • 26 JULY

Ravel Piano Concerto for the Left Hand; **Debussy** La mer
PROM 28 • 4 AUGUST

Saint-Saëns Violin Concerto No. 3
PROM 40 • 12 AUGUST

Debussy Prélude à l'après-midi d'un faune; Nocturnes; **Ravel** Boléro
PROM 44 • 15 AUGUST

Debussy Jeux; **Ravel**, orch. Yan Maresz Violin Sonata in G major
PROM 45 • 16 AUGUST

Ravel Mother Goose; Shéhérazade; L'enfant et les sortilèges
PROM 48 • 18 AUGUST

Ravel La valse
PROM 65 • 31 AUGUST

Dukas La Péri – Fanfare and Poème dansé
PROM 66 • 1 SEPTEMBER

Debussy Sonata for Flute, Viola and Harp; **Ravel** Introduction and Allegro
PROMS AT … CADOGAN HALL 8 3 SEPTEMBER

Berlioz Overture 'Le corsaire'; La mort de Cléopâtre; The Trojans – Royal Hunt and Storm & Dido's death scene; Harold in Italy
PROM 71 • 5 SEPTEMBER

Milhaud Scaramouche
PROM 75 • 8 SEPTEMBER

See also works by Lili Boulanger (feature article, pages 16–17)

The Other Boulanger Girl

Though eclipsed by her older and much longer-lived sister Nadia, Lili Boulanger was a gift to composing whose star burned bright, but all too quickly, as **GAIL HILSON WOLDU** reveals

Portrait of Lili Boulanger (1914) by Pierre Bodard, a fellow resident with the composer at the Villa Medici

In most musical circles, a reference to 'Boulanger' evokes the name Nadia Boulanger (1887–1979), not Lili Boulanger (christened Marie-Juliette Olga, 1893–1918). There are compelling reasons for this. Referred to as 'Mademoiselle', the elder of the Boulanger sisters, Nadia, enjoyed a distinguished career that spanned over 75 years. She was active as an organist, composer, conductor and – perhaps of greatest significance – as a pedagogue. Nadia taught composition at the American Conservatory at Fontainebleau and in her studio in Paris to many of the leading musicians of the 20th century. Among them were composers Aaron Copland and Astor Piazzolla; conductors Leonard Bernstein and John Eliot Gardiner; and the jazz legend Quincy Jones.

By contrast, Lili died at the age of 24 and is remembered entirely as an exceptionally gifted composer whose life was tragically short. Even more precocious than her sister, Lili was able to sight-read music aged 6 and she studied a host of instruments during her early childhood, including violin, cello, harp and organ, as well as piano with Gabriel Fauré. Nadia recalled her sister's precocity, observing: 'From her early childhood up until age 16, she lived in music, singing, playing a variety of instruments, but deciding on nothing in particular. At 16, her soul led her down the path that she would never abandon … she would be a composer.' To that end, in 1909 Lili entered the composition class of Paul Vidal at the Paris Conservatoire to learn the skills that she would need for her life's work.

Four years later, in 1913, Lili Boulanger attracted international attention by becoming the first female composer to win the Prix de Rome in musical composition. To have achieved this distinction at all was remarkable; several noteworthy composers active in the late 19th and early 20th centuries had competed without success, most significantly Maurice Ravel, whose five unsuccessful attempts brought the competition into disrepute. To have achieved this as a chronically ill, 19-year-old woman who had hitherto received not a single First Prize in the competition-driven system of the Conservatoire was extraordinary. She did not exude the confidence of the 'new woman' that had emerged in the early 1900s; indeed, Lili's frailty, her modest demeanour and her conservative clothing were antithetical to this new type. And yet she won the most coveted prize in music composition.

Adjudicators declared her winning submission, the cantata *Faust et Hélène*, 'Sensitive and warm. Poetic. Intelligently orchestrated and coloured.' Claude Debussy noted: 'Mlle Boulanger, who has just won the Grand Prix de Rome … is only 19 years old.' She was given a contract with Ricordi, the prestigious music publishing house, which offered a monthly sum of 500 francs over eight years for the sole rights to her compositions. At age 19, Lili Boulanger was acknowledged as a professional composer in a generally male field.

Boulanger's output includes small- as well as large-scale works. Choral and vocal music were her mainstays, although she also wrote a small body of chamber music, as well as compositions for solo piano and for orchestra. In this sense, her work is similar to Fauré's:

intimate and with a predilection for showcasing the beauty of the human voice. Her choral music, often based on biblical texts, reflects her strong religious faith. She composed several works derived from psalms, including the mournful Psalm 130, 'Du fond de l'abîme', written from 1914 to 1917 and scored for a large orchestra with expanded wind, brass and percussion sections, as well as organ, two harps, a celesta, chorus of mixed voices, and mezzo-soprano and tenor soloists. And there are earlier works: songs composed between 1911 and 1913, on texts by French poets, and other choral works, accompanied by either piano or orchestra. Included in her small catalogue of music for solo piano are the *Trois morceaux*, composed during her first residency at the Villa Medici as a laureate of the Prix de Rome in May and June 1914. These miniatures are very much products of fin-de-siècle France: each bears a descriptive title, they vacillate between contemplative, melancholy and jubilant expression, and they utilise the rich harmonic vocabulary of the early 1900s.

Boulanger composed her last works between 1916 and 1918. These include *La princesse Maleine*, a five-act opera based on the eponymous play by the Belgian playwright Maurice Maeterlinck; *Pie Jesu*, which Lili, too sick to write in her own hand, dictated to Nadia; as well as *D'un soir triste* and its companion, *D'un matin de printemps* – both of which exist in more than one arrangement. They reflect a variety of moods – optimistic joy, the daily realities of living through the First World War – and, certainly, Boulanger's mental state, as she was fully aware at the time that the chronic intestinal maladies that had afflicted her since childhood would soon end her life.

The Villa Medici in Rome (painting, 1685, by Caspar van Wittel), where Lili Boulanger worked and studied as a laureate of the Prix de Rome

How ought we to remember Lili Boulanger? While we cannot ignore the heartbreak of her short life, we must see her legacy in the power and beauty of her music, in her achievement as the first female Prix de Rome winner in composition and, above all, in her determination to become a composer. ●

Gail Hilson Woldu is a musicologist and Professor of Music at Trinity College in Hartford, Connecticut. She has written extensively on French composers Gabriel Fauré, Maurice Ravel and Vincent d'Indy.

D'un matin de printemps;
D'un soir triste
PROM 8 • 20 JULY

Pour les funérailles d'un soldat
PROM 41 • 12 AUGUST

Psalm 130, 'Du fond de l'abîme'
PROM 44 • 15 AUGUST

Nocturne for violin and piano;
Trois morceaux for piano
PROMS AT … CADOGAN HALL 8
3 SEPTEMBER

Fantastic Four

As four major European orchestras mark important anniversaries at the Proms, **PETROC TRELAWNY** explores their distinctive evolution and clear sense of musical footprints

Few orchestras have had such a close association with a single conductor as the Orchestre de la Suisse Romande enjoyed with Ernest Ansermet. He founded the Geneva-based ensemble in 1918 and remained in charge for the next 49 years.

Although Ansermet was succeeded by conductors such as Wolfgang Sawallisch, Armin Jordan and Marek Janowski, his and the orchestra's names are synonymous, from the hundreds of works they recorded together.

'Many people immediately associate us with Ansermet,' says the OSR's General Manager, Magali Rousseau. 'But all the musicians who worked with him have long since retired and the conductors who succeeded him have all had a very clear view of what they wanted for the orchestra. We talk about him, we won't forget about him, but the OSR has moved on and changed.'

The latest chapter in that process was the appointment last year of British conductor Jonathan Nott as Music and Artistic Director. He seems more than happy to salute his illustrious predecessor in a Prom featuring Stravinsky, Ravel and Debussy. 'Ansermet founded the orchestra at the same time as he was conducting for Diaghilev's Ballets Russes,' says Nott. 'He got to know Stravinsky well and developed a great personal knowledge and love of his music, sharing all he knew with his players in Geneva.' He was friends with Ravel and Debussy as well; the music of all three composers became central to the OSR's output – in the concert hall and on disc.

The Orchestre de la Suisse Romande at its home: the Victoria Hall in Geneva

Nott's new appointment follows his 16 years as Principal Conductor of the Bamberg Symphony Orchestra. Both ensembles are subsidised by grants from city and regional government. He plans to spend up to 22 weeks a year in Geneva, a major commitment for a modern conductor. One of the great attractions is the OSR's opera work. 'It spends nearly half its time in the pit of the Grand Théâtre de Genève,' explains Nott. 'That means telling a story through music is something the players have much experience in doing. It's why I have decided to bring Stravinsky's ballet *Petrushka* to the Proms.' He will conduct the original 1911 score, the version that Ansermet would have introduced to his nascent orchestra.

The OSR was not the only ensemble born in 1918. Some 400 miles north, in the Netherlands, a new orchestra was coming together through a rather more democratic process. There was no great maestro behind the Rotterdam Philharmonic Orchestra; rather, it was a collective of professional musicians working in casinos, cinemas and cafés who wanted to get together and play the symphonic repertoire. Led by violinist Jules Zagwijn, they convened on 10 June 1918 and established a new organisation, the principal aim of which was to 'practise good, high-standing musical art'.

Amsterdam's Concertgebouw Orchestra was already well established and The Hague's Residentie Orchestra (founded in 1904) was attracting great names, including Stravinsky, Ravel and Reger. The burghers of Rotterdam had wealth (the city was to become Europe's biggest port), but they needed culture as well.

Yannick Nézet-Séguin conducting the Rotterdam Philharmonic Orchestra at the Proms in 2013

'There is still a great rivalry with Amsterdam to this day,' says the Rotterdam Philharmonic's Artistic Programmer, Floris Don. 'We see ourselves as the eternal second city.' Bruckner's Fourth Symphony will be the focal point of the orchestra's Prom. 'We can't escape the fact that one of the greatest Bruckner orchestras is only an hour away,' he says. 'But we want to say, "Listen to ours!". Surely the Concertgebouw isn't the only one with a call on Bruckner?'

Yannick Nézet-Séguin will direct the performance, in one of his final engagements after 10 years as Chief Conductor. Afterwards, he will continue his work with the Philadelphia Orchestra and in 2020 becomes Music Director at the Metropolitan Opera in New York. Nézet-Séguin's ascendant career trajectory is a good example of the Rotterdam Philharmonic's seeming ability to spot and then appoint great talent early on. The Russian Valery Gergiev was little known in the West when he first worked with the orchestra, later serving as Chief Conductor for 13 years. Simon Rattle was just 25 when he was appointed Principal Guest Conductor. Next season, 29-year-old Israeli musician Lahav Shani, who won unanimous support from the orchestra after his first concert, will become Chief Conductor. 'We are no stranger to young conductors here,' laughs Floris Don.

The focal point for both the Orchestre de la Suisse Romande and the Rotterdam orchestra is their home city. The BBC National Orchestra of Wales has the responsibility of bringing classical music to an entire country.

A Welsh Symphony Orchestra was founded in a blaze of glory in 1923; Adrian Boult and Henry Wood came and conducted concerts. But the organisation soon went bust and it wasn't until the BBC's first Director General, John Reith, stepped in a few years later that Wales had an orchestra again. Wood returned to conduct the opening concert at City Hall, Cardiff, on 12 April 1928, featuring a Berlioz overture and a Mozart symphony.

It was a rocky start: within a few years most of the Corporation's music funding was diverted to the BBC Symphony Orchestra in London and the Welsh ensemble was reduced to just nine players. It took until 1987 before the BBC's Welsh orchestra finally reached full symphonic strength; six years later it took on the name that remains today – the BBC National Orchestra of Wales (BBC NOW).

Though largely funded by the BBC, the orchestra has had a significant partner for over 30 years in the Arts Council of Wales. 'That means we have multiple identities,' says Director Michael Garvey. 'We are a traditional broadcasting orchestra with a crucial relationship with Radio 3 at our heart, but we are also a national orchestra, with a concert season in Cardiff and a commitment to the whole of Wales.'

At BBC Hoddinott Hall, in Cardiff's Wales Millennium Centre, BBC NOW has a home

Thomas Søndergård conducting the BBC National Orchestra of Wales at Venue Cymru, Llandudno, in 2013

that is the envy of many other orchestras: a studio-concert hall with a fine acoustic and a design reminiscent of an intimate non-conformist chapel. However, the players have got used to long hours on coaches as they travel to perform in venues the length and breadth of Wales, often in leisure centres or theatres not best suited to music-making. It's nothing new; in his history of the orchestra, Peter Reynolds recalls Mariss Jansons, Chief Guest Conductor in the mid-1980s, directing a concert at the Classic Cinema in Llanelli.

'We have this enormous responsibility,' says Garvey. 'In Aberystwyth we provide the only professional symphonic music-making, and we only go twice a year. It's very different to a London or Manchester orchestra that plays in the same venue week in, week out.

Bangor is another regular stop for BBC NOW. With the city being situated

a five-hour drive from Cardiff, an overnight visit is out of the question. 'We do a residence,' explains Garvey. 'There are normal orchestral programmes, but we will also work with the music department at the university, giving masterclasses for composition students; we'll work with the local youth orchestra and find ways of engaging with Welsh-language artists, working with BBC Radios Cymru and Wales. In a few days we want to try and give the audience the same breadth of offer that they would get if they lived in Cardiff.'

When one looks through 90 years of BBC NOW archives, the orchestra's commitment to Welsh music becomes immediately clear. Works by Grace Williams, Alun Hoddinott and William Mathias feature a lot; more recently there have been partnerships with Guto Puw and Huw Watkins.

New music has always been at the centre of the London Sinfonietta's artistic manifesto. It gave its first performance in 1968, a year of student and wider social revolution across Europe and America. Flexibility was key to its early ideals; it became a new sort of chamber orchestra, not necessarily reliant on strings. The basic line-up was 12 musicians, but sometimes there would be 45 or more on stage.

'It's a strange thing for a new music ensemble to celebrate its 50th birthday,' says Chief Executive and Artistic Director Andrew Burke. 'The danger is, you start to look more at the past than the future. We may have made our own history, but we remain hungry to explore the music of today – and this longevity proves that the idea of the group is bigger than anyone who worked for it in a particular era.'

Andrew Gourlay conducting the London Sinfonietta at the BBC Proms at … Roundhouse, Camden, in 2016

When the Sinfonietta started, it would often balance new music with earlier 20th-century work by composers such as Stravinsky or Schoenberg. Today, it is the second half of the previous century that provides context. So the music of Sir Harrison Birtwistle, Hans Werner Henze, Wolfgang Rihm and Elliott Carter is placed alongside brand-new works. The Sinfonietta's Prom at Camden's Roundhouse covers music ranging from Ives's haunting *The Unanswered Question* to a quartet of new commissions marking 100 years since the end of the First World War.

'I suppose we are now part of the musical establishment,' admits Burke. 'Good governance and careful planning mean that we are stable, and yet what keeps us relevant and vital is that we are prepared to keep reinventing ourselves and taking risks. We can be a little feral in our outlook,'

All music groups today spend much time attempting to reach out and extend their

audiences. In Rotterdam, a city with a 13 per cent Muslim population and a mayor of Moroccan birth, plans include a major project in which the orchestra will work with musicians from the Maghreb classical tradition. For the London Sinfonietta it is all about harnessing technology, with new apps and online games key to digital outreach. The ensemble's *Clapping Music* app has been downloaded over 200,000 times. 'Forget *Angry Birds* or *2048*. The latest star of a maddeningly addictive iPhone game is the composer Steve Reich,' reported *The New York Times*.

The London Sinfonietta has appeared at the Proms from 1969 to 2016. The BBC NOW and the Rotterdam Philharmonic each made their debuts during the 1970s. But the Orchestre de la Suisse Romande has had to wait until 2018 for its first Proms appearance.

'Given the short time I've been here, I wasn't expecting it to happen quite so soon,' admits

Jonathan Nott. 'Geneva is a small town, we don't have much competition here, so it is vital for the orchestra to be seen at the most important European music festivals. This is exciting and, in our centenary year, a really important gig for us.' ●

Petroc Trelawny presents *Breakfast* on BBC Radio 3, and introduces the BBC Proms on radio and television.

Orchestre de la Suisse Romande

Founded 1918
First music director Ernest Ansermet
Current music director Jonathan Nott
Home Victoria Hall, Geneva

PROM 45 • 16 AUGUST

Rotterdam Philharmonic Orchestra

Founded 1918
First music director Willem Feltzer
Current music director Yannick Nézet-Séguin
Home De Doelen, Rotterdam

PROM 61 • 28 AUGUST

BBC National Orchestra of Wales

Founded 1928 (as Cardiff Station Orchestra)
First music director Warwick Braithwaite
Current music director Thomas Søndergård
Home BBC Hoddinott Hall, Cardiff

PROM 8 • 20 JULY;
PROM 11 • 22 JULY; PROM 17 • 27 JULY;
PROM 24 • 1 AUGUST

London Sinfonietta

Founded 1968
First music director David Atherton
Current artistic director Andrew Burke
Home Southbank Centre, London

PROMS AT … ROUNDHOUSE • 21 JULY

WIGMORE HALL

Intimate concerts featuring internationally acclaimed classical musicians in central London

2018/19 Season

Dame Sarah Connolly Residency

Schumann Song Series

Christian Blackshaw Focus

Angela Hewitt: The Bach Odyssey

Vox Luminis Residency

and much more...

The Wigmore Hall Trust
36 Wigmore Street, London W1U 2BP
Director: John Gilhooly OBE
Registered Charity Number 1024838

Department for Culture Media & Sport

LOTTERY FUNDED

Supported using public funding by
ARTS COUNCIL ENGLAND

www.wigmore-hall.org.uk

"Steinway allows me to unfold the world of imagination."

YUJA WANG
STEINWAY ARTIST

SOUTHBANK CENTRE

Classical Season 2018/19

Featuring

Andris Nelsons
& Gewandhausorchester
Leipzig

Mitsuko Uchida
& Mahler Chamber Orchestra

Stockhausen
Donnerstag aus Licht

Leonidas Kavakos
& Yuja Wang

Philip Glass
The Bowie Symphonies

**Pierre-Laurent
Aimard** & Tamara
Stefanovich

and concerts from our four resident orchestras
London Philharmonic Orchestra
Philharmonia Orchestra
Orchestra of the Age of Enlightenment
London Sinfonietta

LOTTERY FUNDED   Supported using public funding by ARTS COUNCIL ENGLAND

Andante
TRAVELS

~ SMALL GROUPS | FULLY INCLUSIVE | SPECIAL ACCESS | EXPERT LED ~

Spring

Summer

Autumn

Winter

- Milan & La Scala
- Wagner - The Ring Cycle in Leipzig
- Picasso & Modern Art on the French Riviera

- Puccini Opera Festival & Wine
- Rossini Anniversary Opera Festival in Pesaro
- St Petersburg - Palaces & Art

- Verdi Festival in Parma
- Havana & the Ballet Festival
- Wexford - The Opera Festival
- Netherlands - Dutch Painters
- Havana & the Ballet Festival
- Art & Architecture in Veneto

- New York - Opera, Music & Dance
- Florence - The City & its Artists
- Seville - The City & its Arts
- Milan - Masterpieces & the City

TRAVELS IN...
~ART HISTORY~ & ~OPERA & BALLET~

EXCLUSIVE ACCESS, LEGENDARY ARTWORKS & CULTURE ABOUND

Our Travels In... tours invite you to experience your destination in unique ways, from private recitals and culinary adventures, to after-hours visits to renowned galleries. Culture and history can be found in more than just the ground a city stands upon.

SPECIAL ACCESS

From privileged museum access and hands-on experiences at private workshops, to personal encounters with revered artistes and exclusive backstage tours at world-famous venues, our little black book helps us to secure special extras you won't find elsewhere.

Get in touch to see our full range of tours and request a brochure

www.andantetravels.com | tours@andantetravels.com | 01722 713800

EDINBURGH INTERNATIONAL FESTIVAL

3–27 AUGUST

PERFECT SCORES

This year, classical music and opera at the International Festival bring together established superstars alongside some of the world's finest youth orchestras. Join us for an unmissable three weeks of world class music, right here in Edinburgh.

Highlights include **Simon Rattle** and **London Symphony Orchestra**, **Marin Alsop** and **Baltimore Symphony Orchestra**, **Vasily Petrenko** and **Oslo Philharmonic Orchestra**, **Mirga Gražintytė-Tyla** and **City of Birmingham Symphony Orchestra**, **Nicola Benedetti**, **NYO Jazz** and **Dianne Reeves**, **Jérémie Rhorer** and **Théâtre des Champs-Elysées**, **Daniel Harding** and **Swedish Radio Symphony Orchestra**, **Christine Goerke**, **Pierre-Laurent Aimard**, **National Youth Orchestra of Canada**, **Opera de Lyon**, **Gabriela Montero**, **Sir Mark Elder** and **Hallé** and many more.

EIF.CO.UK
#EDINTFEST

·EDINBVRGH·
THE CITY OF EDINBURGH COUNCIL

THE TWELFTH
ENGLISH MUSIC FESTIVAL

The ever-innovative, inspirational and exhilarating English Music Festival returns to Oxfordshire in 2018 with exceptional music-making, fascinating talks and convivial social events. Join us to hear Roderick Williams singing Ivor Gurney; to experience dramatic programmes such as our First World War event or our Ethel Smyth programme; to enjoy Jacob Heringman playing the lute; or to relish such works as the Delius Double Concerto for Violin and Cello, the UK première of Richard Blackford's Violin Concerto, and choral and orchestral works by Vaughan Williams, Finzi, Ireland, Holst, Warlock, Bliss and Dyson.

25-28 MAY 2018
DORCHESTER-ON-THAMES, OXFORDSHIRE
www.englishmusicfestival.org.uk

For further information please contact Festival Director Em Marshall-Luck by email at: em.marshall-luck@englishmusicfestival.org.uk or on 07808 473889.

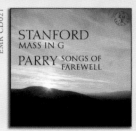

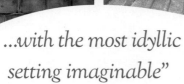
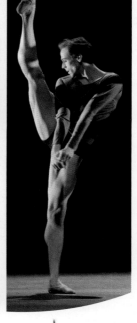

"Opera and dance
in a jewel of a theatre...

...*with the most idyllic
setting imaginable*"

**DANCE AT
THE GRANGE**
WAYNE McGREGOR

SOLD OUT

AGRIPPINA

HANDEL

THE BARBER OF
SEVILLE
ROSSINI

THE ABDUCTION
FROM THE SERAGLIO
MOZART

CANDIDE

BERNSTEIN

SOLD OUT

JUNE 7 — JULY 8 | +44 (0)1962 791 020

THEGRANGEFESTIVAL.CO.UK

THE
GRANGE
FESTIVAL
HAMPSHIRE

An Embarrassment of Gifts

Endlessly talented – as composer, conductor, pianist and teacher – probingly intelligent, charismatic and happy to live out his life in the public gaze, Leonard Bernstein had it all. But it was for his work as a composer, **NIGEL SIMEONE** says, that he most wanted to be remembered

During Leonard Bernstein's time as a student at Harvard University, at least three encounters were decisive in his early development as a composer. He met the writer and lyricist Adolph Green in 1937, beginning a lifelong friendship, the first important consequence of which was Bernstein's debut as a Broadway composer with the musical *On the Town*. In 1939, during his Senior Year at Harvard, Bernstein appeared for the first time as a composer-conductor with his incidental music for a production of Aristophanes' *The Birds*, and he also directed from the piano Marc Blitzstein's agitprop play with music *The Cradle Will Rock*. Blitzstein became a friend and mentor, encouraging Bernstein to write challenging music for the commercial theatre.

Much the most important influence on Bernstein the composer was Aaron Copland: father figure, confidant, and the closest Bernstein came to having a composition teacher. They first met on Copland's 37th birthday, 14 November 1937, at a dance recital in New York and at a party afterwards, where Bernstein's impromptu performance of Copland's *Piano Variations* prompted the start of a close and long-standing friendship. Bernstein graduated from Harvard in 1939 and then studied at the Curtis Institute in Philadelphia (where Fritz Reiner was his conducting teacher), receiving his diploma in May 1941.

It was with his own music that Bernstein hoped to leave his most enduring legacy – composing lay at the core of his creative personality, but finding the time to compose

Bernstein at his home in Fairfield, Connecticut, 1986

was increasingly hard. From his mid-twenties onwards, Bernstein was a busy conductor and this inevitably limited the time he could devote to writing. In 1943, as the newly appointed Assistant Conductor of the New York Philharmonic, Bernstein found himself on the front page of *The New York Times* after standing in at six hours' notice for an ailing Bruno Walter, but the following year, 1944, marked a turning point in his career as a composer: three major premieres heralded the arrival of a significant new voice in American music. The 'Jeremiah' Symphony (No. 1) was premiered by the composer with the Pittsburgh Symphony Orchestra in January (at Reiner's invitation), the ballet *Fancy Free* was given its first performance at the Metropolitan Opera in April, and the musical *On the Town* opened at the Adelphi Theatre on Broadway in December.

Bernstein himself said that 'Jeremiah' was the piece that was most heavily influenced by Copland. This is particularly apparent in the irregular rhythms of the 'Profanation' movement, which owes something to Copland's *El Salón México* – a work Bernstein had arranged for piano. For the other two 1944 works, Bernstein collaborated with others. A gregarious personality who liked to be surrounded by friends and couldn't bear solitude, this was the way he always preferred to work: in 1958 he told *The New Yorker* that he was 'a born collaborator'. *Fancy Free* – with choreography by Jerome Robbins – was greeted with tremendous enthusiasm after the first night on 18 April 1944. John Martin wrote in *The New York Times*: 'The music by Leonard Bernstein utilises jazz in about the same proportion that Robbins's choreography does … It is a fine score, humorous, inventive and musically

interesting.' *On the Town*, with book and lyrics by Bernstein's friends Betty Comden and Adolph Green, was his second collaboration with Robbins and it integrated extended dance numbers into a comic tale of sailors on shore leave in wartime New York – carrying over the same theme as the ballet *Fancy Free*. The score as a whole is one of Bernstein's most spontaneous creations: vibrant, funny, immensely touching – and bursting with the rhythmic energy that was to become such a familiar fingerprint in his music.

> " Composing lay at the core of his creative personality, but finding the time to compose was increasingly hard. "

With these three works – a symphony with solo voice, a ballet and a Broadway musical – Bernstein had arrived as a composer who not only had an immediately recognisable style but also showed extraordinary versatility. His next major work was his Symphony No. 2, 'The Age of Anxiety' (1949). Like 'Jeremiah', it included a soloist – this time a significant piano part. Based on W. H. Auden's 1947 poem, the work was commissioned by Serge Koussevitzky, who conducted the premiere on 8 April 1949 with Bernstein at the piano. Auden apparently disliked the symphony, but its music is some of the most powerful and intense that Bernstein ever wrote for orchestra. Reflecting the form of Auden's poem (in two parts, each comprising three sections) and including in 'The Masque' one of the most dizzying scherzos in the modern

Mean streets of Manhattan: Riff (Russ Tamblyn, *far right*) and fellow Jets corner Bernardo (George Chakiris), leader of the Sharks, in the 1961 film of *West Side Story* – echoing the feuding Montagues and Capulets in Shakespeare's *Romeo and Juliet*

symphonic repertoire, the work ends with a solemn and deeply expressive Epilogue that culminates in what Bernstein himself described as 'a positive statement of the newly recognised faith'.

Bernstein was acutely aware of the tensions between composing and conducting. In April 1950 he wrote to his sister Shirley: 'I've never felt so strongly … how through I am with the conductor-performer life (except where it really matters) and how ready I am for inner living, which means composing.' A month later he wrote to Hans Heinsheimer at the publisher Schirmer: 'Now to do something really important musically. I can see more and more clearly that the conducting side of my life will diminish rapidly, and the writing side augment.' Though this was a wildly inaccurate prediction – he would give more than 1,200 concerts with the New York Philharmonic

alone – Bernstein somehow found the time to compose, and the 1950s were particularly productive. After *Trouble in Tahiti* (1951), an adroit fusion of opera and jazz, Bernstein wrote the musical *Wonderful Town* with Comden and Green (1953), a gloriously breezy score written in just four weeks.

Two pieces from 1954 reveal a sterner side to Bernstein's music. His only original film score was for *On the Waterfront* – the music suggests he was an ideal choice for this gritty crime drama starring Marlon Brando. The *Serenade (after Plato's 'Symposium')* for violin and orchestra is effectively a five-movement violin concerto, inspired by Plato's text exploring aspects of love. According to Bernstein, the musical development of the *Serenade* 'does not depend on common thematic material, but rather on a system whereby each movement evolves out of elements

in the preceding one' and, particularly, the evolution of the opening violin theme that returns in different guises. The premiere was given by Isaac Stern in Venice on 9 September 1954 with Bernstein conducting.

Bernstein was already grappling with *Candide*, a work with a troublesome genesis that eventually opened on Broadway on 1 December 1956, closing two months later. The title-page of the score describes *Candide* as 'a Comic Operetta' and the composer called it his 'Valentine card to European music' – something that is immediately apparent from its effervescent overture. *West Side Story* was first mooted in 1949 but composed in 1955–7 during spells when Bernstein wasn't working on *Candide*. Whereas *Candide* had all sorts of problems, virtually nothing was changed in *West Side Story* between the previews in Washington DC and the premiere at the Winter Garden Theatre in New York on 26 September 1957. In many ways *West Side Story* was the perfect project for Bernstein, bringing together his passion for Latin-American rhythms, his gift for tender melody and his ability to convey senseless violence, all in a Broadway idiom. It has remained the work that, perhaps more than any other, has defined Bernstein the composer. A decade earlier, in 1948, he wrote: 'Most of my scores have been, in one way or another, for theatrical performance, and the others – most of them – have an obvious dramatic basis … Where it will lead I cannot tell; but if I can write one real, moving American opera, that any American can understand (and one that is, notwithstanding, a serious musical work), I shall be a happy man.' He may not have achieved that, but with *West Side Story* Bernstein and his collaborators

LYRICS FOR LENNY

STEPHEN SONDHEIM, writer of the lyrics for *West Side Story*, recalls working with Leonard Bernstein on the show in 1957

I knew some of Lenny's work before we collaborated on *West Side Story*: the musicals *On the Town* and *Wonderful Town*, of course, his film score for *On the Waterfront*, and also his Symphony 'The Age of Anxiety', whose solo piano part I used to play for fun at parties.

Lenny liked to work in a room together and I did not, so we would spend one afternoon at his studio and then two days apart, when I would work at home and get a 'spine' for the lyric, refine things or get other ideas; or he would come up with a musical idea and then we would get together and work them out so that they went with each other (or didn't).

At the time I was a subscriber to *The Listener* because of the puzzles, and I introduced them to Lenny. Every Thursday, when my *Listener* arrived, we'd spend the afternoon doing those puzzles. *West Side Story* might have been finished a couple of months earlier had it not been for that.

For Lenny there weren't enough hours in the day. All his life, whatever he was doing, he wished he were doing the other thing. If he was writing he'd say, 'I don't have any time for conducting'; if he was conducting he'd say, 'I don't have any time to write, to play the piano.'

He had too many gifts – he composed well, he conducted well, he taught well – and he balanced them as best he could. He had time to do it all, he just didn't have time to do as much as he wanted.

(Jerome Robbins, Arthur Laurents and Stephen Sondheim) wrote what is arguably the greatest of all American musicals.

The premiere of *West Side Story* coincided with Bernstein's appointment as Music Director of the New York Philharmonic, but in the summer of 1958 he took a sabbatical, in which he hoped to get down to serious composing. Nothing came of it, and in a letter to the composer David Diamond he even expressed doubts about whether he was cut out to be a composer at all: 'My first free summer in 20 years: and it's been so shocking to have it that I've literally done nothing: not a note … I wonder whether any composer who is *really* a composer could go for two months without composing.'

The 1960s were extremely busy for Bernstein the conductor, but he completed the Third Symphony ('Kaddish') and the *Chichester Psalms* (reworking music mostly salvaged from an abandoned musical based on Thornton Wilder's *The Skin of Our Teeth*). *Mass: A Theatre Piece for Singers, Players and Dancers* was written in 1970–71, after Bernstein had relinquished his post as conductor of the New York Philharmonic. It was followed by the ballet *Dybbuk* (1974), another collaboration with Robbins, and the ill-fated musical *1600 Pennsylvania Avenue*, which ran for just seven performances in 1976. Its music deserved a far better fate and two themes from it were recycled in *Slava! A Political Overture* (1977), dedicated to Mstislav Rostropovich. His largest project in the 1980s was *A Quiet Place*, the closest he came to the American opera he had always longed to write.

In an interview with Paul Baird in 1982 Bernstein said, 'I feel I've written very little … Considering my other activities, it's explicable … but the fact remains that the list is short.' I'm not sure he was right: not only is his music highly individual, but there's also more of it than Bernstein's own assessment might suggest: three symphonies, plenty of other orchestral works, three ballets, two operas, chamber music, piano pieces, songs and choral music – as well as some of the most innovative and memorable scores ever written for the Broadway stage. ●

Nigel Simeone is the author of *Leonard Bernstein: West Side Story* (2009) and editor of *The Leonard Bernstein Letters* (2013).

Candide – overture
PROM 31 • 6 AUGUST
PROM 59 • 27 AUGUST

Symphony No. 1, 'Jeremiah'
PROM 37 • 10 AUGUST

West Side Story
PROMS 38 & 39 • 11 AUGUST

On the Town
PROM 57 • 25 AUGUST

Conch Town *UK premiere;* La bonne cuisine; Fancy Free – 'Big Stuff', *etc.*
PROMS AT … CADOGAN HALL 7
27 AUGUST

Fancy Free – Three Dance Variations
PROM 59 • 27 AUGUST

Slava! A Political Overture;
Symphony No. 2, 'The Age of Anxiety'
PROM 60 • 27 AUGUST

Serenade (after Plato's 'Symposium')
PROM 69 • 3 SEPTEMBER

Podium Passion

Leonard Bernstein often attracted criticism for his effusive conducting style but, as **EDWARD SECKERSON** observes, this only reflected his belief that in order to conduct music you must first become one with it

'Everything I do is *to* the orchestra ... I don't plan any gestures, I've never rehearsed with a mirror': Bernstein at work in Paris, November 1966

Leonard Bernstein's famously theatrical nature all but preordained that his big break as a conductor should play out like a drama of his own making. And so it was that on the afternoon of 14 November 1943, at just a few hours' notice and with no rehearsal – none at all – he stood in for an ailing Bruno Walter at the helm of the New York Philharmonic at Carnegie Hall. That it should have been Bruno Walter – disciple and confidant of the composer Gustav Mahler, a composer Bernstein would take wholly to his heart – was in itself prophetic; but consider the chutzpah of the 25-year-old Assistant Conductor who, as he contemplated the monumental task ahead of him on the day in question, entertained the thought (and we know this from a late interview he gave) that 'one day all this could be yours'. And, of course, it was. He would in time take the New York Philharmonic to the top of the mountain.

Bernstein once said that he could gauge the success or otherwise of any performance he gave by the extent to which he felt as though he was composing the piece himself as he went along. It was his composer's perspective that enabled him to inhabit the music as if it were his own, relishing the gamesmanship of the composition as surely as its storytelling, theatricality and spiritual message. Bernstein's way with the fantastical effects of the Witches' Sabbath from Berlioz's *Symphonie fantastique* always had an air of 'Why didn't I think of that?' about it; Stravinsky's rhythmic angularity found kinship in his own jazzer's soul; Sibelius's deep-sunk bass lines somehow seemed more unfathomable under Bernstein; Copland's wide-open spaces and skyscraping soundscapes rejoiced in that very particular sense of what it meant to Bernstein to be American; and the profound irony of Mahler and Shostakovich was as much a part of his DNA as theirs.

With Bernstein it was always as much about identification as it was about technique and the finer points of interpretation. He was an accomplished pianist who could despatch a Mozart concerto with as much elan as Gershwin's *Rhapsody in Blue* or Ravel's swaggering G major Piano Concerto and *because* he was such an accomplished pianist the central piano part in his Second Symphony, 'The Age of Anxiety' (1948–9), borders on the sadistic in its difficulty. Again, identification. He clearly needed to feel as much at one with the pieces he conducted as the ones he composed.

> 66 He was a small figure made towering by virtue of his charisma. 99

With Mahler, of course, he did. There was a kinship in the nature of their careers: in the perpetual struggle to balance superstardom as conductors with their need to compose, in their Jewishness and in their innate sense of theatre. But where Bernstein always scored points over even the greatest Mahler conductors (including Bruno Walter himself) was in his determination to take Mahler at his word. Mahler's are among the most heavily annotated scores in the history of

Carving a place in history: Bernstein at the Berlin Wall in 1989 (with his assistant Craig Urquhart, *far left*); on Christmas Day Bernstein conducted musicians from East and West Germany and from countries of the four occupying powers in Beethoven's 'Choral' Symphony (No. 9), altering the word 'Freude' (joy) in Schiller's text to 'Freiheit' (freedom)

music and Bernstein understood as few have before or since that there could be no short-changing him, that the drama was in the excess, that Mahler took all the trappings of 18th- and 19th-century Austro-German music and pushed them, really pushed them, to the nth degree. Bernstein never shied away from a perilous shift in tempo, a headlong *accelerando* or a mighty *ritardando* because it was tough to pull off. Indeed, there are moments in Mahler's symphonies that have *never* been as scrupulously realised as they have by him. I think back to the extraordinary performance he gave of the Fifth Symphony with the Vienna Philharmonic at the Proms in 1987 where, in the central Scherzo, he honoured as few do those monumental pauses in which all nature seems to stop and listen. Mahler himself predicted that this movement would have a troubled life, that conductors would invariably take it too fast. He hadn't reckoned upon Bernstein.

Much has been written and spoken about Bernstein's platform antics – his mobile hips, his flying leaps. He was a small figure made towering by virtue of his charisma and a sizeable but irresistible ego. There's a clip of him conducting the finale of Haydn's 88th Symphony using nothing more than his eyebrows. But these 'eccentricities' were not choreographed for effect – rather, they were an integral part of his physical response to the music, his need to communicate *exactly* how he felt about it. Who could ever forget the spectacle of him in the mighty 'Chorus mysticus' at the close of Mahler's Eighth (the 'Symphony of a Thousand') at the Royal Albert Hall, turned sideways on to his audience, one arm summoning the offstage brass at the rear of Gallery, the other urging the many hundreds of performers to reach for the stars, head flung back in that classic Bernstein 'angel of music' pose. The Lenny factor, as it came to be known. And he

THE LEEDS
INTERNATIONAL
PIANO COMPETITION

Experience the very best of The Leeds in 2018

Leeds Piano Festival

The Leeds International Piano Competition, in partnership with our Global Ambassador, Lang Lang, presents our inaugural Festival.

16 May / Lars Vogt

17 May / Sunwook Kim

18 May / Alessio Bax

23 May / Lang Lang International Music Foundation Young Scholars

All 1pm, Wigmore Hall

Tickets on sale 6 February at wigmore-hall.org.uk or 0207 935 2141

2018 Competition

The Leeds International Piano Competition is back in 2018, with every round being live streamed online at Medici.tv.

6-8 September / Second Round

9-11 September / Semi-Finals

14-15 September / Finals with the Hallé Orchestra

At University of Leeds and Leeds Town Hall

Tickets on sale 12 March at leedspiano.com or 0113 376 0318

WIGMORE HALL　　　medici.tv　　　UNIVERSITY OF LEEDS

LEARNING WITH LENNY

A former student of Bernstein's, now a key interpreter of his works, MARIN ALSOP recalls his work as a conductor

Bernstein always told me that our first responsibility as conductors is to the composer. The conductor is the messenger of the composer, and that's a big responsibility. Bernstein talked about how every piece has a story and a moral, and that it's our job to draw out that story and convey it with conviction to the musicians, and through them to the audience.

People often said that Bernstein was too flamboyant or too flashy on the podium, but once you understand that he was truly embodying, almost channelling, the composer, his extraordinary enthusiasm makes perfect sense. When Bernstein conducted a Tchaikovsky symphony, for example, he felt that he really *was* Tchaikovsky. But he knew when he had to be clear with his gestures and always inspired and galvanised the musicians. He was very demanding, but also very warm and generous. Like all great artists, he was a consummate perfectionist.

I'll never forget one time when I was about 20. I was driving and listening to Beethoven's opera *Fidelio* on the radio, and it was just spectacular. I thought: who on earth is conducting this? And of course it was Bernstein. You might assume he'd be great at conducting American music such as that of his teacher, Aaron Copland. But I remember watching Bernstein rehearse Copland's gnarly, 12-tone *Connotations* with the New York Philharmonic. You don't necessarily think of Bernstein conducting avant-garde music like this, but he was open to anything and everything. I was just in awe of his analytical grasp of the piece.

wanted, *needed*, his players to be complicit in that. I remember him blowing a kiss to the late, great Maurice Murphy – Principal Trumpet of the London Symphony Orchestra – for a searing high-stopped note in the finale of Mahler's Second Symphony. Only Bernstein could have stepped outside the music for a split second to acknowledge what it takes to bring such music off the page.

Equally, though, there are awkward rehearsal moments preserved on video: one with the Vienna Philharmonic in which Bernstein exasperatedly vents the suggestion that this of all orchestras should know how to play Mahler (ouch!); and an encounter with the trumpet section of the BBC Symphony Orchestra during rehearsals for Elgar's 'Enigma' Variations – not, by all accounts, the happiest of collaborations and a performance over which we Brits are inclined to draw a veil. 'Nimrod'? That wasn't slow, that was *eternal*.

And yet, few conductors were capable of living 'in the moment' as Bernstein was and maybe that interminable 'Nimrod' didn't feel that way while we were experiencing it 'live'. His now notorious live recording of the closing Adagio of Tchaikovsky's Symphony No. 6 ('Pathétique') is a case in point – almost twice the length of any other recorded performance. I remember speaking to string players from the New York Philharmonic some years later and asking if at the time that last movement felt as poleaxingly slow as the stopwatch confirms it was. The answer in every case was an emphatic 'no'. From 'inside' those performances, the music of that tragic finale quite simply took as long as it needed to. Such was the spell that Bernstein exerted over his players.

Great artists create a sense of occasion, they conjure atmosphere, they change the way the

air moves in the room – and even on a less than inspirational night the expectation of magic would descend the moment Bernstein stepped onto the podium. Even when you didn't, *couldn't*, agree with his choices, he was irritatingly persuasive. But beneath the powerful persona there was integrity, too, a deference to the composers he served. That is less often talked about. Indeed, it is too often assumed that superstars like Bernstein reached a point where there was nothing more to learn and they could simply rest comfortably on their hard-earned laurels. Not so.

Let one anecdote suffice. It was shared with me by Bernstein's last personal assistant, Craig Urquhart. The night before conducting Beethoven's Seventh Symphony in Vienna – a piece he'd conducted countless times before – Urquhart dropped the conductor off at his hotel room, arranging to pick him up as usual for breakfast in the morning. But in the morning Bernstein was still in his robe; he clearly hadn't slept. 'I've been up all night with this,' he said, pointing to the score of the Beethoven. 'I really didn't know it at all, you know.'

Of course, the performance that night was incandescent. But it was Bernstein's acknowledgement that the work was never done – that there was always something more to be unlocked from great music – that makes this story so affecting and indeed further illustrates why history has placed him among the select few. ●

Writer and journalist Edward Seckerson was a critic for *The Independent* and for many years wrote and presented Radio 3's *Stage and Screen* programme. He is a regular contributor to numerous magazines and podcasts.

Recreation of Leonard Bernstein's Prom of 10 September 1987
PROM 50 • 19 AUGUST

Leonard Bernstein analysing his Symphony No. 2, 'The Age of Anxiety', before a class at Tanglewood, 1949

Lifelong Teacher

For Bernstein, teaching was 'probably the noblest profession in the world'. **SOPHIE REDFERN** outlines how his eternal curiosity inspired generations of audiences, making him a household name in the process

Bernstein understood the importance of an inspirational teacher. The great conductors Dimitri Mitropoulos, Fritz Reiner and, above all, Serge Koussevitzky guided him on his way to becoming America's first home-grown maestro, while Aaron Copland occupied a unique place in his life as friend, mentor and 'the closest thing to a composition teacher I ever had'. Bernstein never stopped paying homage to those who had encouraged and influenced him, but he would go on to leave his own formidable educational legacy. And its reach and impact were unrivalled.

A desire to teach and to share was apparent early on: as a teenager Bernstein excitedly regaled friends with tales of his latest musical discoveries. Then, in the 1940s – alongside major successes as a composer and conductor – he made the transition from student to teacher at Tanglewood, the acclaimed music school at the summer home of the Boston Symphony Orchestra, where he studied with Koussevitzky, its founder. Having taken on assistant roles over the years, Bernstein was appointed head of conducting upon Koussevitzky's death in 1951. Other positions followed elsewhere; however, a new, much larger audience beckoned.

In 1954 Bernstein met with television executive Robert Saudek, the man behind CBS's ambitious Sunday-afternoon series *Omnibus*, and, as Saudek remembered: 'Thus was born a new Bernstein – television's star teacher.' From the mid-1950s Bernstein became a regular TV fixture, presenting pioneering original music programmes for adults and children, and leading concert performances broadcast from around the globe. Looking back, he admitted: 'I found a real paradise in the whole electronic world of television.' The medium turned him into America's musical spokesman, and in return he revealed – and revelled in – its power as a tool for the arts.

Launched in 1952, *Omnibus* – hosted by Alistair Cooke (known to British audiences for his radio series *Letter from America*) – had admirable aims. It tapped into a desire for television to be more than mere entertainment and set out 'to raise not only television programme standards but also the general level of American taste and interests'. Bernstein's first programme aired on 14 November 1954 and is still remarkable today. The subject was Beethoven's Fifth Symphony and it opened with the 36-year-old Bernstein standing on a floor-sized blow-up of the first page of Beethoven's score. Over the course of 30 minutes he talked through the composer's sketches, played, sang and hummed musical examples, and conducted a performance of the first movement. By the end, Beethoven's creative process had been laid bare.

It was promptly hailed a triumph. Bernstein was a natural on screen; he spoke with clarity, included familiar references, and never patronised. As he stressed in 1959: 'The public is *not* a great beast, but an intelligent organism, more often than not longing for insight and knowledge.' All a topic needed was the right delivery and, while Bernstein gave the appearance of its being impromptu, the scripts were painstakingly revised until a final version was agreed, often minutes before airing.

Six more *Omnibus* episodes followed over the next four years and he led similar programmes under different names between 1958 and 1962. The subjects reflected his own interests: Beethoven gave way to jazz, while musical theatre, modern music, conducting and opera were also on the agenda. There were some criticisms, such as those highlighted by the composer and writer Gunther Schuller, who, after the 1957 'Introduction to Modern Music' programme, wrote eloquently to Bernstein about how 'sarcastic colouring and inflection' had undermined his objectivity. But there were bold choices too: the 1961 programme 'Drama into Opera: Oedipus rex' saw Bernstein pick apart how Stravinsky transformed Sophocles' tragedy into his 1927 opera-oratorio. More than 50 years on, it remains a daringly aspirational topic for television.

> ❝ Bernstein was a natural on screen; he spoke with clarity, included familiar references, and never patronised. ❞

After his success in educating America's adults, it was to young people that Bernstein next turned his attention. In 1957 he was announced as the incoming Music Director of the New York Philharmonic (taking up the post in 1958) and so was responsible for the Philharmonic's Young People's Concerts. Already broadcast on the radio, with Bernstein at the helm they would reach an unprecedented audience: CBS agreed to air them on television and between 1958 and 1972 he wrote and presented 53 instalments. With the series dubbed into 12 languages and syndicated to 40 countries, Bernstein became the face of music for an entire generation.

LEARN, TEACH, REPEAT

JAMIE BERNSTEIN, the eldest of Leonard Bernstein's three children, talks about her father's abiding desire to teach

No matter what form of communication my father used in life – from composing a piece to rehearsing a symphony to telling a good Jewish joke – it was all the same essential act of grabbing you by the sleeve and saying, 'Listen to this: this is *great*. I have to share this with you!'

Leonard Bernstein's greatest gift of all may have been his ability to convey his own excitement about music. Watching him explain sonata form or the difference between a tonic and a dominant, you had the sense that he was letting you in on a wonderful secret. It was that irrepressible urge to communicate that made my father such a gifted educator – and that gift may have been due above all to his lifelong love of learning. The minute he learnt something exciting, he felt compelled to turn around and share it with others. For him, being a teacher, an artist and a student was one continuous, glorious cycle.

My father never ran out of topics that interested him: not just music but also Shakespeare, the Renaissance, world religions, biology, vaudeville gags, Russian literature, astrophysics – and, best of all, any places where these seemingly disparate topics might overlap. 'The best way to know a thing,' he used to say, 'is through the context of another discipline.'

At the end of his life, he said he was proudest of his achievements as a teacher. And that makes sense – because, as a teacher, Leonard Bernstein was his most complete self.

90th Anniversary KAWAI

'Deep in my heart, I *know* that every person is born with the love of learning': Bernstein sharing his passion and experience with the next generation of music-lovers, *c*1965

His audience may have been young but no subject was out of bounds: he tackled music theory, dissected genres, explored composers, delved into famous works, and, in his first Young People's Concert on 18 January 1958, questioned the very meaning of music. Just as in his programmes for adults, he managed to illuminate a topic without dumbing down. The composer John Adams was a regular viewer and remembered Bernstein's appeal: 'He was like a movie star, only better. Good-looking and fully at ease in the glare of the television lights, he was also persuasive and articulate.' Bernstein's explanations were easy to follow, his enthusiasm was boundless and, importantly, he made the concerts fun.

'It would be easy to assume a high and mighty attitude and to sniff with disdainful hauteur at Leonard Bernstein, television glamour boy, selling music to the kiddies,' wrote the *New York Times* critic Harold Taubman after the first two episodes, 'but it would be wrong.' Some at the *Times* sniped at Bernstein's antics on the podium, but even they could see the merit of his latest venture. The Young People's Concerts reached 3,300 a year in the concert hall but, with television ownership booming (up from less than 400,000 in 1948

to nearly 46 million in 1960), it was music education on a mass scale – and Bernstein was its charismatic leader. 'They're a smash but oh so difficult and tiring!' he wrote to a friend at the time, but he would later consider them 'among the favourite, most highly prized activities of my life'.

At the end of 1971 Bernstein presented his last Young People's Concert and focused on a new project: the series of lectures he would deliver as Charles Eliot Norton Professor of Poetry at his alma mater, Harvard. In accepting the position, given annually to a leading figure in the arts, Bernstein followed not only literary giants including T. S. Eliot and E. E. Cummings, but such musical luminaries as Stravinsky, Hindemith and Copland. This was Bernstein as public intellectual and thinker, and he committed to it wholeheartedly.

Published as *The Unanswered Question* – the title courtesy of a work by Charles Ives – Bernstein's six lectures, delivered in autumn 1973, saw him focus on what he considered the innate qualities of music and its central meaning to us, as human beings. Packed with music and drawing heavily on Noam Chomsky's writings on linguistics, the talks combined ideas from a wide range of disciplines. Expansive in scale and scope, they reached an international audience by being recorded and televised in the USA and on the BBC; and, though there were criticisms, they stand as Bernstein's most extended argument on music.

The television programmes were undoubtedly major milestones, but Bernstein never lost contact with young musicians; almost every year he returned to Tanglewood, to guide and mentor others. It held a special significance, and in films and photographs over the decades

Bernstein can be seen in his element, holding court on the Berkshire lawn surrounded by students and working with aspiring conductors. Among his protégés were Michael Tilson Thomas and Marin Alsop, both of whom have spoken of how he made them see music anew (*see page 41*), but Bernstein always emphasised the impact teaching had on him too: 'When I teach I learn; when I learn I teach' was an oft-repeated phrase.

In 1963 he presented 'A Tribute to Teachers', a deeply personal Young People's Concert in which he praised teachers and explained the debt he owed to his. When in his opening he asked his young audience what teachers had to do with music, there was only one answer: 'Everything!' Bernstein remained dedicated to education until the end of his life: on 14 August 1990 he conducted the Tanglewood student orchestra in a performance of Copland's Third Symphony to mark 50 years since Koussevitzky established the summer school. It was one of his last concerts and a poignant final act as a teacher; and yet, as his programmes, writings and former students continue to inspire and educate, perhaps it wasn't his final act at all. ●

Sophie Redfern is a musicologist specialising in 20th-century American music and dance. She is the author of a forthcoming book on Bernstein and ballet.

The Sound of an Orchestra

What makes an orchestra sound the way it does? In a tribute to Bernstein's TV broadcasts, we explore the orchestra's astonishing variety, as experienced by composers, musicians and listeners
PROM 58 • 26 AUGUST

See also Prom 32 (Inside Shostakovich) and Prom 59 (Relaxed Prom)

Musical Giftedness: Born or Bred?

As the Proms celebrates the multifaceted talents of Leonard Bernstein, lecturer in music psychology **VICTORIA WILLIAMSON** explains what past and present studies reveal about the predictors of musical ability

One of my first school memories is of sitting in our school hall one cold autumn morning, where the desks were laid out for us in rows. The teacher put a cassette tape into the audio system and out came a booming, authoritative voice, of the type that featured on old newsreels. The voice announced that we were going to be tested on our musical ear. We heard chords and guessed how many notes they contained. We were played rhythms and we selected pictures to match. Different instruments played an assortment of notes and we had to say if the pattern was the same or different. I was enjoying myself: school had become more fun over night. Shortly after this test I was selected to begin guitar lessons and so began an accidental but nevertheless passionate love of studying music.

Fast-forward just over a decade and I am sitting in a university lecture for my Music Psychology Master's degree. We are discussing the history of assessing musical talent and my lecturer is playing audio examples from several music tests. Suddenly, I hear that booming voice again. I am thrown back to my old school hall. This is the very test I did back at school.

As a child growing up in the 1980s, I was one of many who had their 'musical potential' or talent level assessed using a standardised test. At the time the prevailing theory was that musical talent was present at birth, a fixed ability that would provide the foundation for later success. Tests were developed to assess levels of the supposed crucial ingredients of musical talent, such as pitch, timbre and rhythm perception.

> **66 In the 1980s the prevailing theory was that musical talent was present at birth. 99**

The controversial aspect of these tests is that the results were – and still are – used as a basis on which to offer further opportunities in terms of musical education, placing top-scoring children above those who perform less well. A quotation attributed to Thomas Jefferson (paraphrasing Plato) is often used as justification for this approach: 'There is nothing so unequal as the equal treatment of people of unequal ability.' Even if this argument sounds convincing, you might question the idea that such a complex ability as musical talent can reveal its full potential at a young age. You wouldn't be alone.

Research in the 1990s challenged the idea that a child's musical talent has predictive power in determining whether they will become a great musician. A series of highly influential studies by John Sloboda, Michael Howe and Jane Davidson looked at highly accomplished musicians and asked what factors determined excellence. The overwhelming answer was nurture: early environmental influences.

The body of research produced by Sloboda, Howe and Davidson largely dismissed the concept of musical talent and instead referred to the benefits of early inspiration, positive youth role models, effective teaching strategies and timely musical opportunities. And, of course, practice – targeted, monitored, efficient and rigorous practice schedules that amount to tens of thousands of hours by the time a student reaches conservatoire level.

AM I MUSICAL?

Recent research shows that musical ability may be more common than was previously thought

Modern musicality assessment began in 1919 with the Seashore Tests of Musical Ability. These tests, developed by psychologist Carl Seashore, measure discrimination of pitch, loudness, tempo, timbre and rhythm. The Seashore Tests of Musical Ability are still used and their design has inspired many similar publications, including the extensive Musical Aptitude Profile (1965) and the Bentley Test (1966).

Recently, a new generation of tests has emerged that has identified musical ability in adults where potential may previously have been dismissed. These include the Goldsmiths Musical Sophistication Index (2011) and the Profile of Music Perception Skills – aptly, PROMS (2012).

The new tests feature at least two improvements. First, they use many more real music samples as well as tones and beats; hence they can determine auditory abilities as well as responses that reflect our complex musical experiences. Secondly, they take account of musical background and listening preferences.

We now know that people with little formal musical training but a strong preference for and responsivity to music will show abilities above those who have little interest in music. The exciting conclusion is that musical potential is lifelong and can be maintained by an active involvement with music – at any age – when we pick up our first instrument or take our first singing lesson. So, if you love music then, yes, you are musical. Specific musical skills can be yours whenever and however you choose to learn.

We now had both sides of the argument on the table: nature *and* nurture as the drivers of musical potential. Are great musicians simply born or can they be made?

By the time I began my Master's degree, Sloboda, Howe and Davidson's work had been digested by the academic community, made it into mainstream education, and was leading the way. The question presented to me was not whether you could train a genius – especially in the area of musical performance – but rather how best to go about the task. Papers emerged on the best teaching styles, the most effective practice strategies and the importance of parental/guardian support. A 'sensitive learning period' was identified that apparently gave an advantage to early-trained over late-trained musicians.

The nature argument, however, would not be laid to rest. There were too many unexplained questions about the reality of musical talent. What, for example, about child prodigies? Where do they come from? There is the often-cited case of Wolfgang Amadeus Mozart, who played for Louis XV aged 7, reputedly wrote out Allegri's *Miserere* from memory, aged 14, after only a single hearing, and composed more than 25 symphonies by the time he was 20. In this Proms season alone we encounter pianist Benjamin Grosvenor (Proms 46 and 56) who, as the youngest ever finalist of BBC Young Musician of the Year in 2004, played Ravel's Piano Concerto in G, aged just 11; and the Messiaen-pupil George Benjamin, who made his Proms debut as a composer aged 20 in 1980, and this year also appears as conductor (Proms at … Roundhouse, 21 July, and Prom 28). The multitalented Leonard Bernstein *(see pages 34–45)* is another example of a musical

Pianist Benjamin Grosvenor who, still only in his mid-twenties, has already been performing for over a decade

high-achiever whose gifts might seem to be explained only by a genetic predisposition. In fact, many highly musical children experience what amounts to professional training from an extremely early age. It may well have been Mozart's upbringing (*ie* nurture) – as the child of Leopold Mozart, a prominent musician and teacher – rather than a genetic gift that set him apart from his peers.

However, this pattern is not seen in, for example, the composers Arnold Schoenberg and Hans Zimmer, Indonesian jazz-piano prodigy Joey Alexander, David Bowie or Jimi Hendrix. Their musicality drives and directs their lives despite little evidence of the early structured, expert guidance thought to be essential in a nurture argument. They are examples of the amazing feats that can be achieved before or even without a rigorous formal musical education. There is no question that musical giftedness shines through in their compositions and performances. I am sure that these musicians would agree with Leonard Bernstein when he said: 'I can't live one day without hearing music, playing it, studying it or thinking about it.'

If we accept that some people are born with a musical gift, then perhaps, conversely, some people are born non-musicians. This would make logical sense if musicality fell along a pattern of typical genetic variation where, in the case of height, for example, a minority are very short or very tall with most of us in the middle.

Indeed, a minority of individuals do struggle with music from early childhood. I spent several years conducting research with the help of people who live with congenital amusia, a rare neurodevelopmental condition in which an otherwise typically developing intelligent adult is unable to process musical sound. These people report no sudden onset to their condition; rather, they have had difficulty understanding music from a young age. In addition, a small number of individuals live with musical anhedonia, in which music perception is fine, but the person reports feeling no pleasure or emotion in response to music.

The slow rise of the nature argument received another boost from the field of genetics. Yi Ting Tan and colleagues at the University of Melbourne reviewed research on the genetic basis of perfect pitch (the ability to identify a given pitch without reference to other pitches), congenital amusia, as well as musical memory, singing, creativity and the kind of basic tone and rhythm skills assessed by music profile tests *(see panel opposite)*. Several individual genes featured prominently in multiple areas of musicality and studies have put the heritability of some musical skills as high as 80 per cent.

Despite these tantalising glimpses of music in our genes, the scientists concluded that the crucial role of epigenetics – the interactions

The 'original' prodigy, Wolfgang Amadeus Mozart: but could his talents be attributed to nurture, not nature?

between gene and environment – remains poorly understood. These complex interactions may hold the key to understanding the best way to nurture people who carry higher than normal potential for musicality.

Having gone full circle, the debate on whether musical talent arises from nature or nurture is settling down to a happy medium. The few genuine antecedents of musical giftedness can now be investigated using the latest tools from the fields of genetics, bio-physiology and neuro-imaging. They take their place alongside the important educational and psychological studies that will tell us the most effective, healthy ways to provide stimulating and enjoyable musical education.

So, what is needed for musical talent to thrive? First, we must accept that a one-off test of talent in a child can easily fail to capture potential. Aptitude tests such as the one I took on that cold autumn morning have a useful role in assessing basic musical skills related to audition and timing. They allow us to determine where individuals may struggle with aspects of musical education, so that instruction and support can be maximally beneficial. However, they should not be used to isolate children from music education on the basis that they have limited talent. This follows Leonard Bernstein's view that 'children must receive music instruction as naturally as food, with as much pleasure as they derive from a ball game, and this must happen from the beginning of their lives'.

Once a rich ground of inclusive musical education is established, then skill acquisition and talent encouragement can be optimised by ensuring that all aspects of musical ability are supported at whatever level they happen to present in early years. For the majority of us who emerge from our education with a love of music and a handful of skills, we take music with us on our life journey, as a companion and a refuge. I sit with my seven-month-old and play her the pieces of classical guitar music that I can still recall – it brings us both great joy.

Musicality, in all its complex forms and levels, is within all of us and is lifelong. Musical talent can emerge in many guises and should be encouraged at any age for the benefit of both the individual and the rest of us eager music-listeners. ●

Victoria Williamson is a lecturer in Music Psychology at the University of Sheffield, where she is also Director of the Music and Wellbeing facility. Her book *You Are the Music* was published in 2014.

Rich Pickings

KIMON DALTAS explores the wide variety of talks, discussions, readings, films and other free events to complement this year's Proms concerts

The Proms is the perfect place to become immersed in music: alongside the concerts there are opportunities to look deeper and learn more about the context, ideas and history behind some of the works performed at the Royal Albert Hall.

Every day of the Proms season you will find a free pre-concert event a stone's throw away at Imperial College Union's Beit Venues. The events range from talks, discussions and readings to film screenings and live recordings of favourite radio programmes. If you're following the season on the airwaves rather than in person, many of the events will be broadcast in the intervals of the main concerts – and will of course remain available to listen to for 30 days afterwards via the BBC Radio 3 website.

Events are programmed for both new audiences looking for entry points to the music and Proms veterans alike, with most of the pre-concert discussions focused on a particular work or composer featured in that evening's concert. Think of them as live programme notes hosted by Radio 3 presenters, inviting you into their conversations with historians, musicologists and artists to enrich your musical experience.

In the main group of discussions around composers and music, one strong strand focuses on Leonard Bernstein in the year marking the centenary of his birth, with events highlighting his enormous contributions to music in parallel roles as conductor, composer, commissioner and educator. The first of these (18 July) takes that evening's performance by the BBC Symphony Orchestra of Messiaen's *Turangalîla Symphony*, which Bernstein conducted at its premiere in 1949, as a launching point for a look at his relationship with and championing – or not – of contemporary composers. *(For other related Bernstein events, see listing at end.)*

The tragically early deaths 100 years ago of two female composers will be marked by the Proms as well as by pre-concert discussions dedicated to them: Morfydd Owen, a prolific Welsh composer, pianist and mezzo-soprano, who died just short of her 27th birthday, will be the subject of 20 July's event; and French composer Lili Boulanger, who became the first woman to win the Prix de Rome composing prize and died at the age of 24, will be celebrated on 15 August.

> 66 Look deeper into the context, ideas and history of the works. 99

The Proms takes great pride in the number of new works presented each season, especially its own commissions. The added benefit of featuring living composers is that they are available for discussion – and who better to introduce the premiere of Joby Talbot's Guitar Concerto on 2 August than the composer himself? Other pre-Prom Q&As include Andrew Norman (23 July), Tansy Davies (25 July) and Philip Venables (17 August).

These live programme notes are complemented by some fascinating talks that take a more lateral angle, such as one inspired by Richard Strauss's *An Alpine Symphony* (30 July). Abbie Garrington, an expert on literary potrayals of mountaineering, will hear from Dan Richards, author of *Climbing Days*, about the enduring appeal of mountains in art, music and writing.

The following day will see novelists John Lanchester and Diana Evans set their own depictions of modern-day London as a sideways introduction to both Haydn's and Vaughan Williams's 'London' Symphonies in the concert that evening.

The literary theme continues into a series of readings, with the 5 September event hosted by journalist Alex Clark introducing an all-Berlioz Prom, including parts of his opera *The Trojans* – by looking to its source material in Homer, Virgil and others. And, while in this case readings will be directly relevant to the works being performed, other events take a more playful approach, such as the selection of humorous prose and verse aiming to capture the jocular spirit of Beethoven's Second Symphony (28 July).

Alternatively, you could take an opportunity to be in the audience of a radio programme, starting on the First Night of the Proms with an 'on location' live edition of *In Tune*. Tom Service presents a special edition of *The Listening Service* (22 July) exploring Mahler's Eighth Symphony and Faustian influences on composers from the early 19th century to the present day. Radio 4 will also get in on the act with the Grand Final of the music quiz *Counterpoint*, presented by Paul Gambaccini, held as a pre-Prom event (4 September).

The BBC Young Musician Prom on 15 July, featuring a host of past winners, will mark 40 years of the famous competition and, ahead of the concert, there will be a screening of a new film about the event's history and the illustrious careers it has helped to build.

On 3 September the winners in the two categories (ages 12–18 and 19-plus) of the 2018 Proms Poetry Competition will be

announced by Radio 3's Ian McMillan, along with Poetry Society Director Judith Palmer and poet Helen Mort. Proms Learning also runs a whole programme of free participatory activities for all ages *(see pages 66 and 78)*.

So, as you read through this guide and plan your Proms 2018 journey, remember to look out for over 70 free pre-concert events – a real chance to learn something new every day. •

Kimon Daltas is a freelance journalist and former editor of *Classical Music* magazine.

Leonard Bernstein Centenary Talks

Nigel Simeone discusses Bernstein as a champion of contemporary music
WEDNESDAY 18 JULY, 5.45PM–6.25PM

Humphrey Burton introduces Aaron Copland's influence on Benjamin Britten and Leonard Bernstein
WEDNESDAY 8 AUGUST, 5.15PM–5.55PM

David Benedict explores *West Side Story*
SATURDAY 11 AUGUST, 6.15PM–6.55PM

Norman Lebrecht investigates Bernstein's relationship with Mahler's music
SUNDAY 19 AUGUST, 6.15PM–6.55PM

Edward Seckerson introduces *On the Town*
SATURDAY 25 AUGUST, 5.45PM–6.25PM

Readings and memories of Bernstein
SUNDAY 26 AUGUST, 5.45PM–6.25PM

Glyn Maxwell and Polly Clark discuss Auden and Bernstein
MONDAY 27 AUGUST, 6.15PM–6.55PM

Performance Art

Every musician strikes a balance between the public act of performing before an audience and the private relationship with their instrument. Photographer and journalist **DAMIEN DEMOLDER** captures the latter in images

COLIN CURRIE *percussion*
PROM 3 • PROMS AT ... CADOGAN HALL 5

The sound this old skin drum made was far bigger than its physical size seemed to suggest, and the visual complexity of textures in the skin only just out-did the sonic richness of its vibrations for variety. Colin was fascinated by its tones and listened intently, absorbed, as it whispered its history into his ear.

JACOB COLLIER
PROM 7

Whatever instrument it is Jacob has picked up, as soon as he starts playing he is completely immersed. I wanted to highlight the connection between his hands and his head to draw attention to the source of his music. Although his face is turned directly to his hands, the positions of those fingers come not by sight but by touch and intuition. For these shots in his London practice room I wanted to get across the physical motion that's involved when he's lost in action. The music creates quite a groove as it flows through his being, making him convulse with the rhythm, whether he's beating, plucking or blowing.

CYNTHIA MILLAR *ondes martenot*
PROM 6

The extraordinary ondes martenot creates a mysterious and other-worldly collection of sounds that suggest messages transmitted from far-flung galaxies, so, when the sun presented us with this spectacular 'shadow manuscript' on the wall it seemed appropriate to take advantage of it. We've slipped into sci-fi – an *X-Files* poster perhaps – as Cynthia seems to tease a reverberating note from this fleeting display of celestial strings that was projected into the room.

GOLDA SCHULTZ *soprano*
PROM 33

Hearing Golda sing in person felt deeply spiritual and affecting. Her mouth opened and the most amazing notes thickened the air. I wanted to show off the wonderful curves of her calm face, and to emphasise where that voice leaves her body. The patterning on the studio wall panels in the background suggests the waves of sound as they emanate into the space.

Discussing pre-performance preparation, Golda explained that she dances backstage when she needs to burn off energy, and does core-strengthening yoga when she needs to build some heat. Balancing her energies is critical so that she can deliver her best by approaching her performance in the right state of mind and body. She finds the 'Warrior' pose particularly useful, but only rarely does she practise it atop a grand piano.

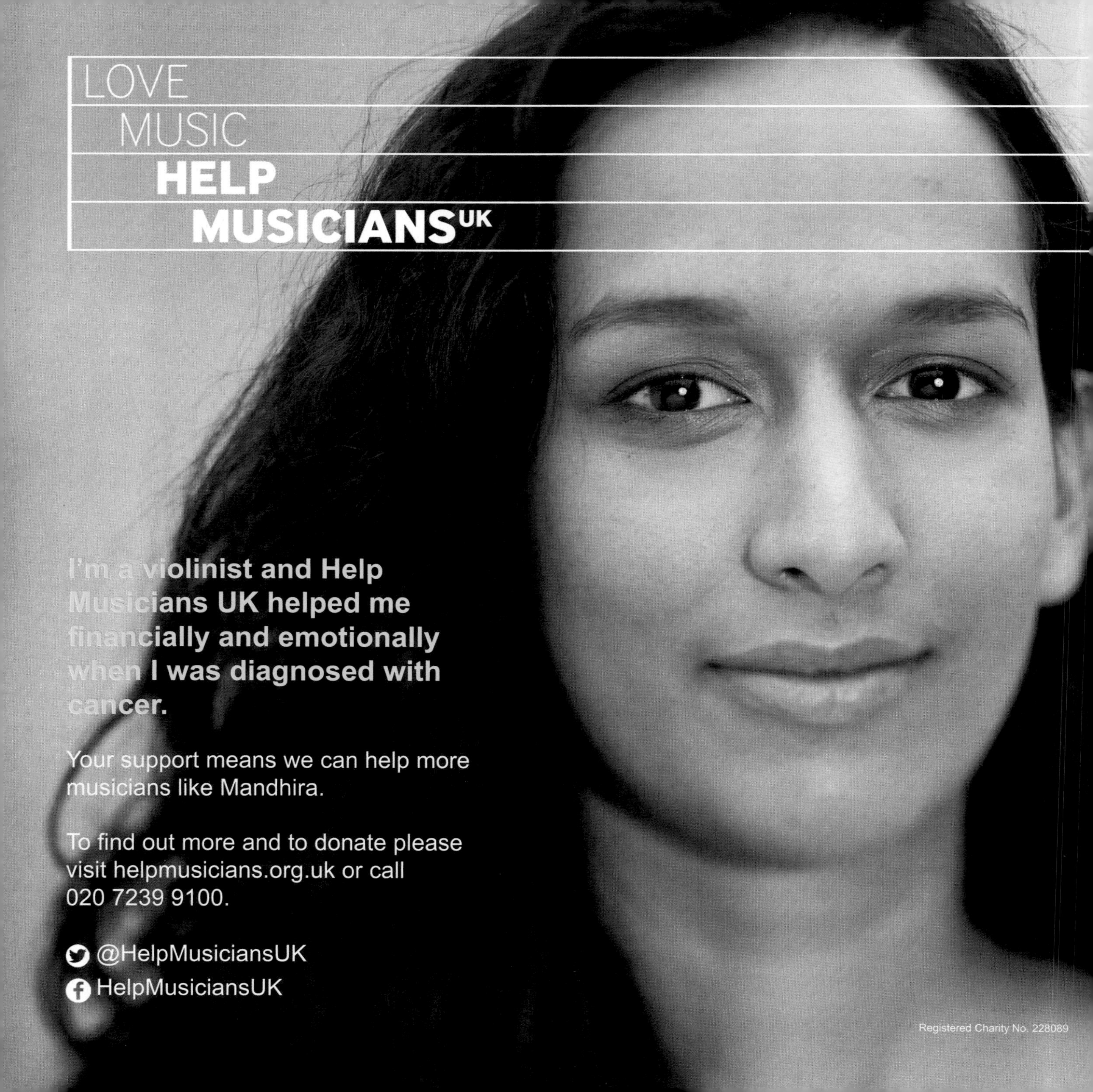
LOVE
MUSIC
HELP
MUSICIANS UK
I'm a violinist and Help Musicians UK helped me financially and emotionally when I was diagnosed with cancer.
Your support means we can help more musicians like Mandhira.
To find out more and to donate please visit helpmusicians.org.uk or call 020 7239 9100.
@HelpMusiciansUK
HelpMusiciansUK
Registered Charity No. 228089

WHERE AMAZING
THINGS HAPPEN

2018 PROGRAMME INCLUDES
MACBETH, ROMEO AND JULIET,
THE DUCHESS OF MALFI AND
A CHRISTMAS CAROL

SUMMER AND WINTER SEASONS
ON SALE NOW

rsc.org.uk

opera north

2018 – 2019

TOSCA Puccini

THE MERRY WIDOW Lehár

SILENT NIGHT Puts

THE MAGIC FLUTE Mozart

KATYA KABANOVA Janáček

DOUBLE BILL
THE RITE OF SPRING Stravinsky
A co-production with Phoenix Dance
GIANNI SCHICCHI Puccini

AIDA Verdi
Concert staging

**TOURING THE NORTH
SEP 2018 – JUN 2019**

For full venue listings and booking:
**OPERANORTH.CO.UK
0844 848 2720**

Calls will cost 7p per minute plus your
telephone company's access charge

Registered Charity Number 511726

Supported using public funding by
ARTS COUNCIL ENGLAND

Leeds CITY COUNCIL

Major Supporter
the emerald foundation

LSO 2018/19 Season
Over 50 concerts with
Sir Simon Rattle and the
LSO's family of artists

Save on your booking
40% off for 12+ concerts
30% off for 8 to 11 concerts
20% off for 4 to 7 concerts

lso.co.uk

ALWAYS MOVING

CITY
LONDON

Supported using public funding by
**ARTS COUNCIL
ENGLAND**

barbican
Resident
Orchestra

London Symphony Orchestra

Musical Memorials

As the Proms marks 100 years since the end of the First World War, **KATE KENNEDY** considers how composers of the time – whether in the field or not – responded with acts of musical remembrance

The First World War is now remembered primarily through its literature. We're all familiar with the war poets: Wilfred Owen, Siegfried Sassoon and their contemporaries. The response of classical musicians to the war – both during and after the conflict – is less familiar, despite the fact that music has a unique and important role to play in commemoration, as well as in inspiring and celebrating camaraderie. For practical reasons, it was more difficult for composers than it was for poets to write while on active service. Although the serving composers who survived wrote their war-related compositions in the decade after their return, the majority of music created during the war was by the composers left at home. Their pieces are a barometer of the needs of the time, serving the public good and also conveying private emotion. Older composers who were not called upon to fight, such as Edward Elgar, Charles Villiers Stanford and Hubert Parry, felt strongly that they should write works that met the general populace's need to mourn, commemorate, celebrate and raise spirits. There were even calls in journals

La mitrailleuse ('The Machine Gun'): Christopher Nevinson's pen-and-ink version of his 1915 Futurist painting

for composers to write 'the piece of the war' that might speak both for and to the British people. *The Musical Times* called for a 'composer of genius' to write a bugle-call symphony, creating 'a work of real national importance by taking three or four of the most expressive [bugle] calls and enlarging symphonically on the meaning which they are supposed to convey'.

Despite such appeals for a single musical utterance, there were as many different musical responses to the conflict as there were varied and changing attitudes to the war. While the imperative to write a musical work of remembrance was one recognised by composers and not simply articulated by the general public or journals, the musical responses were far from uniform in their message and approach. They ranged from works as diverse as Frederick Delius's *Requiem* (composed in 1913–14), Gustav Holst's *Ode to Death* (1919), John Foulds's *A World Requiem* (1919–21) and Arthur Bliss's huge 'symphony on war', *Morning Heroes* (1930), to name just a few.

Some works were, as in the case of *Morning Heroes*, written to exorcise a deeply personal sense of grief or guilt, while still serving the purpose of bringing together large forces to

mourn and contemplate loss en masse. Other composers wrote more intimate works, drawing on their experiences of the war to create pieces that expressed their own very personal relationship to the event. They were not necessarily combatants: war compositions were inspired by civilians' losses as much as by the experience of fighting. Herbert Howells, who was too ill to fight, wrote an *Elegy* for solo viola, string quartet and strings in 1917 in honour of his friend Francis Purcell Warren, a budding composer and accomplished viola player, who had been killed.

> " War compositions were inspired by civilians' losses as much as by the experience of fighting. "

Although he did not serve, Frank Bridge was deeply affected by the war and struggled to reconcile it with his pacifist beliefs. His *Piano Sonata* of 1921–4, dedicated to the memory of his friend, the composer Ernest Farrar, is in stark contrast to his pre-war work. It ushered in a new era for Bridge's composition, just as the war itself altered the society around him

RALPH VAUGHAN WILLIAMS AND THE FIRST WORLD WAR

KATE KENNEDY reveals the composer's attitude to the war and what led to the creation of his *Pastoral Symphony*

Vaughan Williams pictured in 1914 in military uniform, as a private in the Royal Army Medical Corps

When the First World War broke out, Ralph Vaughan Williams volunteered for the Special Constabulary, as did Elgar who, at 57, was far too old to fight. Vaughan Williams was also exempted, being over 40. But after a short while he enlisted for the nearest role he could get to active service, joining a Field Ambulance Unit in the Royal Army Medical Corps. It was a contentious decision. He could easily have remained a civilian and, like Holst, ensured that music-making continued at home.

Hubert Parry was singularly unimpressed:

> As to your enlisting, I can't express myself in any way that is likely to be serviceable. There are certain individuals who are capable of serving their country in certain very exceptional and very valuable ways, and they are not on the same footing as ordinary folks … such folks should be shielded from risk rather than exposed to it.

At first Parry had no cause for concern. Vaughan Williams's flat feet had him limited to duty as a lowly waggon orderly and he remained in England during the first two years of the war, and only sailed for France in the summer of 1916. On the eve of his embarkation, he wrote to his dearest friend, Gustav Holst:

> We are on the eve, all packed and ready – I can't say more. Write to me occasionally … Good luck to you – I feel that perhaps after the war England will be a better place for music than before – largely because we shan't be able to buy expensive performers etc like we did.

He made great friends with men from all kinds of backgrounds, accompanying one Private Harry Steggles, who played the mouth organ and entertained the men with such classics as 'When Father Papered the Parlour'. But by 1 July Vaughan Williams's war had become a serious business. He served during the now infamous Battle of the Somme, in which the British army lost some 60,000 men in the first day alone. He struggled through mud and darkness under fire to bring casualties back from the front line and into his motor ambulance, which had to dodge shell holes as it drove them away to casualty clearing stations. Many soldiers died before the journey was over. The sights and sounds were indescribable, and attempts to record them are notably absent from Vaughan Williams's correspondence. Yet out of this mixture of exhaustion and terror emerged his restrained and sorrowfully beautiful *Pastoral Symphony*.

> It's really wartime music – a great deal of it incubated when I used to go up night after night with the ambulance waggon at Écoivres and we went up a steep hill and there was a wonderful Corot-like landscape in the sunset.

In the autumn of 1916, after months on the Somme, Vaughan Williams was moved to Salonika, where he set up camp in the shadow of Mount Olympus in makeshift tents hung with sacks over the opening, and heated by stoves improvised from old pineapple tins filled with charcoal. There was little for the unit to do and plenty of time to reflect on the losses of the past few months, in particular his dear friend, the composer George Butterworth.

> I sometimes dread coming back to normal life with so many gaps – especially of course George Butterworth … I sometimes think now that it is wrong to have made friends with people much younger than oneself – because soon there will only be the middle aged left.

After a spell as a gunner back in France, Vaughan Williams found his musical abilities officially utilised by the army, who were keen to occupy the men in the tedious months after the armistice was declared, but before they were demobilised. In the summer of 1918 he was appointed Director of Music to the First Army and, by the time the volunteer army was disbanded, he had founded nine choral societies, an orchestra and a band.

irrevocably. In 1915 he had read about the torpedoing of the *Lusitania* and wrote the disturbing *Lament*, dedicated to a girl who had been a passenger on board and had drowned.

Not every composer wrote works that were dark and turbulent. Also in 1915 the public embraced Elgar's hearty setting of Rudyard Kipling's nautical *The Fringes of the Fleet*, musical and ideological worlds apart from Bridge's wartime compositions. A year later Elgar came closest to meeting *The Musical Times*'s demand for a war composition for the public to take to their hearts with *The Spirit of England* (1915–17), dedicated 'To the memory of our glorious men, with a special thought for the Worcesters'. In 1919 Gustav Holst wrote his *Ode to Death*, setting the last section of Walt Whitman's elegy on the death of Abraham Lincoln, 'When Lilacs Last in the Dooryard Bloom'd'. Holst dedicated the work to those he had lost in the war, setting Whitman's vision of resigned calm to slow-moving, luminous harmonies that suggest an infinite sense of space. Holst's great friend Ralph Vaughan Williams considered it to be his most beautiful choral work.

These works, in their different ways, set the standard for the shape of musical mourning in the 20th century. Although Britten was young enough that he barely remembered the First World War, it had a deep impact on him and his *War Requiem* (1961–2) is one of the most famous pieces of music written in connection with war. Britten links it specifically to the First World War with his settings of Wilfred Owen. Other composers' works bear a less obvious connection to the war and, without a text to pin down their meaning, were open to

The RMS *Lusitania* in a painting (1981) by Mike Tregenza: over 1,000 people died when the luxury ocean liner was torpedoed by a German submarine in 1915, prompting Frank Bridge to compose his *Lament*

interpretation. Vaughan Williams returned from serving as a medical orderly *(see opposite page)* and wrote his *Pastoral Symphony* in 1921 with the images of the landscape of northern France still fresh in his memory. The inspiration for the symphony came to him when stood on a small hill behind the lines looking out over the gently undulating landscape, seeing all the beauty and sorrow of a country ravaged by conflict.

Cultural historian Jay Winter believes that it is a misconception to think that societies can learn. For him, they simply contain individuals who remember a traumatic event such as a war and whose memories will, for

the time in which they are living, overlap with others. He writes: 'For this overlap to become a social phenomenon, it must be expressed and shared. In this sense, and in this sense alone, can one speak, again metaphorically, of collective memory.' This sharing takes the form of conversation and also expression, mainly through the arts. Each sculpture, composition, memoir or painting alters or reaffirms what we believed we knew as a society about the war. Each generation, from those returned from the trenches to those learning about the war a century on, will have a different and changing understanding of what the war meant and how it ought to be understood and represented.

MORRISON

2018 Solo Exhibitions

Clarendon Fine Art, London, March.
Scottish Art Portfolio, Dundas St Gallery, Edinburgh, April.
Corrymella Scott Gallery, Newcastle, May.
Castle Gallery, Rothesay, June.
Archway Gallery, Lochgilphead, August.
Walker Galleries, Harrogate, September.
The Glasgow Gallery, Glasgow, October.
Iona House Gallery, Woodstock, November.

Jolomo

www.jolomo.com

An art form that requires a particular collectivity, music brings together audience and performers to share the same experience, and has a special role to play in remembrance: no funeral or memorial ceremony would be complete without some form of music appropriate for the occasion, resonant with memory and connection for the congregation or audience. In the context of a memorial service or event, music is placed strategically between the specifics of the spoken word. It both complements text and serves an alternative purpose, creating mood, helping to stir the emotions of the congregation and allowing an often wordless space in which to contemplate readings and testimonies.

> " Music brings together audience and performers to share the same experience … No funeral or memorial ceremony would be complete without some form of music. "

Grief, when recent, can be overwhelming and boundless. Music acts as a delineated space in which to remember and mourn. It is experienced in real time, unlike a text, which, when read on the page, can be scanned at a glance, interrupted or re-read. Music carries its listener at its own speed and the listener must relinquish control as it is dictated to them, while also having the opportunity to pursue their own thoughts within this controlled space. In a society in which almost every family was mourning a relative, composers had a unique and essential role to play in shaping commemoration.

Music has a Proustian power to return the listener to a past event or time and is thus a particularly powerful tool in the process both of remembering and healing. The journalist H. V. Morton testified to this in 1927, when he witnessed a packed Royal Albert Hall at one of the first Festivals of Remembrance after the Armistice, in which demobilised combatants came together to sing the songs that had sustained them in the trenches and at sea. An ex-combatant himself, he found the power of the event overwhelming.

> We did not realise *until* last night that the songs we sang in the Army were bits of history. In them is embalmed the comic fatalism which carried us through four years of hell. How easily we slipped back into it! Cynicism was blown clean out of us. We were young once more as we can never be again and we went deeper into our memories … Thirteen years fell from us. We ceased to see the Albert Hall and the thousands of faces white in the arc lights; we looked into an abyss of memories where long columns passed and repassed over the dusty roads of France, where grotesque, unthinkable things happened day and night – the brief joys, the sharp sorrows of those days, the insane injustices of fate, and above it all the memory of the men we knew so well … It seemed to me that we had caught the only decent thing in the war – the spirit of comradeship. We had come to the hall as individuals; we were now once more an army marching in our imagination to the old music.

Music can connect and heal, or celebrate and mourn, and the generation of composers caught up in the First World War understood this, perhaps better than any other. Even 100 years on, music can transport us so we can march alongside them in our imagination. ●

Dr Kate Kennedy is a Research Fellow in Life-Writing at Wolfson College, Oxford. She has published widely on the music and literature of the First World War, is a regular broadcaster on the BBC and speaks at literary and music festivals. Her biography *Dweller in Shadows: Ivor Gurney* is due to be published this year.

Adapted from an article in *The Edinburgh Companion to the First World War and the Arts* (ed. Ann-Marie Einhaus and Katherine Isobel Baxter), published by Edinburgh University Press.

Holst The Planets; **Anna Meredith/ 59 Productions** Five Telegrams
BBC co-commission: world premiere
PROM 1 • 13 JULY

Holst Ode to Death;
Vaughan Williams Pastoral Symphony
PROM 17 • 27 JULY

Bridge Lament (Catherine, aged 9, 'Lusitania' 1915)
PROM 40 • 12 AUGUST

Vaughan Williams Dona nobis pacem
PROM 41 • 12 AUGUST

Holst Nunc dimittis; **Parry** Songs of Farewell
PROMS AT … CADOGAN HALL 6
20 AUGUST

Remembering the Dead

Brahms A German Requiem
PROM 33 • 7 AUGUST
Verdi Requiem
PROM 64 • 30 AUGUST
Britten War Requiem
PROM 72 • 6 SEPTEMBER

Inspiring the Future

CHARLOTTE GARDNER goes on the trail of the many ways in which Proms Learning supports emerging talent and participation for all the family this summer

Another year, another Proms Guide to enjoy exploring; and, while you're no doubt scouring these pages to see which international artists and ensembles are appearing, don't forget there is a huge number of young musicians performing alongside the professionals. Notice also the many participatory events for anyone looking to expand their musical knowledge beyond the concerts themselves. Learning and, in particular, developing the next generation of musicians, is central to the Proms' celebration of the best music-making of today.

Take the BBC Proms Youth Choir: comprising up to 300 young singers aged between 16 and 25, this ensemble is drawn from choirs around the country and offers the opportunity to take part in a major Proms performance; past concerts have included Elgar's *The Dream of Gerontius* with Sir Simon Rattle (2015) and John Adams's *Harmonium* with Edward Gardner (2017). Chorus Director Simon Halsey says: 'Every year, I look forward eagerly to meeting the Proms Youth Choir. They have a level of curiosity, engagement, enthusiasm and sheer

A Proms Session from 2017, featuring a masterclass given by Andy Grappy, Chineke!'s tuba player

talent that is deeply thrilling. This lively love for music is what the Proms is all about.'

On the menu for 2018 is Beethoven's Ninth Symphony with the World Orchestra for Peace conducted by Donald Runnicles (Prom 9), preceded by a new *a cappella* commission composed specially by Ēriks Ešenvalds and conducted by Simon Halsey.

> 66 Learning ... is central to the Proms' celebration of the best music-making of today. 99

Take a special look too at the BBC Proms Youth Choir Academy, a new initiative only in its second year. Open to singers aged between 16 and 25, it has the specific purpose of unearthing and developing new singers from all musical backgrounds but without previous experience of classical choral singing. While last year's pilot scheme centred on London and the South-East, this year the focus is on the North-East, with residential rehearsals hosted by Sage Gateshead – all with the aim of helping the

singers become members of the venue's own youth choir.

Turning to non-vocal music, the BBC Proms Youth Ensemble offers young instrumentalists of a high standard from across the UK the chance to perform alongside professional musicians in an all-new Proms commission. In 2017 they joined forces with New York's Bang on a Can All-Stars for the world premiere of Michael Gordon's *Big Space*. This year they'll be on stage at the First Night with the BBC Symphony Orchestra and Chorus, conducted by Sakari Oramo, performing Anna Meredith's First World War-themed *Five Telegrams*. Co-commissioned by the BBC Proms, 14–18 NOW and the Edinburgh International Festival, the work features spectacular digital projections created by 59 Productions.

This is Meredith's second collaboration with the BBC Proms Youth Ensemble, her first being *Smatter Hauler* in 2015 (when the youngsters were paired with the Aurora Orchestra), and she's thrilled to be working with the ensemble once more. 'I'll be aiming to both mesh them in with the BBC players and also give them a separate identity, to show what they can do,' she says. 'For instance, I'm looking beyond traditional orchestral instruments to brass-band players and percussionists, to give the group a slightly different colour.'

It's not just about opportunities for singers and instrumentalists, though. In fact, one of the most exciting Proms Learning opportunities of all is the BBC Proms Inspire Young Composers' scheme, which is celebrating its 20th anniversary this year. At its heart is the BBC Proms Inspire Competition, which offers its prizewinners an opportunity most composers can only dream of: to have their entry performed by professional musicians and broadcast on BBC Radio 3. They also receive a new BBC commission for another high-profile performance, with mentoring throughout the process from a professional composer.

The competition is open to 12- to 18-year-olds, with no restrictions on style or genre, or even requirements for previous experience. 'What we're looking for is imagination, individuality and character: someone who crafts and manages ideas, and technique shouldn't be a block to that,' emphasises composer Fraser Trainer, who has been on the competition's judging panel since its inception. For ultimate fairness, the entrants are also judged anonymously.

This year's entrants will be judged by Trainer himself, with fellow composers Kerry Andrew, Sally Beamish, Anna Meredith, Dobrinka Tabakova and Joby Talbot, plus BBC Proms Director David Pickard. The category winners will then have their pieces performed on 22 August by the Aurora Orchestra conducted by Christopher Stark in a free concert at the BBC Radio Theatre in London that will also feature the premieres of some of the pieces commissioned from last year's winners.

The BBC Proms Youth Choir on stage with the BBC Symphony Orchestra and Chorus at the First Night of the 2017 Proms; this year's First Night features the BBC Proms Youth Ensemble in a new work by Anna Meredith and 59 Productions

The volume of attention that past winners have enjoyed over the course of writing their new commissions is remarkable, as 2014 winner Sarah Gait remembers. 'I was asked to write a piece for small ensemble and solo trombone for BBC Symphony Orchestra players,' she says. 'And early on in the process we were given the chance to workshop various ideas with our instrumental groups; it was literally a case of taking along sketches and ideas and asking, "Can you do this with your instrument?", which doesn't usually happen in a professional context but is massively helpful for a young composer developing their musical vocabulary, writing for an instrument they might not know so well.' Furthermore, Gait attended all the workshops with an assigned mentor: composer Martin Suckling.

Beyond the competition, Inspire currently connects with over 400 young composers across the UK through a thriving online community. Also – crucially – it helps them via a nationwide programme of Inspire Sessions, where any young composer who has engaged with the scheme can receive pointers from professional composers and musicians. In particular, it was an Inspire Session led by composer Paul Griffiths that encouraged 2017 winner Sarah Jenkins to keep composing, after entering the competition in 2015 as an A-level student with limited composing experience. 'I decided to go to one of the Inspire Sessions anyway,' she explains. 'We were a group of about 30 people of all ages, and the day we had writing a piece together as a team felt so warm and open that it inspired me to enter again.' The year after that she was highly commended and the following year she was a winner.

For young musicians after something less intensive within the Proms period itself, there are the BBC Proms Sessions: a series of free workshops and masterclasses with some of the artists appearing at the Proms. The focus of these varies according to the artist, but they range from masterclasses through Q&As to practical music-making sessions. While participants are initially invited via partner groups, any spare places are released through the Proms website. Previous sessions have been led by musicians such as Laura Mvula and Jamie Cullum.

BBC Proms Learning is not all about young musicians, though. For instance, there's the Proms Scratch Orchestra, which anyone aged 16 or over can sign up to. Its 2018 activities include the opportunity to play side by side with members of the BBC Concert Orchestra conducted by Bernstein protégée Marin Alsop as part of the Bernstein centenary celebrations. Likewise, over-16s can sign up for the free Proms Sing events, led by professionals and often with support from members of the BBC Singers.

For younger ones, in addition to the various family and Ten Pieces Proms *(see pages 78–79)*, the participatory initiatives include workshops attached to specific Proms, and also the Proms Family Orchestra and Chorus.

So why not try something beyond concert-going this year? You never know where it may lead. ●

Charlotte Gardner is a freelance writer, journalist and critic. Among the publications she contributes to are *Gramophone*, *The Strad* and *Classical Music*. She is also the author of Touch Press's *Liszt Sonata in B Minor* and *Vivaldi's Four Seasons* apps.

OPPORTUNITIES FOR YOUNG PERFORMERS

BBC Proms Youth Choir for singers aged 16 to 25

BBC Proms Youth Ensemble for instrumentalists aged 16 to 25

BBC Proms Sessions, run in partnership with Royal Albert Hall Education & Outreach, for ages 14 to 25

Proms Family Chorus: *West Side Story*
Saturday 11 August, 10.30am–3.30pm, for ages 12 to 18

Proms Sessions are free but places must be booked in advance. Priority booking opens to partner groups in May and any remaining places can be booked at bbc.co.uk/proms from 10.00am on 22 June.

For further information, visit bbc.co.uk/proms

OPPORTUNITIES FOR YOUNG COMPOSERS

BBC Proms Inspire Scheme, for composers aged 12 to 18

Inspire Competition: deadline for entries is 24 May. Please visit bbc.co.uk/promsinspire for full terms and conditions.

Inspire Day: a full day of workshops and events on 22 August, 10.30am–4.00pm

Inspire Concert: hear the winning pieces from this year's competition on 22 August, 5.00pm–6.00pm

Proms Inspire Day is free but places must be booked in advance. Priority booking opens to partner groups in May and any remaining places can be booked at bbc.co.uk/proms from 10.00am on 22 June.

For further information, visit bbc.co.uk/promsinspire

OPPORTUNITIES FOR ADULTS

Proms Scratch Orchestra
Play Shostakovich side by side with members of the BBC Concert Orchestra conducted by Marin Alsop
Monday 27 August • 3.00pm–4.00pm; 4.30pm–5.30pm

Proms Sing
Folk music
Friday 3 August • 5.30pm–6.30pm

Ravel: L'enfant et les sortilèges
Saturday 18 August • 1.00pm–4.00pm

Music by Bernstein
Saturday 25 August • 1.00pm–4.00pm

Open to ages 16-plus. Events are free but places must be booked in advance. Booking opens at 10.00am on 22 June. Visit bbc.co.uk/proms or call 020 7765 0557

SHOWCASING YOUNG PERFORMERS

Alongside the many schemes led by BBC Proms Learning, there are numerous projects and ensembles working with young musicians from across the UK. With eight youth choirs featuring in 11 Proms and five youth ensembles performing in this season, there's plenty of diverse and remarkable talent to celebrate.

BBC Young Musician 40th Anniversary
Ravel, Saint-Saëns, Iain Farrington, etc.
Prom 3 • 15 July

Southend Boys' Choir and Southend Girls' Choir
Mahler: Symphony No. 8
Prom 11 • 22 July

Hallé Youth Choir
Debussy, Russian folk songs
Prom 16 • 26 July

Ten Pieces Children's Choir
Kerry Andrew, Orff

Creative responses to Elgar, Dvořák, Mason Bates
Proms 19 & 20 • 29 July

Finchley Children's Music Group
Tchaikovsky: The Nutcracker (Act 1)
Prom 25 • 2 August

National Youth Orchestra of Great Britain
Mussorgsky, George Benjamin, Ravel, Ligeti, Debussy
Prom 28 • 4 August

Students from ArtsEd and Mountview
Bernstein: West Side Story
Proms 38 & 39 • 11 August

CBSO Youth Chorus
Debussy: Nocturnes; Mahler: Symphony No. 3
Prom 44 • 15 August & Prom 67 • 2 September

National Youth Jazz Orchestra
Gershwin: Rhapsody in Blue
Prom 46 • 16 August

European Union Youth Orchestra
Agata Zubel, Chopin, Tchaikovsky
Prom 49 • 19 August

Restoration Drama

As the Proms witnesses the renewal of the Victorian Theatre at Alexandra Palace for Gilbert and Sullivan's courtroom comedy *Trial by Jury*, **KATE ROMANO** traces the history of the venue, constructed as part of the People's Palace, and now aptly returned to the people

On 9 June 1873 a devastating fire ripped through Alexandra Palace. The seven-acre glass-and-iron exhibition hall on London's Muswell Hill had only been open for 16 days. At 1.30pm the spectacular domed roof, measuring 53 metres wide, crashed 67 metres to the ground. As it fell, it demolished the huge organ designed by Henry Willis, modelled on his grand Royal Albert Hall organ. Willis was in Alexandra Palace at the time of the fire, risking his life amid falling red-hot shards of glass as he desperately tried to salvage some of the pipework from his creation. The sonic destruction of dome and organ was heard across many miles.

For the stoic, entrepreneurial Victorians, the fire was a setback – but also an opportunity to create a bigger, better recreation centre to rival the Crystal Palace south of the Thames at Sydenham Hill. Undaunted, the Alexandra Palace management team approved its rebuilding while the blackened silhouette of gaping circular windows and hollow triumphal arches still smouldered. The new building would have a concert hall, banqueting suite, lecture rooms, restaurants, galleries, an exhibition space, a small zoo, a new organ – and a huge theatre. North Londoners needed a state-of-the-art People's Palace for pleasure and entertainment, and building work began in earnest.

Meanwhile, a few miles away at the Royalty Theatre in Soho, the impresario Richard D'Oyly Carte was also in need of some fresh entertainment for his public. Lacking a short opera as an afterpiece to Offenbach's

Romantic ruin: the jewel of Alexandra Palace's East Wing, the Victorian Theatre, as it undergoes renovation; this summer the venue is host to a 'Proms at …' concert

La Périchole, he recalled a comic courtroom sketch by playwright W. S. Gilbert that had appeared some years ago in *Fun* magazine and suggested that composer Arthur Sullivan should write the music for it. With characteristic Victorian vim and vigour, the spring of 1875 saw both the reopening of Alexandra Palace – attended by 94,000 people, just 23 months after the fire – and the premiere at the Royalty of Gilbert and Sullivan's *Trial by Jury*, written in a few short weeks.

Trial by Jury, a short one-act comic opera about the defendant Edwin's heinous crime of breaking off an engagement, delightfully combined satire and silliness and was an instant hit. Gilbert drew heavily on his former profession as a barrister and it captured the spirit of the day with its characterful improbability (the Judge ends up offering to marry Edwin's spurned fiancée) and its familiar London setting. Peckham is described as an 'arcadian vale' and Camberwell as a 'bower': these references to prosaic, working-class suburbs drew as many chuckles from the Victorian audience as they might today.

Trial by Jury was the second operetta arising from the ingenious partnership of Gilbert and Sullivan (the score for *Thespis*, written four years earlier, is lost). Their new contract with D'Oyly Carte would prove lucrative, and their prolific output would help overcome the disrepute of Victorian British theatre which, at the time, largely consisted of poorly translated French operettas and badly written, prurient burlesques. Gilbert and Sullivan's 14 comic operas, direct descendants of music hall, were part of this ambition to make theatre a respectable domain for the bourgeoisie. Gilbert later recalled that he and Sullivan

'Put your briefs upon the shelf, I will marry her myself!': the Judge and the Plaintiff come to an irregular agreement in Gilbert and Sullivan's Trial by Jury

'made up our minds to do all in our power to wipe out the grosser element, never to let an offending word escape our characters'.

Alexandra Palace boldly embraced this transitional chapter in British theatrical history: the 1875 East Wing theatre was a huge, boxy space with seating for 2,500. An uneasy hybrid, its design resembled period music hall architecture with the addition of 'theatre style' elements, such as the proscenium arch flanked by classical niches of pilasters and statues. There was an awkwardness about its too-big, too-cavernous, well-meaning dimensions. The acoustics were poor and the sight-lines problematic.

Alasdair Beatson
Aurora Orchestra
(Resident at Kings Place)
Brodsky Quartet
Carducci Quartet
Cédric Tiberghien
Chiaroscuro Quartet
Explore Ensemble
Hugo Ticciati
(Artist-in-Residence)
Icebreaker
Iestyn Davies
Imogen Cooper
Instruments of
Time and Truth
John Tilbury
Lawrence Power
London Sinfonietta
Mary Bevan
Orchestra of the
Age of Enlightenment
O/Modernt
Rex Lawson
Roderick Williams
Songlines Encounters
Sonica Festival
The Sixteen
Víkingur Ólafsson

50+ concerts
100 musicians
1000 years of music

TIME
unwrapped

kingsplace.co.uk/time | follow us: 🐦 f 📷
90 York Way, London N1 9AG | ⊖ King's Cross
Box Office 020 7520 1490

Throughout 2018 at
kings place

But beneath and above the stage lies an entirely different story. The boards hide a complex wood-and-iron *Wunderkammer* (cabinet of curiosities) of rare mechanical devices. There are grave traps and corner traps (for disappearing in a puff of smoke), clever movable sections of stage floor for scenery to be winched on and off, counterweight and pulley systems. Look directly upwards from the central trapdoor (with its innovative 'lock iron' accident-prevention system) and you can see the fly and rigging loft platforms from which painted scenery would have been hoisted up and down and lavishly costumed fairies would have flown.

> 66 A new generation of audiences will enter this extraordinary world of faded grandeur. 99

Ironically, it was the failure of the theatre to be economically viable that ensured the survival of this remarkable box of tricks. Despite an opening succession of extravagant, exuberant music-hall pantomimes, plays and an 1876 production of *Trial by Jury* (with the original cast), it struggled to return a profit. A projection box was installed and from 1910 to 1914 the theatre became a cinema, the stage mechanisms remaining intact mostly through neglect and under use. During the First World War the theatre became a centre for Belgian refugees and, during the Second, an internment camp for German prisoners. It was leased to the BBC in 1935, largely for storage, until the Corporation moved out in 1950. The theatre then went dark.

In 1980 Alexandra Palace suffered another huge fire that raged around the disused theatre, leaving it curiously unharmed. Palace staff tell the story of a firefighter who apparently gave orders for the crew to focus their efforts on saving the theatre. Whether it was a result of this call to arms, the fact that the wind was blowing in their favour or the more plentiful supply of water on the east side of the Palace, the theatre slept on, its gentle process of natural decay uninterrupted.

On Saturday 1 September a new generation of audiences will gain a first glimpse of this extraordinary space before its restoration is fully completed. Thanks to a £26 million East Wing development, the theatre is being painstakingly restored and preserved. The faded pink and cream paint on the walls dates back to a 1922 update but flakes away to reveal ghostly layers of 1875 stencil-work. Crumbling elaborate plaster, time-worn timber boards and the ornate fleur-de-lys pattern on the ceiling carry a visual and emotional imprint of history. The transfiguration of the theatre from youthful ungainliness to mature elegance is as mystical and wondrous as any stage-mechanical illusion.

'There's a fascination frantic, In a ruin that's romantic,' sings Ko-Ko to Katisha in Gilbert and Sullivan's *The Mikado* (1885). The ruin was a romantic notion for the Victorians, a symbol of a previous life, of vulnerability and mortality. But today the modern ruin has a different meaning, with an appeal that comes from its organic quality: a living, tactile entity in contrast to the sleek contemporary towers of glass and steel. Or maybe the special synergy lies in the curious ability of ruins to tell of multiple futures and pasts? They animate and excite us because they offer

untold stories, allowing our imaginations to explore the journey into a parallel world.

Into this highly charged atmosphere comes *Trial by Jury*, still charmingly turning the legal system on its head almost 150 years after its premiere. In its 'Proms at … Alexandra Palace' performance, music that once sought a niche bourgeois audience is performed in a People's Palace created to enrich the lives of thousands. The topsy-turvy world of Gilbert and Sullivan has never seemed so fitting or complete. ●

Kate Romano is a producer, clarinettist and writer. Previously a senior member of academic staff at the Guildhall School of Music & Drama, she is currently the Artistic Director of Goldfield Productions.

Gilbert and Sullivan Trial by Jury
BBC Singers, BBC Concert Orchestra/ Jane Glover
PROMS AT …
ALEXANDRA PALACE • 1 SEPTEMBER

Other 'Proms at …' events

Works by Ives and Stravinsky, plus new commissions by composers from countries that were involved in both sides of the First World War
London Sinfonietta/George Benjamin
PROMS AT …
ROUNDHOUSE, CAMDEN • 21 JULY

Stravinsky's wartime fable *The Soldier's Tale* staged at Lincoln's Grade II-listed former military training centre
Hebrides Ensemble/William Conway
PROMS AT …
LINCOLN DRILL HALL • 4 AUGUST

Contemporary Collaborations

Over the past seven seasons Jules Buckley has performed at the Proms alongside leading musicians ranging from Quincy Jones to Jacob Collier. He talks to TIM RUTHERFORD-JOHNSON about the art of exploring themes for artistic collaboration

Jules Buckley conducting the Scott Walker Prom last summer with the Heritage Orchestra

Performing 'Billie Jean' at the Quincy Jones Prom in 2016 is an obvious highlight in Jules Buckley's association with the Metropole Orkest: Michael Jackson's song marked the climax to a concert Buckley described at the time as one of the greatest honours of his career. Watching the video from that performance today, the grin that breaks out on his face as the keyboardist and vocalist Cory Henry and pianist Jacob Collier begin to play is unmissable. Yet the real tribute to his skills as an arranger (and to Henry's performance) is that it takes the Royal Albert Hall audience a full minute to recognise what they're hearing. Henry's vocal ('Billie Jean is not my lover') is their first clue, and Buckley's arrangement withholds the vamping groove that is the most immediately recognisable feature of Jackson's original until its final verse. That trick makes it more memorable still, and stamps Buckley's imprint on the music.

Buckley began appearing with the Netherlands' Metropole Orkest – a specialist jazz and pop orchestra founded in 1945 by the Dutch conductor Dolf van der Linden – in 2008 and became its Chief Conductor in 2013. Before this, in 2004, he co-founded the Heritage Orchestra with producer Chris Wheeler, and continues as its conductor and principal arranger. His first appearance at the Proms was in 2010, when the BBC Symphony Orchestra supported Jamie Cullum's Proms debut concert, and since then both Heritage and Metropole have made regular appearances, notably in the Urban Classic

Prom in 2013, Radio 1 Ibiza Prom with Pete Tong in 2015 and the Scott Walker Prom last year, as well as sharing the stage with Laura Mvula in 2014.

I call the audience's reaction during that Quincy Jones night a 'tribute', because Buckley's aim with both orchestras is not to produce simple imitations of pop recordings, in the symphony-orchestra-goes-pop mould that was fashionable in the 1970s and 1980s. 'The modern exploratory approach,' he explains to me by phone from his home in Berlin, 'takes into account all the musicians on stage and the potential that comes with that.'

'It's the difference between an orchestra and a classical orchestra,' he goes on. 'With the Pete Tong concert, for example, we didn't invest any classical music into the project. We invested the techniques and methods of players who have a classical background but it was fundamentally not a classical reworking.' So, while Metropole Orkest and the Heritage Orchestra both feature up to 60 trained musicians, divided into groups of wind, strings, brass and percussion – they both look like symphony orchestras, more or less – they don't share the same responsibility to history and tradition as does a classical orchestra.

One big difference is in the orchestras' rhythm sections. This is not something a traditional orchestra will have, yet Metropole Orkest has two, one for jazz and one for pop and rock. The Heritage Orchestra is also built around its rhythm section – 'You can think of the Heritage Orchestra as a massive band,' says Buckley – and it is key to the group's creative process.

'Once we find an artist we want to collaborate with, we thrash out with them a hit list of

Wanna be startin' somethin': Quincy Jones, Jules Buckley and the Metropole Orkest in rehearsal for their 2016 Prom

tunes. Then we go into the studio with our band, Chris Wheeler and I, and we essentially dissect all the core parts of those pieces. Rather than transcribe the songs and just play them, instead we pull apart the track, a bit like pulling apart a car. Every nut and bolt is taken out and looked at. Then we come up with a concept in which we play some parts of these compositions and we build a new car out of them.'

The orchestra's core players are closely involved throughout this phase. 'The next stage is to jam those ideas with the band, then start to arrange them,' Buckley explains. 'It knocks back and forth for

a bit – a bit like making a record, actually.' Although everything is eventually written down in full score – even the drum tracks might be specified in detail – the process is much closer to the collaborative, ad hoc vibe of a recording studio than the lonely composer at their piano. This continues even after the full orchestra is involved. 'Once we've got a master score from those rehearsal tapes we get into the room with everybody and kind of hack it out. All the time we're making changes – almost right up to the concert.'

Other elements start to come into play at this stage, too. The details of how sounds

EXPERIENCE ALL OF LONDON
WITH A PERFECT CHAMPAGNE MOMENT

Visit our website for details on our latest offers
theviewfromtheshard.com

THE VIEW

FROM THE SHARD

Set to stun: the rapper Fazer lives up to his name at the Urban Classic Prom with the BBC Symphony Orchestra in 2013

should blend into one another, for example; the specifics of microphone placement (the Heritage Orchestra always plays amplified); ideas about lighting. The process can get quite archaeological: for last year's Scott Walker Prom, a large part of the process was figuring out exactly what instruments (including mandolins, 12-string guitars, steel guitars and more) had been used on Walker's original recordings and in which combinations – often several at once.

> **66** You shut yourself away, losing friends and weight while you spend months writing out the third clarinet part. **99**

With Walker, the aim was to stay close to the late-1960s originals. 'There are some things you don't want to touch,' says Buckley. 'That

was the thinking behind that Prom – let's not mess with this music because it's incredible [Walker's first four albums were originally arranged by Angela Morley, known then as Wally Stott], and that dark and melancholic sound is something everybody is longing to hear.' In this instance, Buckley's role was much more like that of a traditional arranger. 'You take the vinyl, get the best headphones money can buy and shut yourself away in a top-floor room, losing friends and weight while you spend months painstakingly writing down the third clarinet part,' he jokes.

At the other extreme, however, lie examples such as his 2016 version of 'Billie Jean'. That was an instance, Buckley explains, of trying 'to find a track where I could instantly hear the potential for it to go down another avenue. Of course,' he continues, 'when you're pulling apart "Billie Jean" and you know Quincy Jones is going to be in the house, that's a pretty risky endeavour!' The inspiration in this case came from Henry. 'Cory had a really strong idea for components

that he wanted to put back together. So he reharmonised the song and we slowed it down a bit, then I started working on an orchestral arrangement. We wanted to avoid any comparison to Michael Jackson because no-one is ever going to top that. We felt it really needed to go somewhere else.'

This way of thinking is based in the recording studio, I suggest: building songs out of individual tracks or, in the case of the dance music used in the Pete Tong Prom, groups of samples. 'Yes,' Buckley agrees, 'but, if you look back over the classical repertory, that approach of pulling something apart and putting it back together was as prevalent then as it is today in the studio. That idea of taking raw material and messing with it I think has been around for ever: take Vaughan Williams's *Fantasia on a Theme by Thomas Tallis*. It's just that in the studio the process is documented more – you can read about how Phil Collins made that particular gated snare sound but you can't read about Vaughan Williams's intentions with his Tallis theme.' We wait to hear what Buckley has up his sleeve for his two concerts this year, but in more ways than one both Metropole Orkest and the Heritage Orchestra are fast becoming part of the Proms' long and evolving tradition. ●

Tim Rutherford-Johnson is author of *Music after the Fall: Modern Composition and Culture since 1989* (University of California Press) and editor of the *Oxford Dictionary of Music*, sixth edition. He blogs about contemporary music at johnsonsrambler.wordpress.com.

Jacob Collier and Friends
Metropole Orkest/Jules Buckley
PROM 7 • 19 JULY

New York: Sound of a City
Heritage Orchestra/Jules Buckley
PROM 35 • 8 AUGUST

Magical Moments

Whether you're going on a musical journey in the Ten Pieces Proms, relaxing at a Sunday matinee or participating in a family workshop (whatever your ability), there's something for all the family at this year's BBC Proms, as **ANDREW McCALDON** reveals

S ometimes it grabs you in a mighty hug, sometimes it creeps up on you quietly, sometimes you suddenly realise you've stopped breathing. When a musical experience first sparks your imagination and your emotions, there's no chance of forgetting it: it's going to burn brightly in your life from then on – just try stopping it.

It's a magical moment when you see a young person inspired by music – and there's no better place for them to discover the excitement and power of live classical music than at the BBC Proms. This year's season features some fantastic concerts designed especially for families and young people with a whole bundle of ways for everyone, whatever your age, to participate in making music. With all tickets half-price for under-18s (except for the Last Night of the Proms) and £6.00 Promming (standing) tickets always available on the day, the doors of the spectacular Royal Albert Hall are wide open to everyone.

If you want to see the impact of music on young people, then the Ten Pieces Proms are a great place to start. The BBC's groundbreaking initiative is continuing to help millions of children – fearless, imaginative and already seizing the future of classical music – to discover and create orchestral music throughout the UK. The Ten Pieces website (bbc.co.uk/tenpieces) is a treasure trove of resources that can be explored all year round.

For this year's Ten Pieces Proms the BBC Symphony Orchestra, the ever-amazing Ten Pieces Children's Choir and CBBC presenter

Jessica Cottis conducting the Royal Philharmonic Orchestra at one of last year's Ten Pieces Proms

Naomi Wilkinson will go on an exploration into some exhilarating music. Along with special guests, audiences will be transported to the majestic landscapes of Sibelius's *Finlandia*, party with cowboys and cowgirls in the 'Hoe-Down' from Copland's *Rodeo*, meet a very mysterious creature in Mason Bates's 'The A Bao A Qu' (from his *Anthology of Fantastic Zoology*) and get their spines tingled by Carl Orff's dramatic 'O Fortuna' from *Carmina burana*. At the heart of the concert will be young people themselves, showing the incredible work they have created as part of this year's project.

After its huge success last year, the Relaxed Prom is back. Presented by the Bournemouth Symphony Orchestra in partnership with the Royal Albert Hall's Education & Outreach team, this is a wonderful opportunity to enjoy orchestral music in a more informal setting. Making noise is just fine at this Prom and the audience is free to move about, to dance, sing along or just to listen. Absolutely everyone will feel welcome, including family members of all ages, children and adults with autism, sensory and communication impairments and learning disabilities, as well as individuals who are Deaf or hearing impaired, blind or partially sighted or living with dementia. Staged as part of a weekend celebrating the work of Leonard Bernstein – a constant champion of bringing music to new audiences – the Relaxed Prom presents marvels by Bernstein himself, John Williams, Tchaikovsky and many more, as well as the Bournemouth Symphony Orchestra's trailblazing disabled-led ensemble, BSO Resound.

Starting earlier in the day than the regular evening concerts, the Sunday matinees during the Proms season are a perfect way to bring

Instrumental activity: schoolchildren from Wales on stage with presenter Andy Pidcock at last year's Relaxed Prom

the whole family to concerts full of fabulous and accessible orchestral music. Be dazzled by the inspiring performers of the European Union Youth Orchestra, or hear Mahler conjure music as vast and beautiful as the world itself in his thrilling Symphony No. 3.

As well as listening to music, there are plenty of free opportunities to create it too. Why not get involved and make your debut with the Proms Family Orchestra and Chorus? In these fun family sessions, led by professional musicians, you can make music together with a full orchestra and choir. Bring along an instrument if you've got one but no musical experience is necessary. You could end up singing Kerry Andrew's joyous *No Place Like*, creating your own version of Bach's luminous Brandenburg Concertos or playing at the magnificent Alexandra Palace.

You can also get your hands on some instruments and gain fascinating insights into some of the music featured in the season by heading along to one of the popular Family Workshops held before the concerts. This year's workshops include the chance to rumble with the Jets and the Sharks in Bernstein's pulsating *West Side Story*, and to explore Gypsy dances (with some help

from Liszt and Brahms). Remember, too, if you're watching or listening to the Proms at home, there are lots of online resources to help you enjoy every concert to the full.

With so many ways to get involved, why not bring your family along to the Proms this year and set out on an orchestral adventure? The music is there waiting for you! Get ready to fire your imagination and experience some magical moments of your own. ●

Andrew McCaldon is the writer for the BBC's Ten Pieces project, scripting two films and the three Ten Pieces Proms to date. He has also written two series of BBC Two's *Poetry: Between the Lines*, both of which won a Children's BAFTA.

PROMS FAMILY WORKSHOPS

At Imperial College Union. Family-friendly introductions to the music of the evening's Prom. Bring an instrument or just sit back and take it all in. (Suitable for ages 7-plus.)

Sunday 15 July, 5.15pm–6.00pm

Thursday 2 August, 5.15pm–6.00pm

Monday 6 August, 5.15pm–6.00pm

Saturday 11 August, 1.45pm–2.30pm

Sunday 12 August, 2.15pm–3.00pm

Thursday 23 August, 5.45pm–6.30pm

No booking is necessary. Entry is on a first-come first-served basis. Doors open 30 minutes before the event begins; capacity is limited. Events end one hour before the start of the following Proms concert.

PROMS FAMILY CHORUS

Sunday 29 July, 10.30am–12.00pm:
Kerry Andrew *No Place Like*

PROMS FAMILY ORCHESTRA & CHORUS

Sunday 5 August, 11.00am–1.00pm:
Bach's Brandenburg Concertos

Saturday 1 September, 11.00am–1.00pm:
Alexandra Palace Family Orchestra

At Imperial College Union. Suitable for children aged 7-plus and their families. Entry is free but places must be booked in advance. Booking opens at 10.00am on 22 June. Visit bbc.co.uk/proms, call 020 7765 0557 or email getinvolved@bbc.co.uk. If you are attending a related Prom, tickets must be purchased.

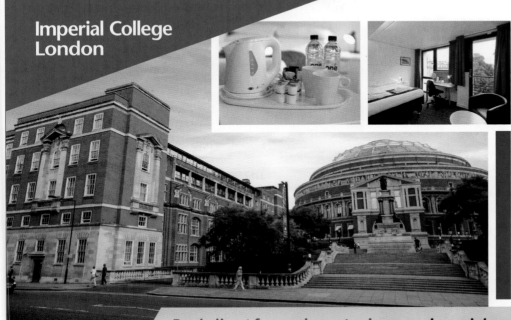

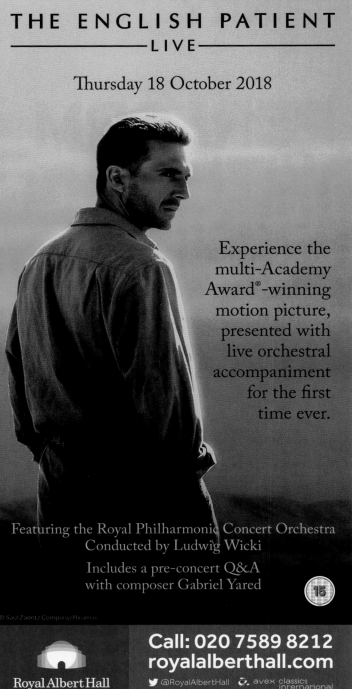

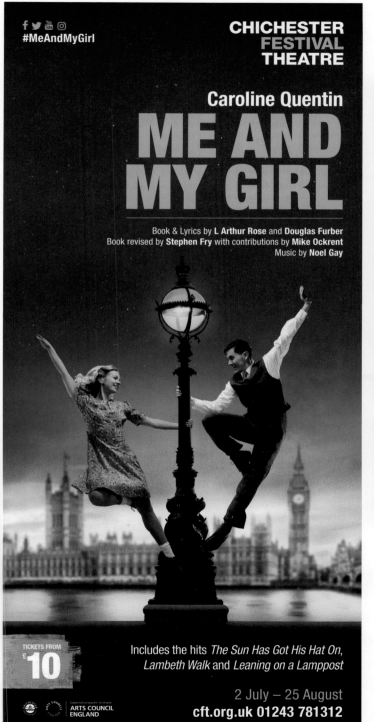

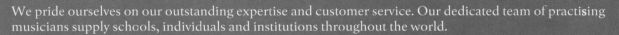

All Types of Beethoven

With orchestras of various sizes and outlooks bringing their individual colouring to Beethoven's symphonies, **TOM SERVICE** looks at how these pillars of the repertoire can stand up to – and even demand – a variety of approaches

A kaleidoscope of interpretations: however you piece the symphonies together, the white-hot inspiration of Beethoven's musical imagination still shines through

Beethoven, O Beethoven! Pity the poor conductor! I know, not words that you hear that often – the maestros up there on the Royal Albert Hall's podium always seem to generate the most applause and the greatest plaudits, despite the fact that they haven't played a single note and yet often seem to have more fun than any of the other musicians on stage. But, when they're about to lead a performance of a Beethoven symphony, I think we should feel some sympathy for our humble (and occasionally not-so-humble) conductors, because they're putting themselves in the most exposing position they can as musicians.

By conducting Beethoven, they are asking for their performances on this particular occasion – this Promenade concert, what's more – to be compared to the entire pantheon of previous interpretations, and not just at the Proms, but in recorded history. These conductors are set on a more Platonic quest as well: to try to reveal something new about Beethoven's symphonies, which have already been turned and polished and illuminated from countless angles. They want to make us feel that we are coming face to face with the white-hot edge of musical inspiration that defines these symphonies, not so much pieces of music as politico-cultural earthquakes in orchestral sound.

So how to prepare your Beethoven if you're a conductor? It's very, very hard. The performances at the Proms this year reveal a range of approaches and ideologies about playing Beethoven's music – and I do mean 'ideologies': the interpretative decisions made by conductors and orchestras are never so freighted with historical consequence as they are with Beethoven's symphonies.

Why is Beethoven's music such a litmus test for conductors? It's because the art of the conductor as interpreter, as modern-day maestro – with all of its sometimes unfortunate associations of ego, power and chicanery – was born in the fiery crucibles of Beethoven's symphonies. In the early decades of the 19th century, as these symphonies began their all-conquering progress over Europe and the rest of the world's concert halls, the first real battles about musical interpretation emerged in classical music, above all in the writings of that noted polemicist, provocateur and ever-controversial composer, Richard Wagner. Wagner's essay 'On Conducting' is, among other things, a plea for the proper performance of Beethoven's music. Astonishingly – or perhaps not, if you know him – Wagner's treatise is a vindication of his flexible, expressive approach to the performance of Beethoven's symphonies, as opposed to the kapellmeisterish inflexibility of Felix Mendelssohn's conducting. He talks about sitting next to Mendelssohn during a performance of Beethoven's Eighth Symphony in Dresden; Mendelssohn approved of the conductor's approach but Wagner talks about hearing 'an abyss of superficiality, a veritable void'. By contrast, Wagner's Beethoven is, in his terms, the real Beethoven.

Yet Wagner's intellectual and musical approach – which also includes a rampant, racist chauvinism – is only one of the most extreme versions of the sort of thing that every conductor ever since has been saying about their vision of Beethoven's symphonies. Most maestros believe, like Wagner, that they are releasing the potential of the notes of the score, divining Beethoven's will, not – heaven forfend! – indulging their own interpretative whims. That's what Gustav Mahler thought he was doing when he retouched Beethoven's orchestrations to make them fit the sound-world of the 20th-century orchestra, something that would make today's paragons of textual fidelity come out in a cold sweat.

> **Interpretative decisions are never so freighted with historical consequence as they are with Beethoven.**

But, you might ask, how is it possible, if everyone is supposedly serving the music first and themselves second, that performances of, say, Beethoven's Fifth Symphony at the Proms can be as different as Daniel Barenboim's with the West–Eastern Divan Orchestra in 2012 – full of orchestral sensuality as well as barnstorming sonic power – and Mirga Gražinytė-Tyla's with the City of Birmingham Symphony Orchestra last year – a performance of punchy energy and lithe textures? Or, from a more distant past, how can performances such as Wilhelm Furtwängler's, whose Ninth Symphony is a massive, cosmic coming-into-being, and Arturo Toscanini's, whose recordings of the same piece are like violent catapults of power and energy, be in the service of the same composer, since they make the supposedly single phenomenon of 'Beethoven's Ninth Symphony' sound like two radically different pieces?

The answer is: they can't! Furtwängler's Beethoven is a different person, a different conception, from Toscanini's, as is Gražinytė-Tyla's from Barenboim's, Sir John Eliot Gardiner's from Nikolaus Harnoncourt's or Sir Roger Norrington's from Riccardo Chailly's. It all means that Beethoven is really 'Beethoven', somebody who is remade in different musical and cultural images by all of these conductors.

The problem in the past was the idea that there was a right way and a wrong way to play Beethoven. And, if Wagner's ideologies held sway for much of the late 19th century into the early 20th, in recent decades there has been another quasi-orthodoxy, which has emerged from the embers of the period-instrument movement. Beethoven was again the touchstone for the sound and seismology of what it meant to hear music performed on the historical instruments for which it was originally written. Leaner and lither than their modern counterparts, these early instruments were played in the 1980s and 1990s by musicians who returned to Beethoven's previously ignored metronome markings. It's a cliché to say that everything got faster, because some movements of his symphonies – including parts of the choral finale of the Ninth – are actually marked to be played slower than we usually hear them. And what was revealed by the avant-gardistes of period-instrument

A panel from the *Beethoven Frieze*, created by Gustav Klimt (1862–1918) for a 1902 Vienna Secessionist exhibition marking the 75th anniversary of the composer's death

Beethoven performance, such as Sir Roger Norrington with the London Classical Players and Sir John Eliot Gardiner with his Orchestre Révolutionnaire et Romantique, wasn't simply a didactic exercise in obeying a metronome: their mission was rather about restoring a sharper, more violent, more shocking Beethoven to our concert halls and to our imaginations.

If previous generations of musicians and listeners wanted their Beethoven to start and end in a place of lofty transcendence, where Furtwängler's performances were always situated and where Christian Thielemann's attempt to reside today, progressive early-music conductors wanted

to emphasise the hard facts of tempo markings and articulation details in new, cleaned-up editions of these symphonies. As well as its practical and technological dimensions – out with the modern, in with the truly new in the sounds of old instruments – the early-music project was about re-grounding Ludwig van Beethoven as a composer of his time and his place, and, therefore, of ours. And what Norrington did for period-instrument ensembles, Nikolaus Harnoncourt achieved with the modern instruments of the Chamber Orchestra of Europe in the mid-1990s, showing that it was possible to cut through the luxurious culture of

conventional orchestral instruments with a sharp-edged musical dagger of sheer, Beethovenian extremity.

For some, this debate about how to play Beethoven amounted to a reductive either/or, so that you were either a signed-up member of the period-instrument camp or a purveyor of so-called 'big-band' Beethoven, the sound-world of the old school of Beethovenian interpretation on their old-fashioned modern instruments. That's what Daniel Barenboim clearly felt in 2012, when he said at a Proms press conference that he refuted what he thought of as the totalitarianism of the period-instrument orthodoxy.

Yet the crucial realisation of recent decades in our collective vision of Beethoven is of a radical multiplicity, in which conductors and audiences are no longer searching for the one true path to Beethovenian enlightenment but, instead, accept the variety of ways in which these pieces can be played and heard: equally definitively, yet always differently. That's also why open-minded musicians such as Daniel Harding, Riccardo Chailly, Marin Alsop and Jonathan Nott refuse distinctions between categories and choose to learn from both – and more – sides of the Beethovenian spectrum of interpretation. That's why today's performances of Beethoven's symphonies, individually and collectively, are arguably more extreme and simultaneously more open-minded than they have been at any point in their history. It may have taken us a couple of centuries or so but we're finally mature enough as a musical culture to accept that the performance history of Beethoven's symphonies is always about 'and' rather than 'or': we listeners are the lucky ones who don't have to decide between these interpretations but can instead relish the revelations of wildly divergent approaches to these pieces. That's where the 'truth' lies, rather than in any single idea or ideology about how these symphonies go.

That richness of musical, intellectual and emotional vision is precisely what the four conductors running the Beethovenian gauntlet at this year's Proms demonstrate. There's a huge diversity of interpretative visions, from Donald Runnicles with the all-star World Orchestra for Peace and the BBC Proms Youth Choir in the Ninth Symphony, a performance of no doubt all-encompassing dimensions and sumptuous sonorities, to Teodor Currentzis with his period-instrument collective from Perm in Russia, MusicAeterna, in the Second and Fifth. Currentzis's music-making always sears with an epiphanic sense of the unexpected and the essential. For him, the spirit of Beethoven's symphonies will be animated by a refusal to take for granted any pre-conceived idea about how this music goes.

Yet the most risky way of performing Beethoven's symphonies at the Proms is arguably the Prom that Joshua Bell will lead with the Academy of St Martin in the Fields. Bell directs the Fourth Symphony from the leader's desk – or, rather, the leader's piano stool – and commands his orchestra with the dynamism, unpredictability and energy of an expanded string quartet, ducking in and out of the *tuttis* as a player, directing and conducting the Fourth Symphony with a spirit of discovery and revelation. 'I had never seen anybody conduct them this way, so I didn't have anything to model it on,' he says. 'It creates a very visceral experience. I choose moments where I drop out and conduct the rest of the orchestra with my bow, and suddenly join them again. Beethoven is so full of contrasts, with *fortissimos* following *pianissimos*, that it's very powerful to be able to dramatise the music like this.'

For Kirill Petrenko, Beethoven's Seventh Symphony is his calling-card at the Proms with his new orchestra, the Berlin Philharmonic. Talk about a chalice brimful of expectation: not only a symphony that Carlos Kleiber and Claudio Abbado made their own but an orchestra that lives by its ownership of the musical tradition whose alpha and omega remain Beethoven's symphonies. There will be no more anticipated performance in this season's Proms, and none more exquisitely pressurised.

Petrenko's Beethoven performance, and all of the symphonies at the Proms this year, will collectively reveal the one truth we can really speak of in the performance history of Beethoven's symphonies: that these pieces remain essential to us because we continually remake and reinterpret them, just as we reshape and refashion ourselves. And there's no more coruscating arena – or Arena – in which to confront this creative renewal than the Royal Albert Hall. ●

Tom Service writes about music for *The Guardian* and since 2003 has been the presenter of Radio 3's flagship magazine programme, *Music Matters*. His two most recent books are *Music as Alchemy* and *Thomas Adès: Full of Noises*.

Symphony No. 9, 'Choral'
BBC Proms Youth Choir, World Orchestra for Peace/Donald Runnicles
PROM 9 • 21 JULY

Symphonies Nos. 2 & 5
MusicAeterna/Teodor Currentzis
PROM 18 • 28 JULY

Symphony No. 4
Academy of St Martin in the Fields/ Joshua Bell (violin/director)
PROM 40 • 12 AUGUST

Symphony No. 7
Berliner Philharmoniker/Kirill Petrenko
PROM 68 • 2 SEPTEMBER

Brandenburgs Old and New

PAUL GRIFFITHS reports on a Swedish-led project to imbue Bach's popular Brandenburg Concertos with new life, spurring a series of partner works commissioned from six of today's most innovative composers

Brandenburg is the region of Germany around Berlin. It is also, of course, a gate in that city. To most readers of this festival guide, though, it will be first and foremost a set of six concertos that Johann Sebastian Bach sent in 1721 to Christian Ludwig, Margrave of Brandenburg, evidently in the hope of employment. As his father's youngest son, Christian Ludwig inherited no throne. He was, however, able to live comfortably in the family capital of Berlin, thanks to the income he received from estates left him by his mother – comfortably enough to maintain a house orchestra, for his main interest in life, apart from soldiering, was music.

We do not know if he had Bach's concertos performed, only that nothing came of the composer's gesture, and Bach had to wait another couple of years before finding a new job, in Leipzig. Meanwhile, the beautifully written-out scores were put away in the margrave's library, sold after his death, and not rediscovered until 1849. They therefore remained unheard right through the lifetimes of everyone from Haydn to Mendelssohn, waiting to amaze a distant age.

Composers of Bach's time commonly wrote instrumental works in sets of six to display variety within uniformity (Bach's own solo pieces for violin and cello provide examples), but the Brandenburg Concertos do not fit this kind of plan. They are at once not various enough, repeating keys (Nos. 1 and 2 are both in F major, Nos. 3 and 4 both in G major),

Frederick the Great playing the flute in a court setting similar to that in which Bach's Brandenburg Concertos may have first been performed: Princess Anna Amalia, who for a period owned the manuscript scores of the Brandenburg Concertos, is seated, second from left (painting by Adolph Menzel, 1815–1905)

Brand-new Brandenburgers: the six composers involved in the Swedish Chamber Orchestra's project (*from left*), Uri Caine, Brett Dean, Anders Hillborg, Steven Mackey, Olga Neuwirth and Mark-Anthony Turnage

and altogether too various, notably in their scoring. While Nos. 3 and 6 are for small groups of strings plus keyboard, the two concertos in F major have prominent parts for woodwind and brass players. All that unites them – and it is enough – is that they fulfilled Bach's criteria for a job application. He had met the margrave two years earlier, on a visit to Berlin with his current employer, Prince Leopold of Anhalt-Cöthen. Now, to impress a prince better placed, he almost certainly looked back through his output of a decade or more to find works of the greatest splendour and energy.

The Brandenburg Concertos were challenging models indeed for Gregor Zubicky, Artistic Manager of the Swedish Chamber Orchestra, to offer to six present-day composers, with the brief that each should write a 'partner work' for one of them, using the same ensemble. The resulting six pieces take their places as partners, sufficiently separate not to be overwhelmed, though in some cases

sneaking sideways looks at the model with which they resonate.

Zubicky left it to the composers to decide what solo instrument or instruments to write for, if any. Mark-Anthony Turnage settled on the cello, and even on a particular cellist, Maya Beiser, whose first name he made his title. He followed the brief in writing for the orchestra of Brandenburg No. 1, though to entirely different effect. In place of the brightness and bounce with which Bach opened his selection, *Maya* offers lament, out of a warm cello darkness that, led by the soloist, is echoed by the orchestra, whose cellos are often in four parts.

The American composer Steven Mackey, charged with partnering the second Brandenburg, takes over the same group of soloists, on piccolo trumpet, flute, oboe and violin, and includes Bach's omnipresent harpsichord. As in the outer movements of

the Bach prototype, the trumpeter is to the fore, but now playing on regular trumpet and suave flugelhorn as well as the spectacular piccolo instrument. Hence the work's title: *Triceros* (three-horned). Concurring with his soloist Håkan Hardenberger that 'no instrument depicts solitary melancholy better than the trumpet', Mackey explores a space between Bach and blues in a single movement of flexible character. He also makes it possible for his piece to follow directly on from its Brandenburg counterpart, the piccolo trumpet projecting a high C from the end of one piece into the beginning of the other.

Anders Hillborg, a fellow countryman of the orchestra's, takes a different view of connection in his *Bach Materia*, quoting from Brandenburg No. 3 and considering its ideas within a wider historical frame. 'There is music from Bach's concerto,' he says, 'as well as music written in his spirit, and my own.' He also expands the resources, from Bach's nine-piece string group to a full body of triple the size, and draws out a solo violin part for Pekka Kuusisto, whose skills as an improviser are given free rein in some passages. At the request of the Swedish Chamber Orchestra's Chief Conductor, Thomas Dausgaard, Hillborg also wrote a slow movement for his Brandenburg, which lacks one, and this music, too, filters into his piece.

As an Austrian, Olga Neuwirth is closest to Bach in geographical terms, and yet her contribution, partnered with Brandenburg No. 4, is surely the wildest. From Bach's solo group of violin and two *fiauti d'echo*, or 'echo flutes', she accepts the flutiness, making hers a virtuoso concerto in which the flautist Claire Chase can skid through new sounds. However, she believes that by 'echo flutes'

Christian Ludwig, Margrave of Brandenburg, for whom Bach wrote his six Brandenburg Concertos

Bach may have meant a double pipe better represented by two trumpets, which she places alongside a string ensemble, harpsichord and – uncommon to Bach – musical wine glasses and a mechanical typewriter. This and the music's dizzying rotations respond to how, as Neuwirth puts it, 'Bach is often very mechanical, especially in the first movement of the Fourth Brandenburg.' As to her title, *Aello*, the reference is to 'a bride of the wind, sent by the gods to restore peace – if necessary even with force', a matter, as she notes, not without contemporary relevance.

Uri Caine, the project's second composer from the USA, is known equally as a pianist and arranger, in both jazz and classical contexts, all of which experience feeds into his take on – or after – Brandenburg No. 5. His solo trio follows that of the Bach – violin, flute and keyboard, this last role written for

himself and partly improvised – and his title, *Hamsa*, makes a nod in the same direction, being the Arabic for 'five'. Moreover, he points out, 'The first and third movements of *Hamsa* use some of Bach's themes from the Brandenburg Concerto, but often transform them rhythmically and harmonically.'

Last on the scene is Brett Dean, with *Approach*, which is exactly that with regard to Brandenburg No. 6, his music not coming to an end but leading directly into the Bach, just as Mackey's *Triceros* has no beginning but emerges from its Bach partner. The Sixth Brandenburg, as one of Bach's double concertos, has solo parts, Dean observes, that are distinct but mutually supportive. It also has a particular appeal to him in that these solo parts are for his own instrument, the viola. His work matches the Bach precisely in its scoring – the only one of the six new works to do so – and makes an 'approach' also to Bachian texture. Noting the 'tight canonic writing' for the soloists in the first movement of his Brandenburg, he felt 'compelled to address this concept of musical counterpoint'. Given that Bach also liked to play the viola, one might imagine in this final piece the two composers sharing the honours. ●

A critic for over 30 years for publications including *The Times* and *The New Yorker*, Paul Griffiths is the author of *A Concise History of Western Music* and *The New Penguin Dictionary of Music* as well as of books on Boulez, Cage and Stravinsky. He also writes novels and librettos.

The Brandenburg Project
Bach's six Brandenburg Concertos, interspersed with new musical responses by Uri Caine, Brett Dean, Anders Hillborg, Olga Neuwirth, Steven Mackey and Mark-Anthony Turnage

PROMS 29 & 30 • 5 AUGUST

New Music

This year, for the first time, the Proms has commissioned a new work for each of the eight Proms at … Cadogan Hall concerts. DAVID KETTLE talks to the composers – all female and all receiving their first Proms commissions

E ight women composers, and eight gloriously contrasting new pieces of music. Each of this year's Proms at … Cadogan Hall concerts features a brand-new work, bringing together an international collection of female voices, 100 years after women in Britain first won the right to vote. What the new creations highlight is the sheer richness and diversity of composition today, straddling a variety of musical genres and styles.

Slovenian Nina Šenk draws heavily on classical traditions in her ensemble work inspired by the qualities and connotations of glass, while Australian Lisa Illean tackles the nature of sound itself in her music – and the inspiration for her new work is the voice of the mezzo-soprano Dame Sarah Connolly, who will give its premiere. New York-born Suzanne Farrin reflects on natural forces at work in Rome, in music for percussionist Colin Currie and the JACK Quartet, while Pulitzer Prize-winning Caroline Shaw is creating two new works for the Calidore String Quartet, tackling the subject of the transformation and manipulation of language.

Jessica Wells explores the virtuosity of fellow Australian Joseph Tawadros in a work for solo oud, and British-Lebanese composer Bushra El-Turk, writing for Canadian mezzo-soprano Wallis Giunta, is on a mission to bring together different musical traditions. Finally, Parisian keyboardist and improviser Eve Risser is creating a new piece for her compatriot, harpsichordist Jean Rondeau, and Birmingham-born singer-songwriter Laura Mvula draws on her love of choral music in a new piece for the BBC Singers inspired by the Black Madonna of Montserrat in Catalonia. ●

David Kettle writes for *The Scotsman, The Daily Telegraph* and *The Arts Desk*, as well as broadly across other publications. He has a special interest in contemporary music and world music.

Bushra El-Turk (born 1982)
Crème Brûlée on a Tree (2018)

PROMS AT ... CADOGAN HALL 7 • 27 AUGUST

'I'm interested in the blurring of things – trying to find the line where one thing dissolves into another.' For London-born composer Bushra El-Turk, that can mean everyday gesture transforming into a new language of movement, as in her recent opera *Woman at Point Zero*, where 'notation also blurs into improvisation', she explains. And, drawing on El-Turk's own Lebanese roots, it can also mean contrasting musical traditions colliding and interpenetrating. 'The opera's wind ensemble is made up of musicians from different ancient traditions,' she explains. 'I've also written a string trio, *Zwareeb*, for violin, Chinese erhu and Azeri kamancha.' She directs her own Ensemble Zar, bringing together 14 musicians from Middle-Eastern and Western traditions.

How does she go about maintaining or blending the different identities of the instruments she uses? 'I try to perceive each instrument and player, from wherever they may be, as carrying the imprint of the tradition of which they're part. In a sense, I'm writing for different personalities. Kahlil Gibran's *The Prophet* inspires the way I strive to make music. In the chapter on marriage, he says: "Let there be spaces in your togetherness … for the pillars of the temple stand apart." That has influenced the way I notate my music for musicians of different traditions: to provide space for musicians in that space to flourish. I sow the seeds and, in the right conditions, they will grow.'

El-Turk's Proms commission is a response to Leonard Bernstein's comic song-cycle of recipes *La bonne cuisine*, for Canadian mezzo-soprano Wallis Giunta, and draws inspiration from Giunta's singing. 'Performers' musical personalities influence the way I think of writing for them,' she explains. 'Pre-echoes of the piece begin to form in this way.'

Suzanne Farrin (born 1976)
new work (2018)

PROMS AT ... CADOGAN HALL 5 • 13 AUGUST

Usually based in New York, where she's a professor at both Hunter College and the Graduate Center of the City University of New York, US composer Suzanne Farrin is currently living in the Italian capital on a Fellowship from the American Academy in Rome. 'It's a quiet place for me to work and reflect, without being distracted by other things – and it's really interesting to be in a city that's so important to human history.'

There's an Italian slant to several of Farrin's works, not least the dramatic cantata *Dolce la morte* setting love poetry by Michelangelo, acclaimed at its 2016 unveiling in New York's Metropolitan Museum of Art. 'For me, writing music is a reflective process,' she explains. 'I wouldn't say there's a particular sound or style that interests me. It's more the chance to reflect on the experience of living, the deep tidal forces in our lives.'

Her BBC Proms commission is for Scottish percussionist Colin Currie and the JACK Quartet: 'I've been corresponding with Colin,' she says, 'but I do know the JACK players personally because they're also based in New York. I'm sort of in awe of their sound, their energy, their powerful openness.'

Her new work, she says, will reflect on her experiences in Italy. 'I've been inspired by how much Rome relates to the natural world – I've been thinking, for example, about the stone pines versus the olive trees, two very thoughtfully planted but contrasting elements in the city. Also on my mind is how powerful a symbol water has been in Rome – how it demonstrates power and success in the city's fountains, for example, but also the destructive forces of the River Tiber that were part of the struggle for the city.'

Lisa Illean (born 1983)
Sleeplessness ... Sails (2018)

PROMS AT ... CADOGAN HALL 4 • 6 AUGUST

Australian-born, London-based composer Lisa Illean is in her final year as a doctoral student at the Royal College of Music, and her music, she says, is often about 'the instability of perception', focusing on the nature of sound itself – through electronics, adapting conventional instruments, even creating sound-works for specific spaces.

'My research arises out of working with non-tempered tuning systems,' she explains, 'paying close attention to sonority, subtly unfolding harmonic forms, auditory phenomena and perspective.' Her BBC Proms commission, *Sleeplessness ... Sails*, is for the very different environment of a song recital, however, where it nestles alongside vocal works by Vaughan Williams, Howells, Britten and others – all, like Illean, with Royal College of Music connections – given by Dame Sarah Connolly and pianist Joseph Middleton.

'The text is a translation of an untitled poem by Osip Mandelstam,' Illean explains. 'It opens with the graceful image of a fleet of ships suspended mid-voyage – resembling cranes in flight – and closes with the thunderous roars and recitations of the encroaching sea.' It's clear that the poem's sonic content is one of the things that attracted her. 'Mandelstam was fascinated by the interplay of language and music, and the sea – here both orator and noise-maker – resounds in elemental sound patterning. It's an incredibly rich poem and the grave, dark roll of the final lines has a striking drama.'

How has she been inspired by the two musicians she's writing for? 'At the moment I've been listening a lot: Sarah's voice (in the fullest sense) and Joseph's playing have been in my ear and my imagination. It's very exciting and inspiring to be working with such wonderful musicians.'

Laura Mvula (born 1986)
The Virgin of Montserrat (2018)

PROMS AT ... CADOGAN HALL 6 • 20 AUGUST

Birmingham-born singer-songwriter Laura Mvula has made three appearances at the BBC Proms, beginning in 2013 with the Urban Classic Prom. But 2018 marks the first time that the classically trained musician is being featured as a composer of music for others – in this case, the BBC Singers, under conductor Sakari Oramo.

Choral music is a medium that Mvula knows intimately. 'I grew up watching my auntie, Carol Pemberton, leading singers in gospel, folk and jazz song all over the world,' she explains. 'Group singing has always been a transcendent and visceral experience for me. I loved singing in gospel choirs and chamber groups as a teenager, mostly for my love of harmony and the challenge of making seemingly independent parts work together as a whole.'

It's far from the first time that Mvula herself has worked with choral ensembles. 'I realised the magnitude of my appetite for choral music when I had the opportunity to write for choir and orchestra for the first time in 2005. I was struck by how individual human voices could together make such a raw, powerful collective sound! Since then, I've been lucky enough to work with the Eric Whitacre Singers, the Town Hall Gospel Choir in Birmingham, Lichfield Gospel Choir, London Contemporary Voices and lots of others.'

For her new work, Mvula is taking inspiration from a controversial religious icon in Spain. 'I visited Mount Montserrat in Catalonia, and I was taken by the whole Black Madonna phenomenon. I was doing some research, and I came across the inscription it at one time carried: *Nigra sum sed formosa*, which means "I am black, but beautiful". It was strange to feel awe and disgust all at once.'

Eve Risser (born 1982)
Furakèla (2018)

PROMS AT ... CADOGAN HALL 2 • 23 JULY

Composer, improviser, harpsichordist, pianist, prepared-piano player and more; Paris-based Eve Risser straddles jazz and contemporary classical in her unconventional, highly distinctive music. 'The music I have in me is very influenced by different scenes,' she says. 'For years I've been trying to get closer to who I am without too much of my intellectual mask. I like to be in a state of listening where I go down into myself, almost into a trance – that's what I'm looking for when I play or listen to or create music.'

The prepared piano – in which objects of various materials are placed between the strings to create a range of unusual sounds – provided a particularly potent route into the kind of direct experience she was looking for, she says. 'It was a completely new vocabulary for me, so I was finally free of any musical education when I explored that side to the piano. It was a very useful experience to find my own way and my own sincerity through music.'

Another keyboard instrument is the vehicle for her BBC Proms commission, however. 'I am a harpsichord lover, for sure!' Risser enthuses. 'I play a vintage electric harpsichord myself and I'm a total fan. It's a good instrument for contemporary music – the sound is close to a computer sometimes.'

Her performer is iconoclastic young French showman Jean Rondeau, in among a recital of Baroque French keyboard music by Couperin, Rameau and Royer. 'I always write for the person in particular,' Risser continues. 'I try to guess their reactions to the music, try to manipulate them through the music, to play with them. I am eager – maybe too much! – to write this piece for such a huge and amazing artist.'

Nina Šenk (born 1982)
Baca (2018)

PROMS AT ... CADOGAN HALL 8 • 3 SEPTEMBER

'With everything that's currently going on about women breaking through the glass ceiling, and other related movements, I found that glass itself had become the inspiration for my new piece.' Slovenian musician Nina Šenk is already well established as a composer, with performances from several major international orchestras and ensembles, and it's soloists from the Berliner Philharmoniker who premiere her new work on 3 September.

Šenk feels strong links with tradition in her music. 'It's about how the music influences the listener, which has been the same for a long time,' she explains. 'Now we're in the 21st century, it doesn't mean that the things the great masters did centuries ago no longer apply. There are elements that are still relevant, and those are the basic pillars of how classical music works. I just like to change them a bit, recompose them in a fresher, more contemporary style.'

But what inspiration has she taken from glass? 'It has a duality – it's very strong, but it's also very fragile. I wouldn't say the piece is going to be overtly political, but those are also qualities I have to have as a mother and an artist – you have to be soft and fragile with your children, but I also have to be hard when I need to work. I'm aiming to convey the cycle of glass's physical states that go from sand to hot, molten glass, then cold, solid glass, and then to the recycling of glass.'

The title of her new piece is *Baca*. 'It's Latin, and it refers to small glass beads, originally made more than 3,000 years ago and still made now. They're fragile but also strong and beautiful; each one is a tiny piece of art. It's also a small, fragile piece of art that I'm creating – it won't change the world, but it will be done with love, and a lot of hard work.'

Caroline Shaw (born 1982)
Second Essay: Echo; Third Essay: Ruby (2018)

PROMS AT … CADOGAN HALL 1 • 16 JULY

'I'm probably the worst person to try and describe my own music.' New York-based composer, vocalist and violinist Caroline Shaw – the youngest ever recipient of the Pulitzer Prize for Music, in 2013 for her *Partita for 8 Voices* – instead points to a whole range of things that inspire her. 'I'm in love with harmony, and that's what has always driven me to make music. I'm in love with radical switches from chaos to order. I love pacing, and organising, time – which I think is what some people call form. I love Buxtehude and [singer-songwriter and rapper] Childish Gambino, and Adele and Gérard Grisey.'

It's no surprise that Shaw mentions contemporary pop names alongside classical composers of all eras: she's remixed tracks by Kanye West, and collaborated with him on others. Does she see different musical genres as separate, interconnected or all part of the same thing? 'Definitely part of the same thing. The more I live and make music, the more I understand what it was that first drew me to these other worlds. I can't really say what it is, because I think it takes a lifetime to begin to understand music.'

For her Proms commission, Shaw has added two further pieces to her *First Essay* (2016), also written for the Calidore String Quartet. 'They're an incredible ensemble, and I'm very lucky to have gotten to write for them already. I used to play in a quartet, in grad school, with their cellist, Estelle Choi. We all knew she was destined for greatness.' But what is the attraction of the idea of an 'Essay'? 'The first piece began as a consideration of essay-writing structures, and the way that some of my favourite writers develop ideas. Ultimately, the music became about the breakdown, deterioration and transformation of language. It was written during the fall of 2016, in the heat of the US election.'

Jessica Wells (born 1974)
Rhapsody for solo oud (2018)

PROMS AT … CADOGAN HALL 3 • 30 JULY

Born in Florida, but based in Australia since the age of 11, Jessica Wells describes herself as 'a bit of a chameleon – I'm just as comfortable working with jazz or contemporary musicians as I am with classical players. I like to cross boundaries between musical genres.' It's an eclecticism borne out in her current projects – from a piece for carillon (an array of bells) and electronics to a cabaret show, by way of a new work for a babies' prom concert at the Sydney Opera House, and also a piece for saxophonist Amy Dickson and string quartet. 'I've always been drawn to orchestral music,' she adds, 'but I also arrange music electronically, and I love writing music for film when I get a chance to.'

Her Proms commission fits in well with her broad-ranging activities: it's a piece for a solo recital by Joseph Tawadros, one of today's most exciting performers of the oud, a lute from the Middle East, Mediterranean and North Africa. 'I was fortunate enough to work with Joe on Nigel Westlake's film score for *Ali's Wedding*, and last year I arranged a full concerto for him to perform with the Melbourne Symphony Orchestra,' Wells explains. 'He's a virtuoso and his performances have great light and shade. He's able to play at lightning speed with great energy, as well as creating a softer, more emotional mood focusing on harmony and colour.'

Wells is also aware of the centuries of tradition that lie behind the instrument she's writing for. 'I'm keen to explore the sound-world of the oud, and to bring out Joe's flair for performance in my ideas. The instrument has many traditions, which are fascinating to explore, but Joe has also shown me in his own writing how you can bring out new styles of playing that are "outside the box".'

Anna Meredith/59 Productions
Five Telegrams†
PROM 1 • 13 JULY

David Bruce Sidechaining*
Iain Farrington Gershwinicity*
Ben Foster new work*
PROM 3 • 15 JULY

Caroline Shaw Second Essay: Echo;
Third Essay: Ruby†
PROMS AT … CADOGAN HALL 1 • 16 JULY

Luca Francesconi new work†
Georg Friedrich Haas new work†
Hannah Kendall new work†
Isabel Mundry new work†
PROMS AT … ROUNDHOUSE • 21 JULY

Ēriks Ešenvalds Shadow*
PROM 9 • 21 JULY

Eve Risser Furakèla*
PROMS AT … CADOGAN HALL 2 • 23 JULY

Andrew Norman new work¥
PROM 12 • 23 JULY

Tansy Davies What Did We See?
(orchestral suite from 'Between Worlds')*
PROM 15 • 25 JULY

Jessica Wells Rhapsody for solo oud*
PROMS AT … CADOGAN HALL 3 • 30 JULY

Georg Friedrich Haas Concerto grosso
No. 1¥
PROM 21 • 30 JULY

Joby Talbot Guitar Concerto*
PROM 25 • 2 AUGUST

Uri Caine Hamsa¥
Anders Hillborg Bach Materia¥
Mark-Anthony Turnage Maya¥
PROM 29 • 5 AUGUST

Brett Dean Approach – Prelude to a
Canon¥
Olga Neuwirth
Aello – ballet mécanomorphe¥
Steven Mackey Triceros¥
PROM 30 • 5 AUGUST

Britten A Sweet Lullaby‡; Somnus‡
Lisa Illean Sleeplessness … Sails*
Mark-Anthony Turnage Farewell‡
PROMS AT … CADOGAN HALL 4
6 AUGUST

Suzanne Farrin new work*
Simon Holt Quadriga‡
PROMS AT … CADOGAN HALL 5
13 AUGUST

David Robert Coleman Looking for
Palestine§
PROM 43 • 14 AUGUST

Philip Venables/Béla Bartók Venables
Plays Bartók*
PROM 47 • 17 AUGUST

Agata Zubel Fireworks¥
PROM 49 • 19 AUGUST

Laura Mvula The Virgin of Montserrat*
PROMS AT … CADOGAN HALL 6
20 AUGUST

Per Nørgård Symphony No. 3¥
PROM 51 • 20 AUGUST

Rolf Wallin Violin Concerto‡
PROM 52 • 21 AUGUST

Bushra El-Turk Crème Brûlée on a Tree*
PROMS AT … CADOGAN HALL 7
27 AUGUST

Alexander Campkin new work§
PROM 59 • 27 AUGUST

Iain Bell Aurora†
PROM 62 • 29 AUGUST

Nina Šenk Baca*
PROMS AT … CADOGAN HALL 8
3 SEPTEMBER

Roxanna Panufnik Songs of Darkness,
Dreams of Light*
PROM 75 • 8 SEPTEMBER

* BBC commission: world premiere   *† BBC co-commission: world premiere*   *‡ world premiere*   *¥ UK premiere*   *§ London premiere*

Love, Faith and Honour

RICHARD WIGMORE introduces Handel's *Theodora*, whose noble Christian heroine, the lover of a Roman convert, dies for her beliefs

''Twas dishonour I declined; Not death': *The Martyrdom of Saint Theodora* (1745) by Giovanni Battista Tiepolo

'Handel has set up an Oratorio against the Operas, and succeeds. He has hired all the goddesses from farces and singers of Roast Beef from between the acts at both theatres, with a man with one note in his voice and a girl without ever an one.' The politician-cum-litterateur Horace Walpole was evidently unimpressed by the cast of Handel's *Samson* at Covent Garden in 1743. But for the composer there was no going back. Oratorio, an unlikely amalgam of Italian opera and English anthem that also drew on Purcellian masque and Greek tragedy, had decisively ousted *opera seria*. Spurred by *Samson*'s success, Handel embarked on a pair of works for the following season, setting the work pattern for the rest of his career.

After the popular triumph of *Judas Maccabaeus* in 1747, Handel allegedly remarked that the English liked music that 'hit them on the drum of the ear'. The 'victory' oratorios inspired by the quashing of the Jacobite rebellion – *Judas*, *The Occasional Oratorio* and *Joshua* – meshed perfectly with the bellicose national mood. But the oratorios that followed, *Susanna*, *Solomon* and *Theodora*, were much less to the public's taste. Least successful of all was *Theodora*, Handel's sole religious drama set in Christian times and the only one not drawn from the Bible. It survived for just three performances in March 1750 and was revived just once, in 1755.

There was, though, a sharp distinction between the reactions of the broader public and those of Handel's friends. On 22 March 1750 Thomas Harris wrote to his brother

James: 'I was last night at *Theodora*, which does not please the generality of people, but I differ widely in my opinion, for I think it has many excellent songs, composed with great art and care.' The Earl of Shaftesbury pronounced *Theodora* 'as finished, beautiful and labour'd a composition as ever Handel made … The Town don't like it at all; but Mr Kelloway [the music teacher Joseph Kelway] and several excellent Musicians think as I do.' Another of Handel's close friends, Mary Delany, wrote to her sister Ann: 'Don't you remember our snug enjoyment of *Theodora*?' Ann responded: 'Surely *Theodora* will have justice at last, if it was to be again performed, but the generality of the world have ears and *hear not*.'

Handel himself shared his friends' special regard for *Theodora*. According to the memoirs of the work's librettist, Thomas Morell, the composer valued it 'more than any Performance of the kind; and when I once ask'd him whether he did not look upon the Grand Chorus in the *Messiah* as his Master Piece? "No," says he, "*I think the Chorus at the end of the 2nd part in Theodora far beyond it.*"' And Handel wryly observed of *Theodora*'s box-office failure: 'The Jews will not come to it (as to *Judas*) because it is a Christian story; and the Ladies will not come because it [is] a virtuous one.'

There may be a grain of truth in Handel's reported witticism, at least as regards the non-attendance of Jewish patrons, hitherto a vital component of his oratorio audiences. But the prime reason behind *Theodora*'s failure was surely its unique inwardness. The story of Christian martyrs in Roman-occupied Antioch inspired music of intense elegiac beauty, suffused with the ageing composer's awareness of human transience. In truth, none

of Handel's oratorios was less calculated to hit listeners 'on the drum of the ear'.

Morell based his libretto on Robert Boyle's 1687 novella *The Martyrdom of Theodora and Didymus*, a lethal blend of prurience and sanctimoniousness. Though no poet, he at least created a coherent narrative from Boyle's discursive ramblings. As a Church of England vicar, he emphasised the power of the Holy Spirit to change lives: Theodora's Roman lover, Didymus, has secretly converted to Christianity; and at the end, in a passage not set by Handel, the Roman officer Septimius likewise becomes a Christian. Didymus and Septimius also enshrine the libretto's concern with freedom of thought and religious tolerance, topical after the wave of anti-Catholic feeling unleashed by the Jacobite uprising.

In Morell's libretto, Theodora emerges as a conventional 'sentimental' 18th-century heroine, first cousin to Samuel Richardson's Clarissa. Through Handel's music she becomes a poignant, vulnerably human figure of immense spiritual strength. Her martyrdom is suffused both with dignity and a sense of agonised loss; and her arias and duets with Didymus give the oratorio its essential tragic colouring.

Although Theodora dominates the oratorio, each of the other characters is a vivid musical portrait. Didymus was the last role Handel created for a castrato, and the most unworldly. The tenderness and glowing spirituality of his music also suffuse the arias for Theodora's confidante Irene, feebly drawn by Morell, but transfigured by Handel.

Not for the first time, Handel enjoyed characterising opposing cultures in his choruses. The Romans emerge not as sadists

Susan Gritton as Theodora and Robin Blaze as Didymus in Glyndebourne's 2003 production, originally directed by Peter Sellars

but as unabashed sensualists, singing to the rollicking strains of trumpets and horns, while the Christian choruses share the rarefied tenderness of Theodora's music. Even the sybaritic Romans are drawn into the Christians' musical orbit in the grave, wondering chorus 'How strange their ends'.

In the final chorus, Morell's words imply an exultant ending. Handel's music – part prayer, part lullaby – confirms that he viewed the fate of Theodora and Didymus as tragic. In his classic study of Handel's oratorios, Winton Dean likened this finale to the closing chorus of Bach's *St Matthew Passion*. We know little about Handel's personal faith, but it is hard to deny that this sublime, valedictory music conveys an intense religious experience and that, for once, Handel and Bach – in many ways musical and spiritual antipodes – meet on common ground. ●

Richard Wigmore is a writer, broadcaster and lecturer specialising in the Classical period and in Lieder. A contributor to *Gramophone*, he has also written *The Faber Pocket Guide to Haydn*.

Handel Theodora
PROM 74 • 7 SEPTEMBER

The Proms on Radio, on TV, Online

Since the BBC took over the festival in 1927 and broadcast the first concerts on radio, it has become easier to access the Proms wherever and whenever you want. Every performance is broadcast live on Radio 3 and in HD Sound online, with many also shown on BBC TV. Take the Proms with you on your mobile, catch up for 30 days via the Proms website or feel part of the festival atmosphere with TV broadcasts on BBC Two and BBC Four throughout the summer.

Listen
Hear every Prom live on BBC Radio 3 on your radio, 90–93FM and DAB, on desktop in HD Sound via the Radio 3 and BBC Proms websites, or on your digital TV service (*eg* Sky, Virgin, NOW TV).

You can take any Prom with you and listen anytime by downloading it from Radio 3 via the iPlayer Radio app.

Proms-related programmes on Radio 3
Listen out for Proms-themed special editions of *In Tune*, *Record Review* and *Composer of the Week*, as well as coverage of pre-Prom talks and events.

Watch
Full concerts on BBC Four on Friday and Sunday nights throughout the season, the First and Last Nights on BBC Two and BBC One. Available to watch for 30 days via iPlayer and on the Proms website.

'Proms Extra' on BBC Two
The Saturday-night preview and review show featuring Proms guests, hosted by Katie Derham.

Proms online
Visit bbc.co.uk/proms for everything you need to know about the Proms, including all the audio and video from the festival, plus articles, quizzes and relevant, in-depth content.

@bbcproms   theproms   bbc_proms

bbc.co.uk/now

CELEBRATING 90 YEARS OF BBC NATIONAL ORCHESTRA OF WALES

Aberystwyth Arts Centre	St David's Hall, Cardiff	Venue Cymru, Llandudno
Theatr Bryn Terfel, Pontio, Bangor	BBC Hoddinott Hall, Cardiff	Hafren, Newtown
Prichard-Jones Hall, Bangor	Sir Thomas Picton School, Haverfordwest	Brangwyn Hall, Swansea

0800 052 1812

@bbcnow

BBC Scottish Symphony Orchestra

2018/19 Season

Thomas Dausgaard
Chief Conductor

Ilan Volkov
Principal Guest Conductor

Matthias Pintscher
Artist-in-Association

John Wilson
Associate Guest Conductor

Donald Runnicles
Conductor Emeritus

Laura Samuel
Leader

Thomas Dausgaard Conducts

Langgaard's *Music of the Spheres* at Glasgow Cathedral

Performances to mark centenaries of Bernstein and Debussy

Composer Roots: Mahler's Symphony No.1 and Klezmer music

Works by Per Nørgård, Simon Steen-Andersen and David Fennessy

Plus

A Portrait of Gloria Coates

Tectonics Festival

Guest soloists including **Elisabeth Leonskaja**, **Barnabás Kelemen**, **Steven Osborne**, and **James Ehnes**

Holst's *The Planets* in its 100th-anniversary year

As well as appearances at the 2018 Edinburgh International Festival and our regular concert series in Aberdeen, Ayr, Edinburgh, and Perth.

bbc.co.uk/ bbcsso

The Bridgewater Hall
Manchester

The 2018/19 Season

On Sale Now

  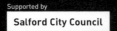

Book now: 0161 907 9000
bbc.co.uk/philharmonic

JOIN THE BBC SYMPHONY CHORUS!

One of the UK's leading choirs, the BBC Symphony Chorus performs with the BBC Symphony Orchestra at the BBC Proms and the Barbican and is regularly broadcast on BBC Radio 3.

If you are an experienced choral singer with a passion for new music as well as key choral works, we'd like to hear from you!

Find out more
bbc.co.uk/symphonychorus
@bbcso   #bbcsc

**BRINGING INSPIRING MUSICAL EXPERIENCES
TO EVERYONE, EVERYWHERE**

bbc.co.uk/concertorchestra

SOUTHBANK
CENTRE
ASSOCIATE

BBC Symphony Orchestra & Chorus

CONCERTS
2018–19

SAKARI ORAMO Chief Conductor
Join us at the Barbican for a bold new season
of thrilling music both new and old.

barbican

Associate
Orchestra

Find out more:
bbc.co.uk/symphonyorchestra

BBC RADIO 3

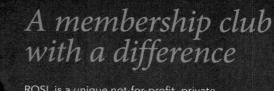

A membership club with a difference

ROSL is a unique not-for-profit, private members' organisation; bringing people together from around the world to meet, socialise and foster an interest in the Commonwealth. This is best realised through our Arts programme that works with young classical musicians and visual artists, and our humanitarian programme of education and enterprise projects. Our members make a difference to people's lives while enjoying the comforts of our London clubhouse overlooking Green Park.

To find out more about becoming a member, or attending our exceptional programme of concerts, exhibitions and book events visit **www.rosl.org.uk** or call **020 7408 0214**.

Royal Over-Seas League
Over-Seas House
Park Place, St James's Street
London SW1A 1LR

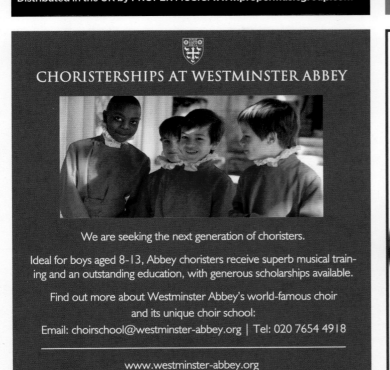

CITY MUSIC FOUNDATION

turning talent into success

Support City Music Foundation as we make plans for our new home in the City of London

At St Bartholomew the Less we will carry out our innovative professional development workshops as well as concerts, mentoring sessions, open rehearsals, CD and video recordings - and we will be sharing our music with St Bartholomew's Hospital patients, relatives and staff.

Wednesday 16th May	Monday 23rd - Friday 27th July
CMF Artists with English Chamber Orchestra	**CMF Summer Residency at Wallace Collection**
Michael Foyle and Mihai Ritivoiu	Featuring Gwenllian Llyr, Lotte Betts-Dean,
Michael Collins, conductor	Rokas Valuntonis and Eblana String Trio
Cadogan Hall, 7.30pm	Daily, 1.00pm

@CityMusicF

www.citymusicfoundation.org

Registered Charity Number: 1148641

Imperial College London

is one of the world's great universities

Discover its outstanding
extra-curricular music and art provision at
www.imperial.ac.uk/music-and-art

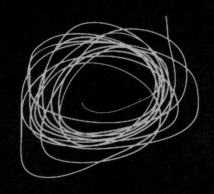

PIERINO

37 Thurloe Place, London SW7 2HP
Tel:0207 581 3770

Monday to Saturday
12 noon – 11.30pm

Sunday
12 noon – 11pm

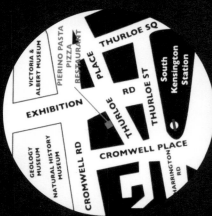

Prompt service guaranteed for you to be in time for the performance

We are within walking distance of the Royal Albert Hall, near South Kensington tube station.

You are welcome before and after the performance.

42 YEARS

EXPERIENCE OF SERVING GENUINE ITALIAN FOOD, HOME-MADE PASTA AND THE BEST PIZZA IN LONDON

Concert Listings

Full details of all the 2018 **BBC Proms concerts** are in this section *(pages 122–159)*. Please note: concert start-times vary – check before you book. You'll also find details in these pages of the free **Proms Plus** talks and other events *(see also pages 66–69 and 78–79)*.

Booking

Online: bbc.co.uk

By phone: 020 7070 4441

General booking
opens at 9.00am on Saturday 12 May. For full booking and access information, *see pages 161–170*.

On Radio, on TV, Online

 Every Prom is broadcast live

 Prom 19 is recorded for future broadcast; Prom 27 is broadcast live

 24 Proms are broadcast on BBC Four, BBC Two or BBC One – look out for this symbol

All Proms are also available for 30 days after broadcast via the BBC Proms website and can be downloaded onto your mobile or tablet via the BBC iPlayer Radio app.

FRIDAY 13 JULY

PROM 1
8.15pm–c10.30pm • Royal Albert Hall

PRICE BAND C
WEEKEND PROMMING PASS *see page 170*

SAKARI ORAMO

First Night of the Proms 2018

Vaughan Williams Toward the
Unknown Region   14'

Holst The Planets   52'

INTERVAL

Anna Meredith/59 Productions
Five Telegrams   c22'
*BBC co-commission with 14–18 NOW and Edinburgh
International Festival: world premiere*

National Youth Choir of Great Britain
BBC Symphony Chorus
BBC Proms Youth Ensemble
BBC Symphony Orchestra
Sakari Oramo conductor

An all-British season launch, featuring two major
figures who composed responses to the First World
War. Holst's much-loved *The Planets* (premiered in
1918) and Vaughan Williams's choral masterpiece
Toward the Unknown Region contrast with a new
work by Anna Meredith and 59 Productions. *Five
Telegrams* draws on communications sent by young
soldiers in 1918 and features specially produced
digital projections, creating a unique spectacle.
*See 'Musical Memorials', pages 60–65; 'Inspiring
the Future', pages 66–69; 'New Music', pages 96–101.*

Broadcast on BBC Two tonight

IN TUNE
5.00pm–7.15pm • Imperial College Union A live Proms
edition of BBC Radio 3's *In Tune*, presented by Sean Rafferty.
*Tickets available from BBC Studio Audiences: bbc.co.uk/
showsandtours/shows. Broadcast live on BBC Radio 3.*

SATURDAY 14 JULY

PROM 2
7.30pm–c9.45pm • Royal Albert Hall

PRICE BAND A
WEEKEND PROMMING PASS *see page 170*

ALAIN ALTINOGLU

Fauré Pavane   5'

Mozart Piano Concerto No. 27
in B flat major, K595   32'

INTERVAL

Ravel Daphnis and Chloe   52'

Francesco Piemontesi piano

BBC Symphony Chorus
Royal Philharmonic Orchestra
Alain Altinoglu conductor

An evening of French music from the Royal
Philharmonic Orchestra opens with Fauré's serene,
gently pulsing *Pavane*, elegantly recalling the French
court dance of the 16th and 17th centuries. Ravel
reaches even further back in time in his mythological
Daphnis and Chloe, written for Diaghilev's Ballets
Russes, and set in a pastoral Greek-island idyll. At the
centre of the concert is Mozart's Piano Concerto
No. 27 – the composer's final piano concerto, and
a work of unusually introspective lyricism. Swiss-born
Francesco Piemontesi, a former BBC Radio 3 New
Generation Artist, is the soloist. *See 'Impressions in
Colour', pages 8–15.*

PROMS PLUS TALK
5.45pm–6.25pm • Imperial College Union Tim Whitmarsh
and Judith Mackrell discuss Longus, author of *Daphnis and
Chloe*, and the premiere production of Ravel's ballet
given by the Ballets Russes in 1912.
Edited version broadcast on BBC Radio 3 during tonight's interval

SUNDAY 15 JULY

PROM 3
7.00pm–c9.45pm • Royal Albert Hall

PRICE BAND B
WEEKEND PROMMING PASS *see page 170*

BBC Young Musician
40th Anniversary

Programme to include:

Saint-Saëns Carnival of the Animals –
excerpts   13'

Ravel Tzigane   10'

Sir James MacMillan Britannia   13'

*plus world premieres of new BBC commissions
by David Bruce, Ben Foster and Iain Farrington*

Nicola Benedetti, Jennifer Pike violins
Nicholas Daniel oboe • **Ben Goldscheider** horn
Alexander Bone, Jess Gillam saxophones
Alexandra Ridout trumpet • **David Childs**
euphonium • **Natalie Clein, Guy Johnston, Sheku
Kanneh-Mason, Laura van der Heijden** cellos
Michael Collins, Emma Johnson clarinets
**Colin Currie, Owen Gunnell, Adrian Spillett,
Sam Walton** percussion • **Martin James Bartlett,
Freddy Kempf, Lara Melda** pianos

BBC Concert Orchestra
Andrew Gourlay conductor

There will be one interval

BBC Young Musician has launched the careers of
scores of artists since it began in 1968. We mark the
competition's 40th anniversary with the help of an
array of previous winners and finalists, joining this
year's finalists; and we take a look at the competition's
rich history. *See 'Musical Giftedness: Born or Bred?',
pages 42–45; 'Performance Art', pages 48–51.*

Broadcast on BBC Four tonight

PROMS FILM
4.55pm–5.55pm • Imperial College Union (Concert Hall)
Ahead of tonight's BBC Young Musician anniversary
celebration, a special screening of a new film marking
40 years of the competition.

PROMS FAMILY WORKSHOP
5.15pm–6.00pm • Imperial College Union (Dining Hall)
Join professional musicians for a family-friendly introduction
to this evening's Prom. Bring your instrument and join in!
Suitable for all the family (ages 7-plus). See pages 78–79 for details.

MONDAY 16 JULY

PROMS AT … CADOGAN HALL 1
1.00pm–c2.00pm • Cadogan Hall

For ticket prices, see page 162

CALIDORE STRING QUARTET

Caroline Shaw Second Essay: Echo;
Third Essay: Ruby   *c15'*
*BBC co-commission with Coretet, the Phillips
Collection, Royal Philharmonic Society and
University of Delaware: world premiere*

Schumann Piano Quintet
in E flat major, Op. 44   *30'*

Calidore String Quartet
Javier Perianes *piano*

There will be no interval

Praised by *The New York Times* for their 'irrepressible
dramatic spirit', BBC Radio 3 New Generation
Artists the Calidore String Quartet make their Proms
debut here in a concert pairing a new work by
Pulitzer Prize-winning American composer Caroline
Shaw with Schumann's richly Romantic Piano Quintet
in E flat major – a buoyant, virtuosic work that
pioneered the piano quintet genre as we know
it today. See 'New Music', pages 96–101.

Every Prom broadcast
live on BBC Radio 3

Thomas Dausgaard
Proms 29, 30, 50 & 51
BBC Scottish Symphony Orchestra

Danish conductor Thomas Dausgaard is a busy
man, with positions at five major international
orchestras. But, among them, the BBC Scottish
Symphony Orchestra holds a special place: he's
recently renewed his contract as Chief Conductor
through to 2022. 'There's a sense of exploration
there that I love,' he explains.

He brings two distinct concerts to the Proms
with the BBC SSO, the first of which contrasts
the Classical elegance of Mozart's Clarinet
Concerto with the might of Mahler's Fifth
Symphony. How do the two composers compare,
does he think? 'They share a duality in their
expression that will forever intrigue us as
performers and listeners,' he explains.
'They share moments of the most sublime
beauty, yet their music is deeply haunting too.'

There's another reason behind this pairing of
works. 'It's a great honour to be conducting this
programme as a tribute to Leonard Bernstein,
who conducted the same works in the first of his
two appearances at the Proms, in 1987 with the
Vienna Philharmonic. It's still an inspiration for
me that I had the privilege of being in Bernstein's
conducting class at the Schleswig-Holstein Music
Festival in 1988. Characteristically, one of
his books is called *The Joy of Music*, not
The Challenge of Music – another important
lesson that I learnt from him.'

Juanjo Mena • Proms 4 & 34
BBC Philharmonic

'Leonard Bernstein is one of the great musicians,'
says Juanjo Mena, who pays tribute to him
in the second of his two Proms with the BBC
Philharmonic (Prom 34). 'As a composer he wrote
such contrasting, extreme music. As a conductor,
he is a reference for the whole idea of music.'

'We're also looking at the connection between
England and America. That's the root of the
programme,' explains Mena. 'So, for example,
we have Britten's *Les illuminations*, which he
started to compose in the USA in wartime.
It was a piece that Bernstein loved. Then *Four
Sea Interludes* was the last piece that Bernstein
conducted in Tanglewood before he died.'

Copland's *Connotations* was another work
that Bernstein loved. 'Nobody plays it now,
but why not?' asks Mena. 'Here Copland is
trying to be dodecaphonic, and it's interesting
to see a composer trying a new language.' Two
scenes from Barber's *Antony and Cleopatra* –
an American composer's tribute to England's
greatest playwright – complete the picture.

It's nine years since Mena took the helm of the
BBC Philharmonic, and these two Proms bring his
final season with the orchestra to a close. 'It's been
one of the most amazing experiences of my life,' he
says. 'It's a luxury to have this commitment from
such high-level musicians. And the Proms is so
special. The first time I went on stage at the Royal
Albert Hall, it was unbelievable.'

MONDAY 16 JULY

PROM 4
7.30pm–c9.50pm • Royal Albert Hall

PRICE BAND Ⓐ

MARK SIMPSON

Magnus Lindberg Clarinet
Concerto   25'

INTERVAL

Shostakovich Symphony No. 7,
'Leningrad'   75'

Mark Simpson clarinet

BBC Philharmonic
Juanjo Mena conductor

In his final season as its Chief Conductor, Juanjo Mena leads the BBC Philharmonic in a concert contrasting darkness and light. Magnus Lindberg's Clarinet Concerto is a modern classic, a glorious collision of tradition and innovation that is at once emotionally direct and ferociously virtuosic; former BBC Radio 3 New Generation Artist and BBC Young Musician winner Mark Simpson is the soloist. Darkness streaks across the second half with Shostakovich's heart-wrenching tribute to the Soviet victims of the Second World War – the powerful 'Leningrad' Symphony.

PROMS PLUS TALK
5.45pm–6.25pm • Imperial College Union An introduction to Shostakovich's 'Leningrad' Symphony with musicologist, presenter and writer Anastasia Belina.
Edited version broadcast on BBC Radio 3 during tonight's interval

TUESDAY 17 JULY

PROM 5
6.30pm–c10.10pm • Royal Albert Hall

PRICE BAND Ⓒ

CHRISTINA GANSCH

Debussy Pelléas et Mélisande   180'
(semi-staged; sung in French, with surtitles)

Christina Gansch *Mélisande*
John Chest *Pelléas*
Christopher Purves *Golaud*
Brindley Sherratt *Arkel*
Karen Cargill *Geneviève*
Chloé Briot *Yniold*

Glyndebourne Festival Opera
London Philharmonic Orchestra
Robin Ticciati conductor
There will be one interval

Debussy's *Pelléas et Mélisande* is an operatic fairy tale played out in the shadowy half-light of the mysterious kingdom of Allemonde. Love, desire, power and violence permeate this luminous score – arguably one of the greatest of the 20th century. This semi-staged performance of Glyndebourne's new production, marking the centenary of the composer's death, is conducted by the company's Music Director Robin Ticciati, with Christopher Purves as the obsessive Golaud and former Kathleen Ferrier Award-winner Christina Gansch as his beloved Mélisande. *See 'Impressions in Colour', pages 8–15.*

PROMS PLUS TALK
4.45pm–5.25pm • Imperial College Union Musicologist Richard Langham Smith introduces Debussy's only completed opera.
Edited version broadcast on BBC Radio 3 during tonight's interval

WEDNESDAY 18 JULY

PROM 6
7.30pm–c9.35pm • Royal Albert Hall

PRICE BAND Ⓐ

ANGELA HEWITT

Gershwin An American in Paris   17'

INTERVAL

Messiaen Turangalîla Symphony   74'

Angela Hewitt piano
Cynthia Millar ondes martenot

BBC Symphony Orchestra
Sakari Oramo conductor

Gershwin's *An American in Paris* – a giddy, gloriously tuneful musical evocation of 1920s Paris – takes a stroll through the bustling City of Light, swept along by the jazz rhythms that were its throbbing pulse. The rhythmic impulse continues through Messiaen's hypnotic orchestral love song, the *Turangalîla Symphony*. Premiered by Leonard Bernstein in 1949, this *Tristan and Isolde*-inspired work is a celebration of sensual pleasure and boundless ecstasy. *See 'Impressions in Colour', pages 8–15; 'Performance Art', pages 48–51.*

PROMS PLUS TALK
5.45pm–6.25pm • Imperial College Union In the centenary year of Leonard Bernstein's birth, the first in a series of talks exploring his life and works. Nigel Simeone, editor of *The Leonard Bernstein Letters*, discusses Bernstein as a champion of contemporary music.
Edited version broadcast on BBC Radio 3 during tonight's interval

THURSDAY 19 JULY

PROM 7
7.30pm–c9.40pm • Royal Albert Hall

PRICE BAND B

JACOB COLLIER

Jacob Collier and Friends

Jacob Collier
Sam Amidon
Take 6

Metropole Orkest
Jules Buckley conductor

There will be one interval

Since becoming an online sensation with his one-man, multi-tracked arrangements of songs such as 'Don't You Worry 'Bout a Thing' and 'Fascinating Rhythm', vocalist and multi-instrumentalist Jacob Collier has been forging a lightning-quick path through the musical world. Last year, aged 23, he picked up two Grammy Awards for his debut album *In My Room*. Having made a guest appearance at the Quincy Jones Prom in 2016, Collier once again teams up with conductor Jules Buckley and his Metropole Orkest in a special collaboration for the Proms, featuring a host of new tracks and a smattering of special guests. See 'Performance Art', pages 48–51; 'Contemporary Collaborations', pages 74–77.

📻 *Broadcast on BBC Four on Friday 20 July*

PROMS PLUS TALK
5.45pm–6.25pm • **Imperial College Union** Musicians from the Metropole Orkest talk about the life and work of the orchestra.
Edited version broadcast on BBC Radio 3 during tonight's interval

FRIDAY 20 JULY

PROM 8
7.30pm–c9.40pm • Royal Albert Hall

PRICE BAND A
WEEKEND PROMMING PASS *see page 170*

BERTRAND CHAMAYOU

L. Boulanger
D'un matin de printemps   5'
D'un soir triste   11'

Mendelssohn Piano Concerto No. 1
in G minor   20'

INTERVAL

Morfydd Owen Nocturne   15'

Schumann Symphony No. 4 (original
version, 1841)   28'

Bertrand Chamayou piano

BBC National Orchestra of Wales
Thomas Søndergård conductor

The BBC National Orchestra of Wales and its Principal Conductor Thomas Søndergård explore the music of two 20th-century female composers whose early deaths cut their careers tragically short: Prix de Rome winner Lili Boulanger and Wales's Morfydd Owen, whose *Nocturne* showcases a sensuous and utterly original musical voice. Bertrand Chamayou makes his Proms debut in Mendelssohn's First Piano Concerto – composed when Mendelssohn was just 22 – while Schumann's jubilant Fourth Symphony is also the work of a composer exploring new musical maturity. See 'The Other Boulanger Girl', pages 16–17; 'Fantastic Four', pages 18–21.

📻 *Broadcast on BBC Four on Sunday 22 July*

PROMS PLUS TALK
5.45pm–6.25pm • **Imperial College Union**
Rhian Davies, Artistic Director of the Gregynog Festival, discusses the life and music of Morfydd Owen.
Edited version broadcast on BBC Radio 3 during tonight's interval

SATURDAY 21 JULY

PROMS AT … ROUNDHOUSE
3.00pm–c4.55pm • Roundhouse, Camden

GEORGE BENJAMIN

Ives The Unanswered Question   6'

Stravinsky Symphonies of Wind
Instruments   9'

Messiaen Et exspecto resurrectionem
mortuorum   35'

plus world premieres of First World War-themed works by Luca Francesconi, Georg Friedrich Haas, Hannah Kendall and Isabel Mundry

Susan Bickley mezzo-soprano

London Sinfonietta
George Benjamin conductor

There will be one interval

The Proms returns to Camden's Roundhouse – a former railway engine shed reinvented as a spectacular contemporary space – with a programme of 20th- and 21st-century works. Composer-conductor George Benjamin directs new-music specialists, the London Sinfonietta – celebrating its 50th anniversary this year – in a concert that continues our series marking 100 years since the end of the First World War. Alongside a quartet of war-themed premieres (co-commissioned with 14–18 NOW), the programme features Stravinsky's homage to Debussy, the elegant *Symphonies of Wind Instruments*; Messiaen's monumental tribute to the dead of both world wars, *Et exspecto resurrectionem mortuorum*, and Charles Ives's *The Unanswered Question*, whose haunting solo trumpet famously raises 'the perennial question of existence'. See 'Impressions in Colour', pages 8–15; 'Fantastic Four', pages 18–21; 'New Music', pages 96–101.

Sakari Oramo • Proms 1, 6, 47, 56 & Proms at … Cadogan Hall 6
BBC Symphony Orchestra

If you want to find Sakari Oramo this summer, best head to the Royal Albert Hall. As Chief Conductor of the BBC Symphony Orchestra, he will be presiding over four Proms, as well as a performance with the BBC Singers at Cadogan Hall. 'I have been with the orchestra for five years now and we are already going back to old friends, like Messiaen's *Turangalîla Symphony* (Prom 6) and Prokofiev's Fifth Symphony (Prom 47),' says Oramo. 'Bruckner's Fifth Symphony (Prom 56) is a completely new venture.'

The Finnish maestro hasn't conducted any Bruckner symphonies during his time in London, but he sees the Royal Albert Hall as the ideal space to hear the Romantic masterpiece that is the Fifth. 'It's one of my favourite Bruckner symphonies. It's not the most popular, but I find it so incredibly deep – and radical in form – that, for me, it is a great masterpiece.'

In his Fifth Symphony, Prokofiev is equally profound. 'It's often considered an orchestral showpiece,' says Oramo. 'I think it's absolutely not that. It's a very strong, humanistic outcry.' Writing in the Soviet era, Prokofiev had to be evasive about his political views and he is a master of hidden meanings in his music. 'It marries very well with the new violin concerto by Philip Venables that we're premiering in the same Prom,' says Oramo.

Thomas Søndergård Proms 8 & 11
BBC National Orchestra of Wales

'It's a lovely way of simply saying thank you for some great years together.' That might be a rather understated way of referring to Mahler's gargantuan Eighth Symphony – not without reason nicknamed the 'Symphony of a Thousand'. But there's no doubt that for Danish conductor Thomas Søndergård, his Proms performance of the symphony (Prom 11) is a fittingly grand, celebratory way to mark his final concert as the BBC National Orchestra of Wales's Principal Conductor. 'Our journey together has been like a celebration of music-making – and I've been incredibly happy with the constant dialogue we've had together to maintain or increase our passions.'

What does he feel the challenges are of conducting such vast forces in such a mammoth symphony? 'I've worked a lot in opera houses, and in some ways a staged opera can be easier! But, if there's anywhere you'd want to perform Mahler's Eighth, it's at the Proms. I really want the audience to let the music's primal force be in control, rather than trying to intellectualise the piece. Sometimes classical music should just overwhelm you.'

He says of the Proms: 'It makes me happy that in today's world, where people are asking if art is even necessary, there's something that shows people are still screaming for tickets.'

SATURDAY 21 JULY

PROM 9
7.30pm–c9.45pm • Royal Albert Hall

PRICE BAND Ⓒ
WEEKEND PROMMING PASS *see page 170*

ERIN WALL

Ēriks Ešenvalds Shadow*   c8'
BBC commission: world premiere

Britten Sinfonia da Requiem   21'
INTERVAL

Beethoven Symphony No. 9
in D minor, 'Choral'   65'

Erin Wall *soprano*
Judit Kutasi *mezzo-soprano*
Russell Thomas *tenor*
Franz-Josef Selig *baritone*

BBC Proms Youth Choir
World Orchestra for Peace
Simon Halsey conductor
Donald Runnicles *conductor*

In the centenary year of the end of the First World War, the World Orchestra for Peace – founded by Georg Solti as an expression of international musical harmony – returns to the Proms with one of classical music's most potent statements of brotherhood and fellowship, Beethoven's Ninth Symphony. Composed in the shadow of the Second World War, Britten's *Sinfonia da Requiem* adds its own emotive warning against war. The concert opens with a new, First World War-themed work by Latvian composer Ēriks Ešenvalds, commissioned for the talented young singers of the BBC Proms Youth Choir. *See 'All Types of Beethoven', pages 88–91; 'New Music', pages 96–101.*

PROMS READING
5.45pm–6.25pm • Imperial College Union An exploration of the narrative voice, with Sarah Dillon and guests.
Edited version broadcast on BBC Radio 3 during tonight's interval

SUNDAY 22 JULY

PROM 10
11.00am–c12.00pm • Royal Albert Hall

PRICE BAND (A)
WEEKEND PROMMING PASS see page 170

IVETA APKALNA

Widor Symphony for Organ No. 5
in F minor – Toccata   6'

Franck Trois Pièces – Pièce héroïque   11'

Fauré, arr. Apkalna Pavane   8'

J. S. Bach Fantasia in G major,
BWV 572 (Pièce d'orgue)   10'

Thalben-Ball Variations on a Theme
by Paganini (A Study for the Pedals)   8'

Thierry Escaich Deux Évocations   13'

Iveta Apkalna organ

There will be no interval

Latvian organist Iveta Apkalna makes her Proms
debut with a programme of French 19th- and
20th-century music. Widor's thrilling Organ
Symphony No. 5, with its famous final-movement
Toccata, offers sprawling, extrovert drama, a mood
it shares with prize-winning French composer-
organist Thierry Escaich's exuberant *Évocations*,
with their nods to Baroque and Renaissance music.
Works by Franck and Bach's great G major Fantasia,
with its 'wonderful variations and foreign tones',
complete the programme given on the Royal Albert
Hall's famous 'Father' Willis organ. See *'Impressions
in Colour'*, pages 8–15.

> Every Prom broadcast
> live on BBC Radio 3

SUNDAY 22 JULY

PROM 11
7.00pm–c8.30pm • Royal Albert Hall

PRICE BAND (C)
WEEKEND PROMMING PASS see page 170

MORRIS ROBINSON

Mahler Symphony No. 8 in E flat major,
'Symphony of a Thousand'   80'

Tamara Wilson *soprano*
Camilla Nylund *soprano*
Joélle Harvey *soprano*
Christine Rice *mezzo-soprano*
Claudia Huckle *contralto*
Simon O'Neill *tenor*
Quinn Kelsey *baritone*
Morris Robinson *bass*

**Southend Boys' Choir and Southend
     Girls' Choir**
BBC National Chorus of Wales
BBC Symphony Chorus
London Symphony Chorus
BBC National Orchestra of Wales
Thomas Søndergård *conductor*

There will be no interval

'It is the biggest thing I have ever done,' said Mahler
of his Eighth Symphony – for which the BBC National
Orchestra of Wales and its Principal Conductor
Thomas Søndergård tonight join forces with no
fewer than five choirs. One of the grandest
symphonic statements of the repertoire, concluding
with a dramatic setting of the mystical closing scene
from Goethe's *Faust*, its mammoth scale matches
the impressive space of the Royal Albert Hall.
See *'Fantastic Four'*, pages 18–21.

THE LISTENING SERVICE
5.25pm–5.55pm • Imperial College Union A special Proms
edition of BBC Radio 3's *The Listening Service*. Tom Service
investigates the grip of the Faust legend over the imaginations
of composers and musicians ever since the early 19th century.
Edited version broadcast later this evening on BBC Radio 3

MONDAY 23 JULY

PROMS AT … CADOGAN HALL 2
1.00pm–c2.00pm • Cadogan Hall

For ticket prices, see page 162

JEAN RONDEAU

Rameau Pièces de clavecin,
Book 1 – Prelude in A minor   5'

Pièces de clavecin, Book 3 – excerpts   12'

Eve Risser Furakèla   c5'
BBC commission: world premiere

F. Couperin Pièces de clavecin,
Book 1 – Sarabande 'La lugubre';
Chaconne 'La Favorite'   9'

Royer Pièces de clavecin, Book 1 –
La sensible; La marche des Scythes   9'

Jean Rondeau *harpsichord*

There will be no interval

Young French harpsichordist Jean Rondeau is a
passionate and quirky champion of his instrument,
with a maverick energy that brings a contemporary
freshness to his period performances. Here, in an
all-French programme, he pairs music by giants of
the French Baroque – François Couperin, Jean-
Philippe Rameau and Joseph-Nicolas-Pancrace
Royer – with a world premiere by genre-crossing
French composer Eve Risser, whose music draws
on jazz and and improvisation to create its edgy
sound-world. See *'Impressions in Colour'*, pages 8–15,
'New Music', pages 96–101.

MONDAY 23 JULY

PROM 12
7.00pm–c9.05pm • Royal Albert Hall

PRICE BAND (A)

ALISA WEILERSTEIN

Beethoven Overture 'Coriolan' 8'

Shostakovich Cello Concerto No. 1
in E flat major 29'

INTERVAL

Andrew Norman new work 6'
UK premiere

Rachmaninov Symphonic Dances 36'

Alisa Weilerstein *cello*

BBC Symphony Orchestra
Karina Canellakis *conductor*

Following her exciting Proms debut with the
BBC Symphony Orchestra last year, rising young
American conductor Karina Canellakis returns to
direct the orchestra in two 20th-century Russian
masterpieces. Although composed just three years
before his death, Rachmaninov's *Symphonic Dances*
pulse with exhilarating rhythmic energy, while
Shostakovich's much-loved First Cello Concerto
features Alisa Weilerstein in the solo part originally
composed for the great cellist Mstislav Rostropovich.
Violence and tenderness battle in Beethoven's
Coriolan overture and a UK premiere by American
composer Andrew Norman completes the
programme. See 'New Music', pages 96–101.

🔲 *Broadcast on BBC Four on Sunday 29 July*

PROMS PLUS TALK
5.15pm–5.55pm • **Imperial College Union** Composer
Andrew Norman introduces his new work ahead of its UK
premiere tonight, and talks about his inspiration and ideas.
Edited version broadcast on BBC Radio 3 during tonight's interval

MONDAY 23 JULY

PROM 13 • LATE NIGHT
10.15pm–c11.30pm • Royal Albert Hall

PRICE BAND (E)

SHIVA FESHAREKI

Pioneers of Sound

Programme to include:

Daphne Oram Still Point c30'
world premiere of revised version

*plus electronic works by Delia Derbyshire
and others, and the world premiere of a
new work for orchestra and electronics*

Shiva Feshareki *turntables/electronics*

London Contemporary Orchestra
Robert Ames *conductor*

There will be no interval

Daphne Oram's visionary *Still Point* fills the cavernous
space of the Royal Albert Hall for the first time in the
premiere of a revised realisation based on recently
discovered archive material. Composed in 1949 –
almost a decade before Oram co-founded the BBC
Radiophonic Workshop – the piece was possibly the
first to combine a live orchestra with live electronic
manipulations, here played via turntables. *Still Point*
forms the centrepiece of a late-night sonic
exploration that features work by Delia Derbyshire –
another Radiophonic Workshop pioneer who
achieved cult status for her electronic arrangement
of the *Doctor Who* TV theme – as well as new works
inspired by the Radiophonic legacy.

🔲 *Broadcast on BBC Four on Friday 27 July*

Every Prom broadcast
live on BBC Radio 3

TUESDAY 24 JULY

PROM 14
7.30pm–c9.40pm • Royal Albert Hall

PRICE BAND (A)

LOUIS LORTIE

Wagner The Mastersingers of
Nuremberg – overture 10'

Schubert, orch. Liszt
Die junge Nonne; Gretchen am Spinnrade;
Lied der Mignon; Erlkönig 13'

Zimmermann Symphony in
One Movement 18'

INTERVAL

Schubert, orch. Liszt Fantasy
in C major, D760, 'Wanderer' 22'

Sibelius Symphony No. 7 22'

Elizabeth Watts *soprano*
Louis Lortie *piano*

BBC Philharmonic
John Storgårds *conductor*

Sibelius's genre-bending Seventh unfolds in a
continuous musical gesture of expansive, if
characteristically enigmatic, nobility. Centenary
composer Bernd Alois Zimmermann's *Symphony
in One Movement* is another assault on tradition
that kicks against Wagner's rousing overture to
The Mastersingers of Nuremberg. Four popular Schubert
songs and his technically formidable 'Wanderer'
Fantasy get a colourful orchestral upscaling.

PROMS PLUS TALK
5.45pm–6.25pm • **Imperial College Union** Horatio Clare
and BBC Radio 3 New Generation Thinker Seán Williams
talk about the inspiration that a wandering life brought to
composers and writers of the 18th and 19th centuries.
Edited version broadcast on BBC Radio 3 during tonight's interval

WEDNESDAY 25 JULY

PROM 15

7.30pm–c9.55pm • Royal Albert Hall

PRICE BAND A

BEN GERNON

Tansy Davies What Did We See?
(orchestral suite from 'Between Worlds') *c20'*
BBC commission: world premiere

Beethoven Piano Concerto No. 5
in E flat major, 'Emperor'   38'

INTERVAL

Brahms Symphony No. 2 in D major   42'

Paul Lewis *piano*

BBC Philharmonic
Ben Gernon *conductor*

Life is celebrated and loss mourned in music
spanning over 200 years. The BBC Philharmonic
and its Principal Guest Conductor Ben Gernon
pair Beethoven's majestic final piano concerto –
for which we welcome back Paul Lewis, who played
all five Beethoven piano concertos in the 2010
season – with Brahms's sunny Second Symphony,
whose lyrical, pastoral spirit harks back to the earlier
composer's own 'Pastoral' Symphony (No. 6).
The concert opens in a more sombre, contemplative
mood with the world premiere of Tansy Davies's
What Did We See? – a meditation on death, healing
and transcendence that builds on material from
the composer's recent 9/11-inspired opera *Between
Worlds*. See 'New Music', pages 96–101.

Broadcast on BBC Four on Sunday 5 August

PROMS PLUS TALK

5.45pm–6.25pm • Imperial College Union Composer
Tansy Davies introduces her new work *What Did We See?*
and talks about her ideas and inspiration.
Edited version broadcast on BBC Radio 3 during tonight's interval

Dame Sarah Connolly
Proms at … Cadogan Hall 4
Songs by Britten, Lisa Illean and
Mark-Anthony Turnage

Dame Sarah Connolly's lunchtime Prom is
inspired by the Royal College of Music and the
composers who studied and taught there. It was
also the place where the British mezzo-soprano
discovered her love of singing, after initially
focusing on the piano. 'I'm extremely lucky to
have been influenced by Sir David Willcocks,'
says Connolly. 'He was a great supporter, and
singing in his chamber choir propelled me into
that sphere.' She joined the BBC Singers, then
embarked on life as an opera singer.

Throughout her career, English song has been
one of Connolly's loves. 'I'm completely proud
of England, the poetic history and Shakespeare,
and I'm impressed by the way composers
responded in song,' she says. 'I particularly
promote English song abroad.'

That's true of this recital, which takes us from
Stanford via Gurney and Bridge to Turnage.
'There's something elegiac about all of these
songs,' says Connolly. 'I see the lineage of these
composers, that's the thing.' The programme
also includes the world premieres of Lisa Illean's
Sleeplessness … Sails and, remarkably, two
'lost' songs by Britten. The composer wrote
'A Sweet Lullaby' and 'Somnus' for *A Charm
of Lullabies*, but ultimately they weren't included
in Britten's final selection.

Gerald Finley • Prom 75
Stanford: Songs of the Sea

It is an 'absolute thrill and an honour' to appear
at the Last Night of the Proms, says Gerald
Finley. There's also a sense of coming full circle
for the Canadian baritone. When he moved to
the UK as a student, one of his very first musical
experiences was going to the Last Night. 'It was
the most exhilarating concert I had ever been
party to,' he recalls. 'It was extraordinary to
see everyone standing, and witnessing this huge
celebration with everyone just having the most
wonderful time.'

Now Finley will take centre-stage at the Royal
Albert Hall, and one of the main items has a
particular meaning for him – Stanford's *Songs of
the Sea*, for baritone solo, chorus and orchestra.
'I began as a chorister in Canada in the English
cathedral tradition and Stanford was my main
introduction to choral music,' he explains. After
a year at the Royal College of Music, he became
a member of the Choir of King's College,
Cambridge. He feels that Stanford's music
embodies the feast of choral singing that first
brought him to the UK.

'*Songs of the Sea* is a perfect piece for the Proms.
It celebrates Britain, its island nature and its
adventurousness over the centuries,' he says.
'It reflects a jaunty, nostalgic view. There's a very
evocative use of chorus, almost mystical voices
coming from the fogs and mists, and the baritone
solo leads the emotion. The writing is amazing.'

THURSDAY 26 JULY

PROM 16
7.30pm–c9.35pm • Royal Albert Hall

PRICE BAND Ⓐ

ANNA STÉPHANY

Wagner Tannhäuser – overture   14'
Debussy La damoiselle élue   20'

INTERVAL

Stravinsky
Song of the Nightingale   20'
The Firebird – suite (1945 version)   31'

Sabine Devieilhe soprano
Anna Stéphany mezzo-soprano

Hallé Choir (female voices)
Hallé Youth Choir (female voices)
Hallé
Sir Mark Elder conductor

Sabine Devieilhe and Anna Stéphany are the soloists in centenary composer Claude Debussy's Wagner-infused, mythical-fantasy cantata *La damoiselle élue*. Wagner's relationship with Paris soured over his opera *Tannhäuser* but Stravinsky was practically adopted by the city. Tonight's second half features two of the latter's most colourful scores, whose striking resemblances result from the fact that Stravinsky broke off work on *The Nightingale* (the opera on which tonight's symphonic poem is based) in order to write his first ballet, *The Firebird. See 'Impressions in Colour', pages 8–15.*

PROMS PLUS TALK
5.45pm–6.25pm • Imperial College Union An exploration of the relationships between birds and humans, with Tim Birkhead and prize-winning author of *H is for Hawk*, Helen Macdonald. *Edited version broadcast on BBC Radio 3 during tonight's interval*

FRIDAY 27 JULY

PROM 17
7.00pm–c9.30pm • Royal Albert Hall

PRICE BAND Ⓐ
WEEKEND PROMMING PASS *see page 170*

TAI MURRAY

Parry Symphony No. 5 in B minor   27'
Vaughan Williams The Lark Ascending   15'

INTERVAL

Parry Hear my words, ye people   15'
Holst Ode to Death   12'
Vaughan Williams Pastoral Symphony (No. 3)   35'

Tai Murray violin
Francesca Chiejina soprano
Ashley Riches bass-baritone

BBC National Chorus of Wales
BBC National Orchestra of Wales
Martyn Brabbins conductor

As well as being the composer of that Last Night favourite, *Jerusalem*, Hubert Parry (died 1918) was in many ways the father of contemporary English music, teaching both Vaughan Williams and Gustav Holst. Tonight's celebration of his legacy features Parry's own hope-filled Fifth Symphony alongside Vaughan Williams's elegiac *The Lark Ascending* and two memorials inspired by the First World War: Holst's *Ode to Death* and Vaughan Williams's *Pastoral Symphony. See 'Musical Memorials', pages 60–65.*

Ⓞ *Broadcast on BBC Four tonight*

PROMS PLUS TALK
5.15pm–5.55pm • Imperial College Union Writers Melissa Harrison and John Lewis-Stempel contemplate contemporary British landscapes and the challenges of rural life today. *Edited version broadcast on BBC Radio 3 during tonight's interval*

SATURDAY 28 JULY

PROM 18
7.30pm–c9.10pm • Royal Albert Hall

PRICE BAND Ⓒ
WEEKEND PROMMING PASS *see page 170*

TEODOR CURRENTZIS

Beethoven Symphony No. 2 in D major   32'

INTERVAL

Beethoven Symphony No. 5 in C minor   31'

MusicAeterna
Teodor Currentzis director

This is Beethoven, but not as you know it. One of the boldest, most exhilarating new voices in classical music, Greek-Russian conductor Teodor Currentzis, and his period-instrument ensemble MusicAeterna are together ripping up the classical rulebook with thrilling, award-winning results. In the ensemble's hands a classic programme of Beethoven symphonies – the vivacious, 'smiling' Second and the emotionally charged Fifth – becomes something altogether more punk and provocative. *See 'All Types of Beethoven', pages 88–91.*

PROMS READING
5.45pm–6.25pm • Imperial College Union Shahidha Bari introduces a series of the best comic readings from literature to tie in with the 'musical jokes' in Beethoven's Second Symphony. *Edited version broadcast on BBC Radio 3 during tonight's interval*

SUNDAY 29 JULY

PROMS 19 & 20
1.00pm–c3.00pm & 5.00pm–c7.00pm
Royal Albert Hall

PRICE BAND (H)
WEEKEND PROMMING PASS *see page 170*

Ten Pieces Prom

Music by Kerry Andrew, Mason Bates, Joseph Bologne (Chevalier de Saint-Georges), Copland, Dvořák, Elgar, Orff, Purcell, Sibelius, Stravinsky and Tchaikovsky

Naomi Wilkinson *presenter*

Ten Pieces Children's Choir
BBC Singers
BBC Symphony Orchestra
Rafael Payare *conductor*

There will be one interval

Join CBBC's Naomi Wilkinson in a thrilling musical adventure for all the family inspired by the BBC's Ten Pieces project, including Copland's foot-stomping 'Hoe-Down' from *Rodeo*, the dramatic 'O Fortuna' from Orff's *Carmina burana*, the lyrical Largo from Dvořák's 'New World' Symphony and a selection of colourful portraits from Elgar's 'Enigma' Variations. Along with the Ten Pieces Children's Choir, young performers and some very special guests, discover the characters and stories behind some spectacular orchestral pieces and watch the imaginations of a new generation of music-makers take flight.
See 'Magical Moments', pages 78–79.

British Sign Language-interpreted performances

📻 *Broadcast live on BBC Radio 3 (Prom 20); recorded for future broadcast on BBC Radio 2 (Prom 19)*

PROMS FAMILY CHORUS
10.30am–12.00pm • Imperial College Union Bring all the family along to sing Kerry Andrew's Ten Pieces song *No Place Like*. No experience of singing required. *Suitable for all the family (ages 7-plus). See pages 78–79 for details.*

PROMS CHILDREN'S 'PRESS CONFERENCE'
3.15pm–4.00pm • Imperial College Union A chance for children to pose questions to leading musicians from across the Proms season and to find out more about what it takes to make it in music! *Suitable for all the family, ages 7-plus. For more information, visit bbc.co.uk/proms. A number of places will be allocated to schoolchildren from across the UK.*

MONDAY 30 JULY

PROMS AT ... CADOGAN HALL 3
1.00pm–c2.00pm • Cadogan Hall

For ticket prices, see page 162

JOSEPH TAWADROS

Ancient Rituals and New Tales

Programme to include:

Jessica Wells Rhapsody for solo oud c5'
BBC commission: world premiere

Joseph Tawadros *oud*
There will be no interval

Cairo-born, longtime Sydney-resident oud virtuoso Joseph Tawadros has reimagined the range of music accessible to his instrument, the ancient Middle-Eastern lute. Steeped in traditional Arabic music (his grandfather was a respected composer, oud player and violinist) but also an avid collaborator with a diverse array of musicians, he draws equally on jazz and folk styles in a kaleidoscopic celebration of his instrument. His debut at the Proms embraces traditional Arabic taqsim (improvisation) and maqam (pieces based on traditional scales) as well as his own compositions, and the world premiere of a BBC commission by Australian composer Jessica Wells.
See 'New Music', pages 96–101.

┌──────────────────────┐
│ **Every Prom broadcast** │
│ **live on BBC Radio 3** │
└──────────────────────┘

MONDAY 30 JULY

PROM 21
7.30pm–c9.45pm • Royal Albert Hall

PRICE BAND (A)

ILAN VOLKOV

Mozart Notturno in D major, K286   17'
Georg Friedrich Haas Concerto grosso No. 1   30'
UK premiere

INTERVAL

Strauss An Alpine Symphony   50'

Hornroh Modern Alphorn Quartet
BBC Scottish Symphony Orchestra
Ilan Volkov *conductor*

A concert of sonic scope and spectacle from the BBC Scottish Symphony Orchestra and its Principal Guest Conductor Ilan Volkov climaxes in Strauss's dramatic *An Alpine Symphony*, which paints a vivid picture of a day's hiking in the Bavarian mountains. The Alps also make their way into Georg Friedrich Haas's *Concerto grosso* in the form of four alphorns – enormous wooden horns, whose other-worldly overtones also inspired Rossini and Berlioz. The concert opens with Mozart's *Notturno*, an unfinished Salzburg carnival serenade, whose four separate instrumental groups will be dispersed around the Royal Albert Hall for maximum acoustic drama.
See 'New Music', pages 96–101.

PROMS PLUS TALK
5.45pm–6.25pm • Imperial College Union
Abbie Garrington and Dan Richards discuss the appeal of the mountains and how wild landscapes have inspired creativity.
Edited version broadcast on BBC Radio 3 during tonight's interval

Miloš Karadaglić • Prom 25
Joby Talbot: Guitar Concerto

Pekka Kuusisto • Prom 47
Philip Venables: Venables Plays Bartók

'I wanted fireworks of sound and expression, and no compromises!' Guitarist Miloš Karadaglić had high expectations of the brand-new Guitar Concerto written for him by British composer Joby Talbot. And he's thrilled with the result. 'It's a really exciting piece, a very imaginative, programmatic work. Joby is a true magician of sound and colour, and working with him has been one of the most inspirational creative processes of my professional life.'

The two men met after Karadaglić heard Talbot's score for the Royal Ballet's *Alice's Adventures in Wonderland*. 'It left me speechless and I was determined to find a way to work with him. His talent for spine-tingling intimacy and sweeps of extraordinary drama felt like the perfect match for the subtle but capricious nature of the guitar – and for my own style as a player.'

There was one technical issue that Talbot and Karadaglić had to resolve, however: balance. 'We'll carefully position speakers within the orchestra, so that the guitar sound feels amplified but natural – that way we can preserve a full orchestral size for maximum effect on stage.'

A hand injury has forced Karadaglić to take a break from playing since 2016. How does it feel to be back performing again? 'That period was scary. But I'm returning to the stage renewed and re-energised, never more determined to follow my dreams and ideals.'

'I had the time of my life,' says Pekka Kuusisto, recalling his Proms debut in 2016, playing Tchaikovsky's Violin Concerto and an encore that got the whole audience singing. 'It's going to be very difficult to have more fun! I'm completely prepared for my future Proms career to be a swift downhill.' This seems unlikely, however, given that the Finnish violinist returns this summer with two concertos – one brand-new, one a UK premiere – both tailor-made for his unique brand of virtuosity and playfulness.

One is a BBC commission by Philip Venables, with whom Kuusisto started working last year. 'We hit it off very well. He is a composer whose music doesn't feel familiar from anything else,' says the violinist. 'We spoke about what we felt was missing in the concerto repertoire.'

'I come from the land of the Sibelius Violin Concerto, and that's the blueprint,' explains Kuusisto, who in 1995 became the first Finn to win the International Jean Sibelius Violin Competition. 'I started thinking about the role of the soloist: are they channelling something, speaking about their own emotions, or part of the orchestra? With the Venables we want to give the soloist a new challenge.'

Kuusisto also features in Anders Hillborg's *Bach Materia* (Prom 29), a recent companion piece for Bach's Brandenburg Concerto No. 3. 'It's a real wild animal when you let it out of its cage.'

TUESDAY 31 JULY

PROM 22
7.00pm–c8.55pm • Royal Albert Hall

PRICE BAND **A**

ANDREW MANZE

Haydn Symphony No. 104 in D major, 'London'   29'

INTERVAL

Vaughan Williams A London Symphony (Symphony No. 2)   50'

BBC Scottish Symphony Orchestra
Andrew Manze conductor

Following on from the Hallé's Paris-inspired programme (Prom 16) comes a corresponding focus on London. Andrew Manze and the BBC Scottish Symphony Orchestra open with Haydn's lively, assertive final symphony – composed and first performed in London during the composer's second triumphant residency. First performed in March 1914, Vaughan Williams's *A London Symphony* evokes the chimes of Westminster, a chilly November in Bloomsbury and the bright lights of the Strand in a city that would soon be scarred by war. *See 'Musical Memorials', pages 60–65.*

PROMS PLUS TALK
5.15pm–5.55pm • Imperial College Union Novelists John Lanchester and Diana Evans discuss depicting contemporary London in their fiction.
Edited version broadcast on BBC Radio 3 during tonight's interval

TUESDAY 31 JULY

PROM 23 • LATE NIGHT
10.15pm–c11.30pm • Royal Albert Hall

PRICE BAND **E**

MISTA SAVONA

Havana Meets Kingston

Mista Savona *keyboards/samples*
Randy Valentine *vocals*
Solís *vocals*
Julito Padrón *trumpet/vocals*
Stepper *saxophone*
Bopee *guitar*
Rolando Luna *piano*
Mafia & Fluxy *drums/electric bass*
Yaroldys Abreu *percussion*
Brenda Navarette *percussion/vocals*

There will be no interval

Australia's leading reggae and dancehall producer Mista Savona (aka Jake Savona) has gathered together some of Cuba's and Jamaica's most influential musicians to create a fresh, unifying take on the music of both cultures. Drawing from the styles of roots reggae, dub and dancehall on the one hand and son, salsa, rumba and Afro-Cuban on the other, Havana Meets Kingston sees a top-flight group of musicians come together in an effortless meeting of genres. Energetic and passionate vocals in Spanish, English and Jamaican patois twist and turn over distinctly Cuban rhythms and melodies, while the typically deep bass lines of Jamaica pulse beneath.

⬤ *Broadcast on BBC Four on Friday 3 August*

Every Prom broadcast
live on BBC Radio 3

WEDNESDAY 1 AUGUST

PROM 24
7.00pm–c9.20pm • Royal Albert Hall

PRICE BAND **A**

OTTO TAUSK

Smyth The Wreckers – On the Cliffs of Cornwall (Prelude to Act 2) 8'
Dvořák Cello Concerto in B minor 42'

INTERVAL

Strauss Ein Heldenleben 45'

Daniel Müller-Schott *cello*

BBC National Orchestra of Wales
Otto Tausk *conductor*

Triumphant horns and a flirtatious, vivacious solo violin set the tone for Strauss's vivid autobiographical tone-poem *Ein Heldenleben* – 'A Hero's Life', outwardly inspired by 'an ideal of great and manly heroism'. The orchestra is also at the forefront in Dvořák's Cello Concerto, sounding as an equal partner to the soloist – German cellist Daniel Müller-Schott, who returns to the Proms under tonight's debut conductor Otto Tausk – in an intensely personal work that marries a pervasive sense of longing with real passion. In the centenary year of British women gaining the right to vote, Ethel Smyth's evocative Act 2 Prelude from *The Wreckers* celebrates a key British composer who, as a suffragette, spent two months in Holloway Prison. See 'Fantastic Four', pages 18–21.

PROMS PLUS TALK
5.15pm–5.55pm • Imperial College Union
Ahead of tonight's performance of Dvořák's Cello Concerto, famously played by Mstislav Rostropovich at the Proms 50 years ago as Soviet tanks entered Prague, Sir John Tusa discusses the cultural repercussions started by the upheaval across the Iron Curtain.
Edited version broadcast on BBC Radio 3 during tonight's interval

---

THURSDAY 2 AUGUST

PROM 25
7.00pm–c9.00pm • Royal Albert Hall

PRICE BAND **A**

ALEXANDER VEDERNIKOV

Glinka Summer Night in Madrid (Spanish Overture No. 2) 10'
Joby Talbot Guitar Concerto c25'
BBC commission: world premiere

INTERVAL

Tchaikovsky The Nutcracker – Act 1 40'

Miloš Karadaglić *guitar*

Finchley Children's Music Group
BBC Symphony Orchestra
Alexander Vedernikov *conductor*

Guitarist Miloš Karadaglić is the soloist in a new concerto written especially for him by Joby Talbot. Taking inspiration from Karadaglić's Montenegrin heritage, Talbot's typically rhythmic piece incorporates Balkan dances into its propulsive flow. Dance also runs through both Glinka's heat-soaked *Summer Night in Madrid,* accompanied by pulsing castanets, and the expansive waltzes of Tchaikovsky's ballet *The Nutcracker,* whose complete Act 1 is here performed for the first time at the Proms. See 'New Music', pages 96–101.

PROMS PLUS TALK
5.15pm–5.55pm • Imperial College Union (Concert Hall)
Joby Talbot introduces his Guitar Concerto ahead of its world premiere tonight.
Edited version broadcast on BBC Radio 3 during tonight's interval

PROMS FAMILY WORKSHOP
5.15pm–6.00pm • Imperial College Union (Dining Hall)
Join professional musicians for a family-friendly introduction to this evening's Prom. Bring your instrument and join in!
Suitable for all the family (ages 7-plus). See pages 78–79 for details.

THURSDAY 2 AUGUST

PROM 26 • LATE NIGHT
10.15pm–c11.30pm • Royal Albert Hall

PRICE BAND E

ANNA PROHASKA

Purcell
Dido and Aeneas – excerpts 15'
The Fairy Queen – Chaconne: Dance for Chinese Man and Woman 3'

Graupner Dido, Queen of Carthage – excerpts 8'

Sartorio Julius Caesar in Egypt – excerpts 3'

Locke The Tempest – Curtain Tune 5'

Handel Julius Caesar in Egypt – 'Che sento? Oh Dio! … Se pietà di me non senti' 8'

Castello Sonata No. 15 in D minor 5'

Cavalli Dido – 'Rè de' Getuli altero … Il mio marito' 3'

Hasse Mark Antony and Cleopatra – 'Morte col fiero aspetto' 4'

Handel Concerto grosso in C minor, Op. 6 No. 8 15'

Anna Prohaska soprano

Il Giardino Armonico
Giovanni Antonini conductor

There will be no interval

Austrian soprano Anna Prohaska joins Italy's leading early music ensemble for a programme that takes inspiration from two great queens, Cleopatra and Dido, who proved endlessly fascinating to Baroque composers. Operatic arias are framed by some of the period's most vital instrumental works.

FRIDAY 3 AUGUST

PROM 27
7.30pm–c9.45pm • Royal Albert Hall

PRICE BAND B
WEEKEND PROMMING PASS *see page 170*

JULIE FOWLIS

Folk Music around Britain and Ireland

Julie Fowlis
Jarlath Henderson
Sam Lee

ALAW
The Unthanks

BBC Concert Orchestra
Stephen Bell conductor

In a Prom that celebrates the history and evolution of the folk music scene in Britain and Ireland, the BBC Concert Orchestra collaborates with some of the folk world's leading musicians who are pushing the boundaries of traditional music, and bringing with them a new breed of folk fan. With performers from England, Scotland, Wales and Ireland, this Prom reflects the diversity of a genre of music that, while steeped in tradition, is constantly evolving and reinventing itself through the generations.

There will be one interval

Broadcast on BBC Four tonight
Broadcast on BBC Radio 2 on Sunday 10 August

PROMS SING
5.30pm–6.30pm • Imperial College Union (Metric Bar)
Join us for a rousing session of folk songs from across the British Isles. No experience of singing is required.
Suitable for ages 16-plus. See pages 66–69 for details.

PROMS PLUS TALK
5.45pm–6.25pm • Imperial College Union (Concert Hall)
Poets Gillian Clarke and Peter Mackay discuss the folk tales of the islands of the United Kingdom.
Edited version broadcast on BBC Radio 3 during tonight's interval

SATURDAY 4 AUGUST

PROMS AT…LINCOLN DRILL HALL
3.00pm–c4.15pm & 7.30pm–c8.45pm

For ticket prices, see page 162

WILLIAM CONWAY

Stravinsky The Soldier's Tale 65'

Hebrides Ensemble
William Conway conductor

Following the success of last year's 'Proms at …' concert in Hull, the BBC Proms once again travels outside London, this time to Lincoln. The city's 19th-century Drill Hall – home to the Fourth Battalion of the Lincolnshire Regiment, deployed to the Western Front in 1914 – is the evocative setting for a staged performance of Stravinsky's First World War music-theatre piece The Soldier's Tale. William Conway conducts the Hebrides Ensemble in this tale of a young man who sells his soul (and his violin) to the Devil in exchange for untold wealth – or so it seems.

There will be no interval

Broadcast live on BBC Radio 3 (3.00pm performance)

> Every Prom broadcast live on BBC Radio 3

SATURDAY 4 AUGUST

PROM 28
7.30pm–c9.45pm • Royal Albert Hall

PRICE BAND A
WEEKEND PROMMING PASS *see page 170*

TAMARA STEFANOVICH

Mussorgsky,
arr. Rimsky-Korsakov A Night on the
Bare Mountain   12'

George Benjamin Dance Figures   16'

Ravel Piano Concerto for the
Left Hand   19'

INTERVAL

Ligeti Lontano   12'

Debussy La mer   23'

Tamara Stefanovich *piano*

National Youth Orchestra of Great Britain
George Benjamin *conductor*

The National Youth Orchestra of Great Britain
return to conjure a series of vivid worlds, both real
and imagined. The sea roars and shimmers in
Debussy's *La mer*, Mussorgsky paints eerie visions of
a Witches' Sabbath, while Ligeti's *Lontano* summons
the 'dream worlds of childhood'. Ravel's brooding
Concerto for the Left Hand was commissioned by
a pianist who lost an arm in the First World War.
See 'Impressions in Colour', pages 8–15.

📻 *Broadcast on BBC Four on Sunday 12 August*

NYO TEEN HANGOUT
5.25pm–6.25pm • Imperial College Union (Metric Bar)
Join musicians from the National Youth Orchestra of Great
Britain at this unique and friendly event for teenagers hosted
by the NYO's Young Promoters – a great chance to find
out about the music in this evening's Prom.
*Suitable for ages 12–18. The first 100 young people to attend the
event will have the option of buying a guaranteed Promming ticket
for this evening's concert.*

SPOTLIGHT
DRAMATIC HEROINES

Louise Alder • Prom 74
Theodora

Louise Alder first heard Handel's *Theodora*
when she was 10, at Glyndebourne. 'I vividly
remember Dawn Upshaw as Theodora, but also
Lorraine Hunt Lieberson as Irene was so
unbelievable,' says Alder. 'I was so lucky to go,
which happened because my mother played in
the Orchestra of the Age of Enlightenment. I
come from a family of musicians and I grew up
with a lot of Handel.' Now, just over 20 years
on, with a clutch of prizes in hand, including
from BBC Cardiff Singer of the World and the
International Opera Awards, the British soprano
is taking the title role in the oratorio.

'*Theodora* is one of the most extraordinarily
dramatic oratorios ever written,' says Alder. 'The
story is gripping, real and true. It can be put in
modern-day terms too: a group of worshippers
from a religious community being persecuted
and put to death still happens all over the world.'

The story of the Christian martyr Theodora is
tragic but, says Alder, Handel sees her as an
incredibly serene and calm character. 'He writes
very lyrically for her. She has beautiful airs and
soul-searching music.'

Alder always starts with the text. 'Especially
with a Handel oratorio, when the libretto isn't
necessarily so clear to the modern English
speaker, I try to put it into my own words,' she
says, adding: 'In opera and oratorio, Handel is a
real favourite of mine.'

Christina Gansch • Prom 5
Mélisande

'Every time I work on it or listen to it, I feel
more pulled into its world of watery mystery
and magic.' Austrian soprano Christina Gansch
is talking about her title-role in Debussy's opera
Pelléas et Mélisande, with which she makes
her Proms debut (Prom 5) in a production
direct from Glyndebourne. 'It's just wonderful,
and you have the feeling that the opera really
sucks you in.'

It's the first time the already acclaimed young
singer has taken on the iconic but hard-to-pin-
down role of Mélisande, an enigmatic figure who
is discovered by Golaud wandering aimlessly in
the woods. What has Gansch found challenging
about it? 'The most important thing has been
time: Mélisande isn't a role that you can learn
quickly. Musically, there's nothing like it. It sits
quite low in the soprano voice, and it's almost
like notated speech – it feels like Debussy wanted
to put fragility and maybe even vulnerability in
the voice by setting it so low.'

Despite the event marking her first Prom as a
performer, she's already had plenty of Proms
experiences as a listener. 'When I came to
London as a student, one of the first things my
friends recommended was that I should go
Promming. At first I was a bit confused about
what that was. But how awesome is it that, for
an international festival, anyone can just turn
up and queue, and get a ticket?'

SUNDAY 5 AUGUST

PROM 29
3.00pm–c5.40pm • Royal Albert Hall

PRICE BAND **B**
WEEKEND PROMMING PASS *see page 170*

The Brandenburg Project – 1

Bach Brandenburg Concerto No. 1
in F major   20'

Mark-Anthony Turnage Maya   12'
UK premiere

Bach Brandenburg Concerto No. 3
in G major   10'

Anders Hillborg Bach Materia   18'
UK premiere

INTERVAL

Bach Brandenburg Concerto No. 5
in D major   21'

Uri Caine Hamsa   28'
UK premiere

Pekka Kuusisto *violin*
Antje Weithaas *violin*
Maya Beiser *cello*
Fiona Kelly *flute*
Uri Caine *piano*
Mahan Esfahani *harpsichord*

Swedish Chamber Orchestra
Thomas Dausgaard *conductor*

Over two concerts in one day, Thomas Dausgaard and the Swedish Chamber Orchestra present Bach's six Brandenburg Concertos – each with its own different and distinctive orchestration – alongside six newly commissioned companion works, to create a brand-new musical cycle spanning almost three centuries, heard here for the first time in the UK. *See 'Brandenburgs Old and New', pages 92–95; 'New Music', pages 96–101.*

PROMS FAMILY ORCHESTRA & CHORUS
11.00am–1.00pm • Imperial College Union Join professional musicians to create your own music inspired by this afternoon's Prom. *Suitable for all the family (ages 7-plus). See pages 78–79 for details.*

SUNDAY 5 AUGUST

PROM 30
7.30pm–c9.50pm • Royal Albert Hall

PRICE BAND **B**
WEEKEND PROMMING PASS *see page 170*

The Brandenburg Project – 2

Bach Brandenburg Concerto No. 4
in G major   15'

Olga Neuwirth Aello – ballet
mécanomorphe   18'
UK premiere

Brett Dean Approach – Prelude to
a Canon   18'
UK premiere

Bach Brandenburg Concerto No. 6
in B flat major   17'

INTERVAL

Bach Brandenburg Concerto No. 2
in F major   12'

Steven Mackey Triceros   18'
UK premiere

Antje Weithaas *violin*
Brett Dean, Tabea Zimmermann *violas*
Claire Chase *flute*
Fiona Kelly *flute*
Mårten Larsson *oboe*
Håkan Hardenberger *trumpet*

Swedish Chamber Orchestra
Thomas Dausgaard *conductor*

The Second, Fourth and Sixth of Bach's Brandenburg Concertos appear alongside present-day responses by Steven Mackey, Olga Neuwirth and Brett Dean. The soloists include star Swedish trumpeter Håkan Hardenberger, German violinist Antje Weithaas and violist Brett Dean himself. *See 'Brandenburgs Old and New', pages 92–95; 'New Music', pages 96–101.*

PROMS PLUS TALK
5.45pm–6.25pm • Imperial College Union
BBC New Generation Thinker and poet Sandeep Parmar and poet Sean O'Brien scrutinise contemporary reworkings of classical stories.
Edited version broadcast on BBC Radio 3 during tonight's interval

MONDAY 6 AUGUST

PROMS AT … CADOGAN HALL 4
1.00pm–c2.00pm • Cadogan Hall

For ticket prices, see page 162

Stanford A soft day   2'

Parry Weep you no more, sad fountains   3'

Vaughan Williams The House of
Life – 'Love-Sight'   4'

Gurney Thou didst delight my eyes   2'

Somervell Into my heart an air
that kills   2'

Bridge Come to me in my dreams   4'

Howells Goddess of Night   2'

Bridge Journey's End   4'

Britten A Sweet Lullaby   c5'
world premiere

Britten Somnus   c2'
world premiere

Holst Journey's End   3'

Britten A Charm of Lullabies   11'

Mark-Anthony Turnage Farewell c2'
world premiere

Lisa Illean Sleeplessness … Sails   c6'
BBC commission: world premiere

Dame Sarah Connolly *mezzo-soprano*
Joseph Middleton *piano*

There will be no interval

Lullabies and dreams, sleep and insomnia are themes that drift through this night-inspired recital of English song. British mezzo-soprano Dame Sarah Connolly makes her Proms recital debut in a programme that combines familiar favourites – Britten's cycle *A Charm of Lullabies* and songs by Vaughan Williams and Howells – with world premieres by Mark-Anthony Turnage and Lisa Illean, as well as of two songs Britten initially intended for *A Charm of Lullabies*. Hubert Parry's 'Weep you no more' marks the centenary of his death and all the composers studied or taught at the Royal College of Music. *See 'Musical Memorials', pages 60–65; 'New Music', pages 96–101.*

MONDAY 6 AUGUST

PROM 31
7.00pm–c9.00pm • Royal Albert Hall

PRICE BAND Ⓑ

OSMO VÄNSKÄ

Bernstein Candide – overture   5'
Gershwin Piano Concerto in F major   31'
INTERVAL
Ives Symphony No. 2   37'

Inon Barnatan *piano*

Minnesota Orchestra
Osmo Vänskä *conductor*

A great American orchestra marks Leonard Bernstein's 100th-anniversary year with a concert of 20th-century American classics that represent Bernstein in his multiple guises as composer, conductor and pianist. The breathless exuberance of Bernstein's *Candide* overture is extended by Inon Barnatan in Gershwin's Concerto in F major, which filters the composer's popular jazz idiom through classical structures and Lisztian virtuosity. Premiered by Bernstein and the New York Philharmonic in 1951, Ives's attractive Second Symphony melds European techniques with an all-American sound-world. *See 'An Embarrassment of Gifts', pages 30–33.*

PROMS FAMILY WORKSHOP
5.15pm–6.00pm • Imperial College Union (Dining Hall)
Join professional musicians for a family-friendly introduction to this evening's Prom. Bring your instrument and join in! *Suitable for all the family (ages 7-plus). See pages 78–79 for details.*

PROMS PLUS TALK
5.15pm–5.55pm • Imperial College Union (Concert Hall)
An introduction to Ives's Symphony No. 2 with musicologist J. P. E. Harper Scott.
Edited version broadcast on BBC Radio 3 during tonight's interval

MONDAY 6 AUGUST

PROM 32 • LATE NIGHT   ☽
10.15pm–c11.30pm • Royal Albert Hall

PRICE BAND Ⓔ

NICHOLAS COLLON

Inside Shostakovich

Shostakovich Piano Concerto No. 2 in F major   20'
Tom Service and Nicholas Collon present Shostakovich's Symphony No. 9, with live excerpts 20'
Shostakovich Symphony No. 9 in E flat major   26'

Denis Kozhukhin *piano*
Tom Service *presenter*

Aurora Orchestra
Nicholas Collon *conductor*
There will be no interval

The Aurora Orchestra's Proms visits are always a highlight of the season – less a concert than a musical event. This year Nicholas Collon and the orchestra tackle their boldest challenge yet – performing Shostakovich's Ninth Symphony from memory. This concert presentation sees Radio 3 broadcaster Tom Service and conductor Nicholas Collon unpack this carefully constructed work, with its fleet-footed melodies and dance-filled rhythms, before the musicians put it back together again in a complete performance. This is a rare opportunity to experience a great symphony – one that Leonard Bernstein featured in one of his famous Young People's Concerts – from the inside out.

> **Every Prom broadcast live on BBC Radio 3**

TUESDAY 7 AUGUST

PROM 33   ▣
7.30pm–c9.35pm • Royal Albert Hall

PRICE BAND Ⓑ

JOHAN REUTER

Thea Musgrave Phoenix Rising   23'
INTERVAL
Brahms A German Requiem   68'

Golda Schultz *soprano*
Johan Reuter *baritone*

BBC Symphony Chorus
BBC Symphony Orchestra
Richard Farnes *conductor*

Inspired by the death of his mother, Brahms's tender, consoling *A German Requiem* couldn't be further from Verdi's and Berlioz's settings of the standard Latin Mass text. It's the first of three Requiems this season (*see also Proms 64 and 72*) marking 100 years since the end of the First World War. Richard Farnes makes his Proms debut directing the BBC Symphony Orchestra and Chorus, along with soloists Golda Schultz and Johan Reuter. Thea Musgrave's *Phoenix Rising* (marking the composer's 90th birthday this year) also traces a journey from darkness to light, enacting the conflict both spatially and musically in some of the composer's most dramatic writing. *See 'Musical Memorials', pages 60–65; 'Performance Art', pages 48–51.*

▣ *Broadcast on BBC Four on Friday 10 August*

PROMS PLUS TALK
5.45pm–6.25pm • Imperial College Union The Revd Lucy Winkett introduces Brahms's *A German Requiem*.
Edited version broadcast on BBC Radio 3 during tonight's interval

John Chest • Prom 5
baritone

'Debussy's *Pelléas et Mélisande* is this opera that's been circling round me,' says John Chest, the American baritone who came to international attention as a finalist in last year's BBC Cardiff Singer of the World competition, 'Since I was 18, people I've sung or auditioned for have said I needed to learn it.'

And now Chest has a date in the diary for singing that title-role in Glyndebourne's production of Debussy's only complete opera, which will also be semi-staged at this year's Proms. Learning the score felt like putting on a glove, he reflects. 'Britten's Billy Budd was the same. I felt it was my role.'

That said, Debussy's writing isn't without its challenges. 'The part of Pelléas lies quite high as it's written for a voice type that doesn't really exist,' explains Chest. 'And the music is so ethereal. It's not even the phrases that are hard, it's the intervals. There's no tune that just jumps off the page and is immediately singable. It has to seep down inside of you.'

'*Pelléas et Mélisande* is one of the most original pieces of music that exist,' Chest says – and few would disagree. This 1902 masterpiece has been hailed as a landmark in operatic history, notable for its elusive plot and remarkable musical style. 'Enigmatic is a good word for the whole story,' says Chest. 'The whole thing is a maze to try and figure out.'

Seong-Jin Cho • Prom 49
piano

'Chopin is one of the most important composers to me.' From South Korean pianist Seong-Jin Cho, winner of the 2015 International Chopin Piano Competition, and whose debut recording was an all-Chopin disc, that might hardly come as a surprise. 'He's a composer I feel very close to – his music is so dramatic, and sometimes poetic. And nostalgic too. Because he left his country when he was only 20, there's always a sense of nostalgia in his music at some point.'

It was with Chopin's First Piano Concerto that Cho won the prestigious contest, but it's the Second that he performs at his Prom. There are similarities between the two concertos, however, Cho feels. 'He wrote both concertos in Warsaw when he was around 20, so he was very young. I find the Second Concerto very fresh and passionate. It's very romantic but it's a very pure romanticism, because the composer still feels very young in it.'

Conducting the European Union Youth Orchestra for Cho's Prom will be Gianandrea Noseda, with whom Cho recorded Chopin's First Piano Concerto in 2016. 'It was a wonderful experience for me because Maestro Noseda is so experienced at conducting opera. Chopin's music is a little bit like opera at times – his melodies are always singing, and I also need to be flexible with my rhythms. Noseda was very sensitive to my playing – it was fantastic to work with him.'

WEDNESDAY 8 AUGUST

PROM 34
7.00pm–c9.05pm • Royal Albert Hall

PRICE BAND **A**

SALLY MATTHEWS

Walton Overture 'Portsmouth Point' *7'*
Copland Connotations *19'*
Britten Les illuminations *23'*

INTERVAL

Barber Two Scenes from 'Antony and Cleopatra' *18'*
Britten Four Sea Interludes from 'Peter Grimes' *16'*

Sally Matthews *soprano*

BBC Philharmonic
Juanjo Mena *conductor*

In Bernstein's centenary year, Juanjo Mena and the BBC Philharmonic celebrate with a transatlantic Prom, uniting music by British and American composers connected not just by generation but in many cases by personal friendship. Commissioned and premiered by Bernstein, Copland's *Connotations* is a portrait of 'the tensions, aspirations and drama inherent in the world today'. Its knotty confrontations find contrast in the sensuous beauty of Britten's orchestral song-cycle *Les illuminations*, while the sea provides inspiration both for Walton's bustling, bonhomous *Portsmouth Point* overture and Britten's boldly dramatic *Four Sea Interludes*. Two extracts from Samuel Barber's opera *Antony and Cleopatra* complete the programme.

PROMS PLUS TALK
5.15pm–5.55pm • Imperial College Union Film-maker and biographer Humphrey Burton explores Aaron Copland's influence on Benjamin Britten and Leonard Bernstein.
Edited version broadcast on BBC Radio 3 during tonight's interval

WEDNESDAY 8 AUGUST

PROM 35 • LATE NIGHT 🌙 ▣
10.15pm–c11.30pm • Royal Albert Hall

PRICE BAND **F**

SERPENTWITHFEET

New York: Sound of a City

Hercules & Love Affair
serpentwithfeet
Sharon Van Etten

Heritage Orchestra
Jules Buckley *conductor*

There will be no interval

Celebrating the music of a modern New York, the Heritage Orchestra and conductor Jules Buckley present their take on the sound of NYC today. With guest artists drawn from across the Big Apple, this Late Night Prom features new music from some of the city's rising stars, plus classic tracks by established acts that have changed the city's soundscape. Expect anything from pagan-gospel and disco-punk to feminist rap or DIY indie … the panoply of musical talent that continues to emanate from New York means anything could happen. *See 'Contemporary Collaborations', pages 74–77.*

▣ *Broadcast on BBC Four on Friday 10 August*

> **Every Prom broadcast live on BBC Radio 3**

THURSDAY 9 AUGUST

PROM 36
7.30pm–c9.45pm • Royal Albert Hall

PRICE BAND **B**

ESA-PEKKA SALONEN

Webern Five Pieces for Orchestra, Op. 10 — 6'
Mahler Symphony No. 10 – Adagio — 24'
INTERVAL
Wagner Die Walküre – Act 1 — 66'

Anja Kampe *Sieglinde*
Robert Dean Smith *Siegmund*
Franz-Josef Selig *Hunding*

Philharmonia Orchestra
Esa-Pekka Salonen *conductor*

The Philharmonia Orchestra and its Principal Conductor Esa-Pekka Salonen take a musical journey from aphorism to epic. Barely six minutes long, Webern's Five Pieces for Orchestra distils expression down to its most concentrated form, every musical gesture carrying infinite weight and colour. By contrast, Wagner's *Die Walküre*, the second instalment of his monumental *Ring* cycle, explores musical expansion and amplitude, offering an all-consuming vision of illicit love. At the midpoint is the Adagio from Mahler's 10th Symphony — music that grasps towards eternity and immortality but that was to remain tragically unfinished at the composer's death.

PROMS PLUS TALK
5.45pm–6.25pm • Imperial College Union Musicologist John Deathridge introduces Wagner's *Die Walküre*.
Edited version broadcast on BBC Radio 3 during tonight's interval

FRIDAY 10 AUGUST

PROM 37
7.30pm–c9.35pm • Royal Albert Hall

PRICE BAND **C**
WEEKEND PROMMING PASS *see page 170*

SIR ANTONIO PAPPANO

Haydn The Creation – Chaos — 6'
Bernstein Symphony No. 1, 'Jeremiah' — 25'
INTERVAL
Mahler Symphony No. 1 in D major — 56'

Elizabeth DeShong *mezzo-soprano*

Orchestra of the Academy of Santa Cecilia, Rome
Sir Antonio Pappano *conductor*

The Bernstein centenary celebrations continue in a programme that pairs his 'Jeremiah' Symphony with music by two composers he admired and championed. Appearing at the Proms for the first time in five years, Rome's Santa Cecilia Orchestra (of which Bernstein was Honorary President for almost a decade) and its Music Director Sir Antonio Pappano perform Bernstein's youthful First Symphony, charged with political anxiety and dread, alongside another symphonic debut, Mahler's dramatic First. The evening opens with Haydn's arresting musical vision of primordial chaos. *See 'An Embarrassment of Gifts', pages 30–33.*

PROMS PLUS TALK
5.45pm–6.25pm • Imperial College Union
Chaos and doom as featured in the Old Testament are examined by BBC Radio 3 New Generation Thinker Joe Moshenska and novelist Salley Vickers.
Edited version broadcast on BBC Radio 3 during tonight's interval

SATURDAY 11 AUGUST

PROMS 38 & 39 • 3.30pm–c5.40 &
8.00pm–c10.10 • Royal Albert Hall

PRICE BAND **D**
WEEKEND PROMMING PASS *see page 170*

JOHN WILSON

Bernstein West Side Story   76'
(concert performance)

Cast to include:

Sierra Boggess *Maria*
Ross Lekites *Tony*

Students from ArtsEd and Mountview
John Wilson Orchestra
John Wilson *conductor*

There will be one interval

West Side Story bursts with violent, sensual rhythms
and big-hearted melodies. This performance of the
theatre score (authorised concert version) marks the
first time the complete musical has been performed
in concert in the UK. A top-flight cast is joined by an
ensemble of students from leading London theatre
schools. See *'An Embarrassment of Gifts'*, pages 30–33.

 Broadcast live on BBC Radio 3 (Prom 39)

PROMS SING
10.30am–3.30pm • Imperial College Union (Metric Bar)
Join us to explore the songs and story of Bernstein's *West Side
Story. Suitable for ages 12–18. See pages 66–69 for details.*

PROMS FAMILY WORKSHOP
1.45pm–2.30pm • Imperial College Union (Dining Hall)
Join professional musicians for a family-friendly introduction
to this evening's Prom. Bring your instrument and join in!
Suitable for all the family (ages 7-plus). See pages 78–79 for details.

PROMS PLUS TALK
6.15pm–6.55pm • Imperial College Union (Concert Hall)
Critic and broadcaster David Benedict introduces Bernstein's
West Side Story.
Edited version broadcast on BBC Radio 3 during tonight's interval

---

SUNDAY 12 AUGUST

PROM 40
4.00pm–c6.00pm • Royal Albert Hall

PRICE BAND **B**
WEEKEND PROMMING PASS *see page 170*

JOSHUA BELL

Mendelssohn A Midsummer Night's
Dream – overture   12'

Saint-Saëns Violin Concerto No. 3
in B minor   29'

INTERVAL

Bridge Lament (Catherine, aged 9,
'Lusitania' 1915)   5'

Beethoven Symphony No. 4
in B flat major   34'

Academy of St Martin in the Fields
Joshua Bell *violin/director*

The Academy of St Martin in the Fields returns to
the Proms with director and soloist Joshua Bell in
a wide-ranging programme, rich in melody and
narrative. Saint-Saëns's Third Violin Concerto is the
Romantic display concerto par excellence but shares
its light-footed musical grace with Beethoven's Fourth
Symphony and Mendelssohn's overture. Bridge's
Lament is an elegy for those who died following the
torpedoing of the RMS *Lusitania*. See *'Impressions in
Colour'*, pages 8–15; *'Musical Memorials'*, pages 60–65;
'All Types of Beethoven', pages 88–91.

PROMS FAMILY WORKSHOP
2.15pm–3.00pm • Imperial College Union (Dining Hall)
Join professional musicians for a family-friendly introduction
to this afternoon's Prom. Bring your instrument and join in!
Suitable for all the family (ages 7-plus). See pages 78–79 for details.

PROMS PLUS TALK
2.15pm–2.55pm • Imperial College Union (Concert Hall)
Historians Saul David and Laura Rowe talk about the causes
and effects of the First World War and the sinking of the
RMS *Lusitania. Edited version broadcast on BBC Radio 3 during
this afternoon's interval*

SUNDAY 12 AUGUST

PROM 41
8.00pm–c9.55pm • Royal Albert Hall

PRICE BAND **A**
WEEKEND PROMMING PASS *see page 170*

SOPHIE BEVAN

L. Boulanger Pour les funérailles
d'un soldat   9'

Elgar Cello Concerto in E minor   28'

INTERVAL

Vaughan Williams Dona nobis
pacem   36'

Sophie Bevan *soprano*
Neal Davies *bass-baritone*
Jean-Guihen Queyras *cello*

BBC Symphony Chorus
BBC Symphony Orchestra
Edward Gardner *conductor*

War casts its long shadow over this Prom given by
Edward Gardner and the BBC Symphony Orchestra
and Chorus – part of this season's musical survey
suggested by the centenary of the end of the First
World War. A precursor to Britten's *War Requiem*
(see *Prom 72*), Vaughan Williams's cantata *Dona nobis
pacem* is a heartbreakingly beautiful exploration of
the violence of war, its expansive lyricism a natural foil
for the compressed drama of Lili Boulanger's choral
miniature *Pour les funérailles d'un soldat*. Elgar's
much-loved Cello Concerto, composed in the
wake of the conflict, completes this emotive concert,
with French cellist Jean-Guihen Queyras as soloist.
See *'The Other Boulanger Girl'*, pages 16–17; *'Musical
Memorials'*, pages 60–65.

 Broadcast on BBC Four on Sunday 2 September

PROMS PLUS TALK
6.15pm–6.55pm • Imperial College Union Musicologist
Kate Kennedy introduces Vaughan Williams's 1936 cantata.
Edited version broadcast on BBC Radio 3 during tonight's interval

MONDAY 13 AUGUST

PROMS AT ... CADOGAN HALL 5

1.00pm–c2.00pm • Cadogan Hall

For ticket prices, see page 162

JACK QUARTET

Xenakis Rebonds B	6'
Simon Holt Quadriga	c16'
world premiere	
Suzanne Farrin new work	c10'
BBC commission: world premiere	
Xenakis Tetras	17'

Colin Currie percussion
JACK Quartet

There will be no interval

Award-winning British percussionist Colin Currie joins forces with dynamic contemporary music specialists, the JACK Quartet, for a programme of 20th- and 21st-century works, including world premieres by Simon Holt and Suzanne Farrin. These are joined by two virtuosic Xenakis chamber works – the impossibly demanding *Rebonds B* for solo percussion and the 1983 string quartet *Tetras* with its eerie, woodwind-like sound manipulation and unsettling rhythmic patterning. *See 'Performance Art', pages 48–51; 'New Music', pages 96–101.*

Every Prom broadcast live on BBC Radio 3

Elizabeth DeShong • Prom 37

mezzo-soprano

'The audience should not so much hear my words as be consumed by the feeling of them.' American mezzo-soprano Elizabeth DeShong is clear that, despite making her Proms debut as soloist in Bernstein's 'Jeremiah' Symphony in Prom 37, she's simply not the focus. 'It's not about the singer – it's about unbridled, sincere expression of emotion.'

The emotions it conveys, she explains, are hugely powerful ones. 'The symphony draws its musical and textual material from Jeremiah's Book of Lamentations. The first two movements are instrumental and set the emotional tone for the third, in which I join the orchestra to voice Jeremiah's cries of mourning for Jerusalem, which has been dishonoured and destroyed by corruption. The vocal writing is sublime – Bernstein's setting of the text utilises the full expressive range of the mezzo voice.'

Despite its biblical origins, however, DeShong sees a far broader significance in Bernstein's immensely moving work. 'It seems fair to say that many of us feel misrepresented by our leaders and are crying out for unity and peace. The third movement provides me with the unique opportunity to channel that desperation and heartbreak, and perhaps, in a small way, channel the voice of the masses who wish to return safely home, be welcomed into a new home or have honour restored to the place they call home.'

Otto Tausk • Prom 24

conductor

'I had my very first Proms experience as a conductor a few years ago, but actually I never made it to the stage – although I was even wearing my concert suit ...' What was it that prevented Dutch conductor Otto Tausk from making his Proms debut in 2003? 'At the time I was Assistant Conductor to Valery Gergiev and, being the stand-in for the busiest conductor in the world, I was always more than prepared to take over! But he did finally arrive, and I remember a phenomenal Berlioz *Symphonie fantastique* with the Rotterdam Philharmonic.'

Tausk makes his official Proms debut in Prom 24, conducting one of his favourite concertos. 'Dvořák's Cello Concerto makes a heroic statement in the way that the cello is in musical conversation with the orchestra – although the orchestra is much stronger, the cello is a completely equal voice in its musical and emotional expression.'

The heroic theme continues in Richard Strauss's *Ein Heldenleben*. '"A Hero's Life" is not just Strauss celebrating himself but a work that puts the orchestra's musicians in the spotlight. Every one of them is a hero in this piece – as we all are in our own lives.' Tausk is delighted, too, to be appearing with the BBC National Orchestra of Wales, with which he's enjoyed a long history. 'It's one of the most versatile orchestras I've had the privilege and joy of joining.'

MONDAY 13 AUGUST

PROM 42
7.30pm–c9.40pm • Royal Albert Hall

PRICE BAND **B**

KHATIA BUNIATISHVILI

Arvo Pärt Symphony No. 3   25'
Grieg Piano Concerto in A minor   29'

INTERVAL

Sibelius Symphony No. 5
in E flat major   32'

Khatia Buniatishvili *piano*

Estonian Festival Orchestra
Paavo Järvi *conductor*

A concert with a Nordic flavour from Paavo Järvi and the Estonian Festival Orchestra (making its Proms debut) pairs music by Grieg and Sibelius with Estonia's own national composer, Arvo Pärt. Celebrated Georgian pianist Khatia Buniatishvili – a former BBC Radio 3 New Generation Artist – performs one of the great Romantic piano concertos. Beloved for its generous melodies and dramatic gestures, Grieg's concerto is matched for sonic drama by Sibelius's stirring Fifth Symphony. Arvo Pärt's eclectic Third Symphony, with its echoes of Renaissance polyphony and Orthodox chant, opens the concert.

Broadcast on BBC Four on Friday 17 August

PROMS PLUS TALK
5.45pm–6.25pm • Imperial College Union
BBC Radio 3 New Generation Thinker Leah Broad introduces Sibelius's Fifth Symphony.
Edited version broadcast on BBC Radio 3 during tonight's interval

TUESDAY 14 AUGUST

PROM 43
7.30pm–c9.40pm • Royal Albert Hall

PRICE BAND **D**

LISA BATIASHVILI

Brahms Violin Concerto in D major   38'
David Robert Coleman Looking
for Palestine   20'
London premiere

INTERVAL

Scriabin The Poem of Ecstasy   22'

Elsa Dreisig *soprano*
Lisa Batiashvili *violin*

West–Eastern Divan Orchestra
Daniel Barenboim *conductor*

Daniel Barenboim and his pioneering West–Eastern Divan Orchestra return to the Proms for a concert marrying passion and politics. One of the best-loved Romantic works in the repertoire – Brahms's colourful, dance-filled Violin Concerto, performed here by Georgian violinist Lisa Batiashvili – is paired with Scriabin's ecstatic, orgiastic *The Poem of Ecstasy*, an attempt to bridge the divide between spirituality and sexuality in music. At the centre of the concert is David Robert Coleman's *Looking for Palestine* for soprano and orchestra, a work commissioned by the ensemble, and one that speaks to its uniquely political identity. *See 'New Music', pages 96–101.*

PROMS PLUS TALK
5.45pm–6.25pm • Imperial College Union BBC Radio 3 New Generation Thinkers Jules Evans and Hetta Howes compare figures from the past and present who have searched for a sense of transcendence and experienced ecstatic states.
Edited version broadcast on BBC Radio 3 during tonight's interval

WEDNESDAY 15 AUGUST

PROM 44
7.30pm–c9.25pm • Royal Albert Hall

PRICE BAND **A**

JUSTINA GRINGYTĖ

Debussy Prélude à l'après-midi d'un
faune   10'
L. Boulanger Psalm 130, 'Du fond
de l'abîme'   25'

INTERVAL

Debussy Nocturnes   25'
Ravel Boléro   15'

Justina Gringytė *mezzo-soprano*

CBSO Youth Chorus
CBSO Chorus
City of Birmingham Symphony Orchestra
Ludovic Morlot *conductor*

The CBSO and Ludovic Morlot mark two major centenaries in this all-French programme. In the centenary of his death, Debussy is celebrated in the languorous beauty of *Prélude à l'après-midi d'un faune*, as well as the *Nocturnes* with their shifting, shimmering play of musical light. Lili Boulanger, whose death in 1918 at the age of just 24 cut short a career of extraordinary promise, is represented by her powerful setting of Psalm 130 – a musical howl of grief composed at the height of the First World War. Ravel's *Boléro* closes the evening with its hypnotic Spanish dance rhythm and swirling orchestral colours. *See 'Impressions in Colour', pages 8–15; 'The Other Boulanger Girl', pages 16–17.*

PROMS PLUS TALK
5.45pm–6.25pm • Imperial College Union French music specialist Caroline Rae introduces Lili Boulanger's *Du fond de l'abîme* and talks about the composer's life and music.
Edited version broadcast on BBC Radio 3 during tonight's interval

THURSDAY 16 AUGUST

PROM 45
7.00pm–c9.00pm • Royal Albert Hall

PRICE BAND **B**

JONATHAN NOTT

Debussy Jeux   19'

Ravel, orch. Yan Maresz Violin
Sonata in G major   19'
UK premiere of this orchestration

INTERVAL

Stravinsky Petrushka (1911 version)   34'

Renaud Capuçon *violin*

Orchestre de la Suisse Romande
Jonathan Nott *conductor*

Geneva's renowned Orchestre de la Suisse Romande celebrates its 100th anniversary by making its Proms debut under its English Music Director Jonathan Nott. The orchestra continues this season's strand of French music with works by Debussy and Ravel – the mercurial dance-fantasy *Jeux*, Debussy's last orchestral work, and a new orchestration of Ravel's jazz-infused Second Violin Sonata with soloist Renaud Capuçon – as well as a Russian piece synonymous with Paris: Stravinsky's colourful folk-ballet *Petrushka*, heard here in its original version. *See 'Impressions in Colour', pages 8–15; 'Fantastic Four', pages 18–21.*

See 'Impressions in Colour', pages 8–15; 'Fantastic Four', pages 18–21.

PROMS PLUS TALK
5.15pm–5.55pm • Imperial College Union Ahead of tonight's concert, writer and broadcaster Gavin Plumley talks about the life and work of the Orchestre de la Suisse Romande, which makes its Proms debut.
Edited version broadcast on BBC Radio 3 during tonight's interval

---

THURSDAY 16 AUGUST

PROM 46 • LATE NIGHT
10.15pm–c11.30pm • Royal Albert Hall

PRICE BAND **F**

NATIONAL YOUTH JAZZ ORCHESTRA

Programme to include:

Gershwin, arr. F. Grofé Rhapsody
in Blue (original jazz band version)*   17'

Benjamin Grosvenor *piano*

National Youth Jazz Orchestra
*Guy Barker *conductor*
Mark Armstrong *conductor*

There will be no interval

Classical music gets a swing in its step in this all-American concert by the UK's National Youth Jazz Orchestra. Former BBC Radio 3 New Generation Artist Benjamin Grosvenor is the soloist in Gershwin's intoxicating *Rhapsody in Blue* – an exhilarating mix of jazz rhythms and classical virtuosity. This upbeat programme also showcases the popular side of Leonard Bernstein – who was, like Gershwin, renowned as both jazz pianist and composer. Expect dazzling performances from some of this country's finest young musicians.

> Every Prom broadcast
> live on BBC Radio 3

FRIDAY 17 AUGUST

PROM 47
7.30pm–c9.35pm • Royal Albert Hall

PRICE BAND **A**
WEEKEND PROMMING PASS *see page 170*

SAKARI ORAMO

Elgar Introduction and Allegro for
Strings   14'

Venables/Bartók Venables Plays
Bartók   c25'
BBC commission: world premiere

INTERVAL

Prokofiev Symphony No. 5 in
B flat major   44'

Pekka Kuusisto *violin*

BBC Symphony Orchestra
Sakari Oramo *conductor*

Maverick Finnish violinist Pekka Kuusisto made a memorable Proms debut in 2016. Now he returns to premiere a new violin concerto written especially for him by award-winning young British composer Philip Venables. The piece grows out of a recording the composer found of himself as a teenager playing one of Bartók's *Hungarian Sketches* to his teacher's teacher, Rudolf Botta, a Hungarian refugee – and the journey that ensued. The concerto is framed by two works suffused with sunny optimism – Elgar's lovely *Introduction and Allegro* for strings and Prokofiev's Fifth Symphony, a piece that rejoices in 'the strength and beauty of the human spirit'. *See 'New Music', pages 96–101.*

See 'New Music', pages 96–101.

PROMS PLUS TALK
5.45pm–6.25pm • Imperial College Union Composer Philip Venables introduces his new work, *Venables Plays Bartók*, ahead of its world premiere this evening.
Edited version broadcast on BBC Radio 3 during tonight's interval

Hornroh Modern Alphorn Quartet • Prom 21

alphorns

Swiss alphorn player Balthasar Streiff is keen to dispel any misconceptions about his instrument. 'The way we think of it today, as a folk instrument, only comes from the second half of the 20th century. It was invented early in the 19th century in the countryside around Berne. Before then there were lots of smaller, similar instruments such as natural horns, which were kind of early mobile phones: used for communication between people, calling cattle, or even to earn a few coins for shepherds in the winter.' Streiff is one quarter of the Hornroh Modern Alphorn Quartet, whose focus is on the sonic possibilities of their remarkable instruments. 'We started in 2000 and we've always been very interested in contemporary music and ways of thinking about the instruments' tuning.'

Accordingly, the work that brings this alphorn quartet to the Proms – *Concerto grosso* No. 1 by Georg Friedrich Haas – has nothing to do with yodelling mountain-dwellers but rather combines the alphorns with an orchestra. 'All the musicians have to really listen hard – we all play in different tunings, sometimes in quarter-tones, and the orchestra also has to play the alphorns' pitches. The most important aspect of the alphorn is its pure tuning – its sound is awesome and it's the perfect instrument for contemporary music.'

Joseph Tawadros Proms at … Cadogan Hall 3

oud

Joseph Tawadros fell in love with the oud thanks to a film he came across when he was growing up. 'I saw it in an Egyptian movie that my parents were watching,' he recalls. 'I loved the sound. My grandfather had played it too, so I guess I felt there was a link to my heritage.'

Born in Cairo, raised in Australia and now living in London, Tawadros is on a mission to bring the oud to a new audience. The instrument is an ancestor of the lute, and common across the Arab world. 'My interest lies in collaboration,' says Tawadros. 'I very much believe in the instrument, not in an exotic or ethnic way but as an instrument that holds its own in many different types of music. The compositions I present bring the oud into a new light.'

With 14 albums to his name, Tawadros has worked with artists in a host of genres, including jazz musicians John Abercrombie and John Patitucci, the Australian Chamber Orchestra and the Academy of Ancient Music. Last year he played at the inaugural BBC Proms Dubai, both with his own quartet and performing symphonic arrangements of his music with the BBC Symphony Orchestra.

'I'm trying to find new ways to present the instrument that are not clichéd,' he says. 'I think, if people come to a show they will be surprised.'

SATURDAY 18 AUGUST

PROM 48

7.30pm–c9.40 • Royal Albert Hall

PRICE BAND C
WEEKEND PROMMING PASS see page 170

SIR SIMON RATTLE

Ravel	
Mother Goose (ballet)	30'
Shéhérazade*	17'

INTERVAL

Ravel L'enfant et les sortilèges	44'

(concert performance; sung in French, with surtitles)

Magdalena Kožená *mezzo-soprano*/Child
Patricia Bardon *Mother/Shepherd/Dragonfly*
Jane Archibald *Fire/Nightingale/Princess*
Anna Stéphany *Chair/White Cat/Chinese Cup/Squirrel*
Elizabeth Watts *Shepherdess/Bat/Owl*
Sunnyboy Dladla *Teapot/Little Old Man/Tree-Frog*
Gavan Ring *Grandfather Clock/Black Cat*
David Shipley *Tree/Armchair*

London Symphony Chorus
London Symphony Orchestra
Sir Simon Rattle conductor

Ravel's magical opera *L'enfant et les sortilèges* follows his fairy-tale ballet *Mother Goose* and the oriental aura of *Shéhérazade*. See 'Impressions in Colour', pages 8–15.

Broadcast on BBC Four on Sunday 26 August

PROMS SING
1.00pm–4.00pm • Imperial College Union
Join Mary King and the BBC Singers to sing excerpts from Ravel's *L'enfant et les sortilèges*. Experience in sight-reading or a knowledge of the piece is an advantage but not essential. *Suitable for ages 16-plus. See pages 66–69 for details.*

PROMS PLUS TALK
5.45pm–6.25pm • Imperial College Union
Composer and author Kerry Andrew and writer Katherine Langrish explore the symbolism in fairy stories.
Edited version broadcast on BBC Radio 3 during tonight's interval

SUNDAY 19 AUGUST

PROM 49
11.00am–c1.15pm • Royal Albert Hall

PRICE BAND Ⓐ
WEEKEND PROMMING PASS *see page 170*

GIANANDREA NOSEDA

Agata Zubel Fireworks 7'
UK premiere

Chopin Piano Concerto No. 2
in F minor 34'

INTERVAL

Tchaikovsky Symphony No. 5
in E minor 45'

Seong-Jin Cho *piano*

European Union Youth Orchestra
Gianandrea Noseda *conductor*

Winner of the 2015 International Chopin
Competition, Seong-Jin Cho makes his Proms debut
as soloist in Chopin's lyrical and much-loved Second
Piano Concerto. The Polish theme that begins in the
mazurkas that swirl through the concerto continues
with the UK premiere of Agata Zubel's *Fireworks*, a
celebration of freedom and of the present moment,
written to mark the 100th anniversary of Polish
independence. In the second half, Gianandrea
Noseda and the European Union Youth Orchestra
turn up the intensity with one of the great Romantic
symphonies, Tchaikovsky's stirring Fifth. See 'New
Music', pages 96–101.

SUNDAY 19 AUGUST

PROM 50
8.00pm–c10.25pm • Royal Albert Hall

PRICE BAND Ⓑ
WEEKEND PROMMING PASS *see page 170*

ANNELIEN VAN WAUWE

Mozart Clarinet Concerto in A major,
K622 28'

INTERVAL

Mahler Symphony No. 5
in C sharp minor 75'

Annelien Van Wauwe *clarinet*

BBC Scottish Symphony Orchestra
Thomas Dausgaard *conductor*

Recreating a Proms concert conducted by Leonard
Bernstein in 1987, the BBC Scottish Symphony
Orchestra and Chief Conductor Thomas Dausgaard
pair two of the best-loved and most beautiful works
in the repertoire. Mozart's Clarinet Concerto, with
its sublime slow movement, is the composer at his
sunniest and most mellow, despite the fact that he
was to die two months after its completion. Mahler's
Fifth Symphony, by contrast, is the urgent work of
a composer starting a new adventure, charged with
new musical possibilities and a new love, expressed
with impossible tenderness in its famous Adagietto.
See 'Podium Passion', pages 34–37.

Ⓘ *Broadcast on BBC Four tonight*

MONDAY 20 AUGUST

PROMS AT … CADOGAN HALL 6
1.00pm–c2.00pm • Cadogan Hall

For ticket prices, see page 162

SAKARI ORAMO

Bridge Music, when soft voices die 3'
Vaughan Williams Rest 4'
Holst Nunc dimittis 4'
Laura Mvula The Virgin of
Montserrat c8'
BBC commission: world premiere

Parry Songs of Farewell 32'

BBC Singers
Sakari Oramo *conductor*

There will be no interval

Endings – whether of a day, a relationship or a
lifetime – are the thread that runs through this
beautiful programme of English choral music
performed by the BBC Singers. Poetry by Donne,
Shelley, Campion and Rossetti is reimagined in
evocative settings by Bridge, Vaughan Williams and
centenary composer Hubert Parry, whose choral
cycle *Songs of Farewell* is the powerful statement of
a man nearing the end of his life, while Holst's *Nunc
dimittis* offers a night-time prayer. Singer-songwriter
Laura Mvula's new commission is inspired by the
Black Madonna in a Catalonian mountain monastery.
See 'Musical Memorials', pages 60–65; 'New Music',
pages 96–101.

⌐ **Every Prom broadcast**
  live on BBC Radio 3 ⌐

PROMS PLUS TALK
6.15pm–6.55pm • Imperial College Union Writer and critic
Norman Lebrecht investigates Leonard Bernstein's
relationship with the music of Mahler.
Edited version broadcast on BBC Radio 3 during tonight's interval

MONDAY 20 AUGUST

PROM 51
7.30pm–c9.30pm • Royal Albert Hall

PRICE BAND Ⓐ

MALIN BYSTRÖM

Wagner Parsifal – Prelude to Act 1   *12'*

R. Strauss Four Last Songs   *22'*

INTERVAL

Per Nørgård Symphony No. 3   *50'*
UK premiere

Malin Byström *soprano*

London Voices
National Youth Chamber Choir of Great Britain
BBC Scottish Symphony Orchestra
Thomas Dausgaard *conductor*

Premiered in 1976, Per Nørgård's Third Symphony
is one of the great contemporary symphonies – a
Danish classic that has never before been performed
in the UK. Suffused with glowing microtones and
thick, textural beauty, the eclectic score draws
on everything from plainchant to Latin-American
rhythms to spin its extraordinary narrative.
Thomas Dausgaard and the BBC Scottish Symphony
Orchestra preface it with two works of equal sonic
breadth: Wagner's exquisite musical meditation, the
Prelude to Act 1 of *Parsifal*, and the autumnal warmth
of Strauss's *Four Last Songs*, sung by Swedish soprano
Malin Byström. *See 'New Music', pages 96–101.*

PROMS PLUS TALK
5.45pm–6.25pm • Imperial College Union Ahead of the
UK premiere of Per Nørgård's Third Symphony, broadcaster
and writer Stephen Johnson discusses the composer and
his music.
Edited version broadcast on BBC Radio 3 during tonight's interval

TUESDAY 21 AUGUST

PROM 52
7.00pm–c9.00pm • Royal Albert Hall

PRICE BAND Ⓑ

ALINA IBRAGIMOVA

Wagner The Flying Dutchman –
overture   *11'*

Rolf Wallin Violin Concerto   *c25'*
world premiere

INTERVAL

Sibelius Symphony No. 2 in D major   *45'*

Alina Ibragimova *violin*

Bergen Philharmonic Orchestra
Edward Gardner *conductor*

A concert with a Nordic flavour from Edward
Gardner and the Bergen Philharmonic Orchestra
climaxes in Sibelius's Second Symphony, whose
folk-like melodies are a musical celebration of Finnish
life and identity. Violinist Alina Ibragimova is the
soloist in Norwegian composer Rolf Wallin's
concerto – the second of two new violin concertos
premiered this season *(see also Prom 47)*. And the
evening opens with Wagner's propulsive overture
to *The Flying Dutchman*, an opera set along the coast
of Norway from the orchestra's base in Bergen.
See 'New Music', pages 96–101.

PROMS PLUS TALK
5.15pm–5.55pm • Imperial College Union
Composer Rolf Wallin introduces his new Violin
Concerto and talks about his influences and ideas.
Edited version broadcast on BBC Radio 3 during tonight's interval

TUESDAY 21 AUGUST

PROM 53 • LATE NIGHT   🌙 ▣
10.15pm–c11.30pm • Royal Albert Hall

PRICE BAND Ⓕ

YOUSSOU NDOUR

Youssou Ndour & Le Super Étoile de Dakar

There will be no interval

Senegalese cultural icon Youssou Ndour makes
his Proms debut in a special late-night appearance.
This largely acoustic performance spotlights Ndour's
characteristic soaring vocals and the smooth
instrumental colours brought to life by his group
Le Super Étoile de Dakar. For over 40 years Ndour
has been thrilling audiences around the world with an
eclectic mix of Cuban rumba, hip hop, jazz, soul and
music of the West African griot tradition. In addition
to his prodigious performing career – which has
embraced more than 30 albums and a Grammy
Award – he has also played a political role, having
campaigned for the release of Nelson Mandela,
performed at concerts for Amnesty International
and served as a UNICEF Goodwill Ambassador.

▣ *Broadcast on BBC Four on Friday 7 September*

> **Every Prom broadcast**
> **live on BBC Radio 3**

WEDNESDAY 22 AUGUST

PROM 54

7.30pm–c9.40pm • Royal Albert Hall

PRICE BAND C

ANNA LUCIA RICHTER

Enescu Suite No. 1 – Prélude à
l'unisson   9'

Bartók Music for Strings, Percussion
and Celesta   28'

INTERVAL

Mahler Symphony No. 4 in G major   57'

Anna Lucia Richter *soprano*

Budapest Festival Orchestra
Iván Fischer *conductor*

The intoxicating energy of their performances makes
any appearance by Iván Fischer and the Budapest
Festival Orchestra a highlight of the season. In the
first of their two Proms together, they pair Mahler's
best-loved symphony – the vivacious Fourth, with
its jingling sleighbells and child's-eye vision of
heaven – with two works exploring the unusual
relationship between strings and percussion: Bartók's
dynamic *Music for Strings, Percussion and Celesta* and
Enescu's *Prélude à l'unisson*, with its slow-build tension.

INSPIRE CONCERT

**5.00pm–6.00pm • BBC Radio Theatre, Broadcasting
House** Christopher Stark conducts the Aurora Orchestra
in the winning pieces of the 2018 BBC Proms Inspire Young
Composers' Competition *(see 'Inspiring the Future', pages
66–69). Tickets available from BBC Studio Audiences: bbc.co.uk/
showsandtours/shows.*

PROMS PLUS TALK

5.45pm–6.25pm • Imperial College Union Musicologist
Jeremy Barham introduces Mahler's Fourth Symphony.
Edited version broadcast on BBC Radio 3 during tonight's interval

Jess Gillam • Proms 3 & 75
saxophones (Proms debut: 2017)

Seeing Jess Gillam take to the stage with her
saxophone this year, it will be easy to forget that
she is now an Albert Hall 'veteran', having made
her debut at 19 with her striking and assured
performance in 2017's John Williams Prom,
featuring the BBC Concert Orchestra. For her,
focusing only on the music is the key to this
remarkable confidence. 'The most nerve-racking
thing for me is actually walking out onto the
stage,' she says. 'As soon as I start playing, I
become completely immersed in the music and
enjoy the thrill of performing.'

This time round sees her take part in a roll call
of BBC Young Musician alumni (Prom 3). It's
a competition that Gillam sees as having been
crucial to her musical development. 'It has been
an amazing platform for me and has provided
me with a lot of exposure and opportunities.
It also gave me the chance to meet some fantastic
musicians and some very dedicated and
supportive people.'

As if one major concert wasn't enough for
her, she also features in this year's Last Night,
displaying her versatility with a performance
of Milhaud's *Scaramouche*. Gillam describes
it as an 'absolute joy to play', and relishes its
diversity. 'It consists of three quite contrasting
movements – the first being lively and bright,
the second very beautiful and gentle, whilst
the third is fantastically energetic and very
reminiscent of a carnival!'

Karina Canellakis • Prom 12
conductor (Proms debut: 2017)

'Beethoven's *Coriolan* overture starts the
programme off with a punch in the face!'
American conductor Karina Canellakis can't
wait to explore the contrasts and sheer drama
of her Prom with the BBC Symphony Orchestra
– beginning with Beethoven's forceful opener.
'I love it – that intensity, the struggle between
right and wrong, major and minor.' She sees
connections, too, between Beethoven and
Shostakovich, whose First Cello Concerto
continues the programme. 'The idea of defiance
and rebelliousness, of shaking the fist at the
oppressor, is something they have in common –
I find their music goes very well together. Our
soloist is Alisa Weilerstein, who's not only a
colleague but also a friend – I feel a deep
musical connection with her.'

Those musical connections continue in the
new work of the evening, by award-winning
California-born composer and Andrew Norman.
'I know him personally, and I'm a huge supporter
and fan. I think to have those three composers –
Beethoven, Shostakovich and Norman – and
then to be able to plunge into the luxurious
bath of Rachmaninov's *Symphonic Dances* is
so refreshing. It's a fiendishly difficult piece
for all concerned, but I decided on it because
I was thinking about the virtuosity of the
BBC Symphony Orchestra, their almost debonair
attitude towards such virtuosic music. They're
not fazed by anything!'

THURSDAY 23 AUGUST

PROM 55
7.30pm–c9.40pm • Royal Albert Hall

PRICE BAND C

Liszt Hungarian Rhapsody No. 1 in C sharp minor — 14'

Brahms Hungarian Dance No. 1 in G minor — 4'

Liszt Hungarian Rhapsody No. 3 in B flat major — 5'

Sarasate Zigeunerweisen — 9'

Brahms Hungarian Dance No. 11 in D minor — 4'

INTERVAL

Brahms Symphony No. 1 in C minor — 46'

József Lendvay Sr violin
József Lendvay Jr violin
Jenő Lisztes cimbalom

Budapest Festival Orchestra
Iván Fischer conductor

Hungarian folk tunes run through the veins of Iván Fischer and the Budapest Festival Orchestra, while Gypsy rhythms set their pulses dancing. This concert – a true celebration of Hungary's national music – traces the development of folk songs and dance, from their colourful, rough-hewn originals into virtuosic concert-hall reimaginings by Liszt, Brahms and Sarasate. In the second half comes Brahms's dramatic First Symphony, whose darkness and drama eventually give way to an ending of transcendent musical triumph.

Broadcast on BBC Four on Friday 24 August

FRIDAY 24 AUGUST

PROM 56
7.30pm–c9.55pm • Royal Albert Hall

PRICE BAND B
WEEKEND PROMMING PASS *see page 170*

BENJAMIN GROSVENOR

Mozart Piano Concerto No. 21 in C major, K467 — 29'

INTERVAL

Bruckner Symphony No. 5 in B flat major — 75'

Benjamin Grosvenor piano

BBC Symphony Orchestra
Sakari Oramo conductor

Former BBC Young Musician winner Benjamin Grosvenor may only be 26 but this exceptional pianist is an artist of startling emotional and technical maturity. Here he joins the BBC Symphony Orchestra and its Chief Conductor Sakari Oramo as the soloist in Mozart's Piano Concerto No. 21 (sometimes known by the nickname 'Elvira Madigan'), with its trickling slow movement and good-humoured *buffo* levity. Bruckner's Fifth Symphony, with its astonishing fugal finale, offers a more serious counterpoint in the second half.

SATURDAY 25 AUGUST

PROM 57
7.30pm–c9.55pm • Royal Albert Hall

PRICE BAND D
WEEKEND PROMMING PASS *see page 170*

JOHN WILSON

Bernstein On the Town — 106'
(concert performance)

Cast to include:

Nathaniel Hackmann *Gabey*
Louise Dearman *Hildy*

London Symphony Orchestra
John Wilson conductor
Martin Duncan stage director

There will be one interval

On what would have been Leonard Bernstein's 100th birthday, and launching a bank-holiday Bernstein weekend at the Proms, John Wilson returns to conduct his second Bernstein musical of the season. Following the adventures of three sailors on shore leave in New York City in 1944, *On the Town* was an instant Broadway hit, featuring classic songs including 'New York, New York' and 'Lonely Town'. See 'An Embarrassment of Gifts', pages 30–33.

Broadcast live on BBC Four

PROMS FAMILY WORKSHOP
5.45pm–6.30pm • Imperial College Union (Dining Hall)
Join professional musicians for a family-friendly introduction to this evening's Prom. Bring your instrument and join in! *Suitable for all the family (ages 7-plus). See pages 78–79 for details.*

PROMS PLUS TALK
5.45pm–6.25pm • Imperial College Union (Concert Hall)
An introduction to Gypsy, Roma and Traveller culture and heritage with writers Louise Doughty and Damian Le Bas. *Edited version broadcast on BBC Radio 3 during tonight's interval*

PROMS PLUS TALK
5.45pm–6.25pm • Imperial College Union Conductor and musicologist John Butt introduces Bruckner's Symphony No. 5. *Edited version broadcast on BBC Radio 3 during tonight's interval*

PROMS SING
1.00pm–4.00pm • Imperial College Union
Join us to sing music by Bernstein. No experience of singing is required. *Suitable for ages 16-plus. See pages 66–69.*

PROMS PLUS TALK
5.45pm–6.25pm • Imperial College Union
An introduction to Bernstein's *On the Town* with Broadway expert Edward Seckerson. *Edited version broadcast on BBC Radio 3 during tonight's interval*

SUNDAY 26 AUGUST

PROM 58
7.30pm–c9.40pm • Royal Albert Hall

PRICE BAND (A)
WEEKEND PROMMING PASS *see page 170*

JOSHUA WEILERSTEIN

The Sound of an Orchestra

Royal Philharmonic Orchestra
Joshua Weilerstein *conductor*
Gerard McBurney *creative director*
Mike Tutaj *projection design*

There will be one interval

What happens – on stage, in the air, in the listener's mind – when an orchestra plays together? In a tribute to Leonard Bernstein's televised presentations, which brought classical music to generations of new audiences, we pay homage to his pioneering work in this area. The first half of our journey into 'The Sound of an Orchestra' presents a vivid tapestry of words, projections and music, leading us from the primal anarchy of tuning-up to the dynamic complexity of Stravinsky's *The Rite of Spring*. In the second half we explore a kaleidoscope of works spanning almost 250 years – from the unsettling echo chamber of Ligeti's *Apparitions*, through Bernstein in Broadway mode, to Debussy's shimmering seascape *La mer* and Beethoven's resolute *Egmont* overture. A scintillating multi-sensory journey for novices and experts alike. See 'Lifelong Teacher', pages 38–41.

PROMS READING
5.45pm–6.25pm • Imperial College Union An audience with Lenny: readings and memories of Leonard Bernstein.
Edited version broadcast on BBC Radio 3 during tonight's interval

MONDAY 27 AUGUST

PROMS AT ... CADOGAN HALL 7
1.00pm–c2.00pm • Cadogan Hall

For ticket prices, see page 162

WALLIS GIUNTA

Bernstein La bonne cuisine   5'
Bushra El-Turk Crème Brûlée on a Tree   c5'
BBC commission: world premiere

Bernstein Fancy Free – 'Big Stuff'   3'
Bernstein Conch Town   12'
UK premiere

Copland Pastorale   3'
Barber Hermit Songs, Op. 29 – 'Sea Snatch'; 'The Monk and His Cat'   3'
Blitzstein 'Modest Maid'; 'Stay in My Arms'   4'
Stephen Sondheim A Little Night Music – 'The Miller's Son'   4'
Bernstein Trouble in Tahiti – 'What a movie!'   3'

Wallis Giunta *mezzo-soprano*
Michael Sikich, Iain Farrington *pianos*
Toby Kearney, Owen Gunnell *percussion*

There will be no interval

Our Bernstein series continues with a recital of gems by Bernstein and his associates. The concert also features a new song by British-Lebanese composer Bushra El-Turk, written in response to Bernstein's witty recipe settings, *La bonne cuisine*. Scored for two pianos and percussion, the early, unfinished ballet *Conch Town* – containing the song now better known as 'America' in *West Side Story* – has now been completed using other material by Bernstein. See 'An Embarrassment of Gifts', pages 30–33.

MONDAY 27 AUGUST

PROM 59
4.15pm–c5.30pm • Royal Albert Hall

For ticket prices, see page 162

JAMES REDWOOD

Relaxed Prom

Programme to include music by Bernstein, Holst, Rachmaninov and Tchaikovsky, plus the London premiere of a new work by Alexander Campkin

James Redwood *presenter*

BSO Resound*
Bournemouth Symphony Orchestra
Sian Edwards *conductor*
***James Rose** *conductor*

There will be no interval

The Bournemouth Symphony Orchestra, in partnership with Royal Albert Hall Education & Outreach and Proms Learning, present orchestral music in an informal setting. Everyone is welcome: family members of all ages, children, young people and adults with autism, sensory and communication impairments and learning disabilities, as well as individuals who are Deaf or hearing impaired, blind or visually impaired, and those living with dementia. There is a relaxed attitude to movement and noise, plus 'chill-out' spaces outside the auditorium. The Prom features picture communication systems on large screens, audio description and British Sign Language interpretation. The orchestra is joined by its groundbreaking disabled-led ensemble, BSO Resound. See 'Magical Moments', pages 78–79.

This concert will be filmed and available to watch at bbc.co.uk/proms

---

PROMS SCRATCH ORCHESTRA
3.00pm–4.00pm, 4.30pm–5.30pm • Maida Vale Studios
Play Shostakovich side by side with members of the BBC Concert Orchestra, conducted by Marin Alsop.
Open to ages 16-plus. See pages 66–69 for details.

SPOTLIGHT
OPERETTA AND MUSICALS

Jane Glover
Proms at … Alexandra Palace
conductor

Conductor Jane Glover wouldn't even call herself a Gilbert and Sullivan specialist. 'It's not in my normal repertoire line at all. I only ever seem to do it at the Proms! This will be my third time conducting Gilbert and Sullivan at the Proms, and actually only my fourth ever. But they're such fun to do. We'll be having a huge amount of fun – however, it's going to be rigorously prepared.'

Following *Iolanthe* in 2000 and *The Yeomen of the Guard* in 2012, she returns this year with *Trial by Jury*. 'It's pretty much the first thing that Gilbert and Sullivan did together – they're sort of inventing themselves in it, and that's what makes it so interesting. They're almost eyeing each other with curiosity and seeing if this partnership is going to work. Little did they know that their immense popularity all over the world was going to stem from this 45-minute piece.'

Does Glover feel any sense of approaching G&S with her tongue slightly in her cheek? Not a bit of it, she says. 'You have to treat it incredibly seriously and make it all sound as wonderful as possible. I always approach these things as if I'm doing an unknown Mozart opera. I think you do have to take it absolutely at face value and embrace it wholeheartedly. And always with a smile. You cannot but smile when you perform this music.'

John Wilson
Proms 38, 39 & 57
conductor

There could be no better centrepiece to a Proms centenary celebration of the great Leonard Bernstein than *West Side Story* (Proms 38 & 39), and who better to present it than John Wilson – a man who has the work in his blood, having first conducted it aged 16. 'It's a great piece to get your hands on,' the conductor says. 'Everything in the score is there for a good dramatic reason. It's this wholeness that gives it operatic dimensions and makes it such a satisfying piece.'

Its groundbreaking and eclectic nature is another feature of the work that most enthuses Wilson, who leads his own orchestra in this rare outing of the authorised concert version based on the theatre score. 'It takes all of the great traditions of the American musical – like show songs in the vernacular – and melds them with other elements: ballet, modern "art" music. The result is a piece which has a further reach than most stage musicals written up to that point.'

Along with *West Side Story*, Wilson will also conduct another Bernstein stage and film musical set in the Big Apple – *On the Town* (Prom 57), this time featuring the London Symphony Orchestra. And, for him, this year's Bernstein anniversary couldn't have come at a better time. 'With every passing year, Bernstein's reputation as a composer of significance grows. All of his music is being played, all over the world.'

PROM 60
8.00pm–c10.20pm • Royal Albert Hall

PRICE BAND Ⓒ
WEEKEND PROMMING PASS *see page 170*

JEAN-YVES THIBAUDET

Bernstein Slava! (A Political Overture)   4'

Bernstein Symphony No. 2, 'The Age of Anxiety'   35'

INTERVAL

Shostakovich Symphony No. 5 in D minor   51'

Jean-Yves Thibaudet *piano*

Baltimore Symphony Orchestra
Marin Alsop *conductor*

Marin Alsop, a protégée of Leonard Bernstein, returns to the Proms with the Baltimore Symphony Orchestra for a politically charged climax to our bank-holiday Bernstein weekend. The concert culminates in Shostakovich's ambiguous Fifth Symphony, whose triumphant finale can be heard either as political protest or capitulation to Stalin's Soviet regime. Pianist Jean-Yves Thibaudet joins the orchestra for Bernstein's 'The Age of Anxiety' – a musical quest for faith in a broken, post-war world – and the evening opens with the boisterous *Slava!*, a 'political overture' dedicated to cellist Mstislav Rostropovich. See 'An Embarrassment of Gifts', pages 30–33.

◉ *Broadcast on BBC Four on Friday 31 August*

PROMS PLUS TALK
6.15pm–6.55pm • Imperial College Union
An examination of W. H. Auden's 1947 poem 'The Age of Anxiety' with poets Glyn Maxwell and Polly Clark.
Edited version broadcast on BBC Radio 3 during tonight's interval

TUESDAY 28 AUGUST

PROM 61
7.30pm–c9.45pm • Royal Albert Hall

PRICE BAND **B**

YANNICK NÉZET-SÉGUIN

Liszt Piano Concerto No. 2 in A major *21'*

INTERVAL

Bruckner Symphony No. 4
in E flat major, 'Romantic' *68'*

Yefim Bronfman *piano*

Rotterdam Philharmonic Orchestra
Yannick Nézet-Séguin *conductor*

The Rotterdam Philharmonic Orchestra celebrates
its 100th anniversary with its first visit to the Proms
in five years, under the baton of Chief Conductor
Yannick Nézet-Séguin. Subtitled the 'Romantic' by
the composer, Bruckner's Fourth Symphony draws
deeply on the German Romantic tradition of Weber
and Wagner for its colourful musical drama. Yefim
Bronfman is the soloist in Liszt's Second Piano
Concerto, a work originally conceived as a 'concerto
symphonique', which offers a fascinating reimagining
of the traditional relationship between soloist and
orchestra. See 'Fantastic Four', pages 18–21.

PROMS PLUS TALK
5.25pm–6.25pm • Imperial College Union Award-winning
author Sebastian Faulks talks about his new novel *Paris Echo*.
Edited version broadcast on BBC Radio 3 during tonight's interval

WEDNESDAY 29 AUGUST

PROM 62
6.00pm–c8.15pm • Royal Albert Hall

PRICE BAND **A**

VASILY PETRENKO

Elgar In the South (Alassio) *19'*

Iain Bell Aurora *c17'*
BBC co-commission: world premiere

INTERVAL

R. Strauss
Das Rosenband; Ständchen;
Wiegenlied; Zueignung *13'*

Bartók Concerto for Orchestra *35'*

Diana Damrau *soprano*

Royal Liverpool Philharmonic Orchestra
Vasily Petrenko *conductor*

Soprano Diana Damrau joins Vasily Petrenko and
the Royal Liverpool Philharmonic Orchestra for a
concert that moves from the lush, late-Romantic
soundscapes of Strauss's songs and the sweeping
melodic generosity of Elgar's Italy-inspired overture
In the South to the leaner, more percussive intensity
of Bartók's *Concerto for Orchestra* – a virtuosic
showcase for the Royal Liverpool Philharmonic
Orchestra. The concert also includes the world
premiere of Iain Bell's concerto for coloratura
soprano and orchestra, *Aurora*, composed especially
for Damrau. See 'New Music', pages 96–101.

PROMS PLUS TALK
4.15pm–4.55pm • Imperial College Union
Nathan Case and Melanie Windridge discuss the latest
scientific research into the *aurora borealis* with BBC New
Generation Thinker Eleanor Rosamund Barraclough.
Edited version broadcast on BBC Radio 3 during tonight's interval

WEDNESDAY 29 AUGUST

PROM 63 • LATE NIGHT ☽ ▣
9.30pm–c12.00am • Royal Albert Hall

PRICE BAND **C**

SIR ANDRÁS SCHIFF

J. S. Bach The Well-Tempered
Clavier – Book 2 *145'*

Sir András Schiff *piano*

There will be no interval

The two volumes of Bach's *The Well-Tempered
Clavier* are a window onto an extraordinary musical
imagination – an infinitely varied, beguiling series
of musical reflections and questions. Following his
complete performance of Book 1 last year,
distinguished pianist and Bach specialist Sir András
Schiff returns to perform the complete Book 2.
Much more than just a musical sequel, this volume
pushes harmony and counterpoint further than ever
before in its fascinating and uniquely challenging
sequence of works.

▣ *Broadcast on BBC Four on Friday 31 August*

> **Every Prom broadcast
> live on BBC Radio 3**

THURSDAY 30 AUGUST

PROM 64
7.30pm–c9.05pm • Royal Albert Hall

PRICE BAND **C**

ANDRÉS OROZCO-ESTRADA

Verdi Requiem   84'

Lise Davidsen *soprano*
Karen Cargill *mezzo-soprano*
Dmytro Popov *tenor*
Tomasz Konieczny *bass*

London Philharmonic Choir
London Philharmonic Orchestra
Andrés Orozco-Estrada *conductor*

There will be no interval

Rising conductor Andrés Orozco-Estrada continues this season's sequence of Requiems with Verdi's mighty concert-hall setting – an 'opera in church vestments'. Embracing the full gamut of human emotion, from the most tender and fragile of hopes to the visceral terror of the Day of Judgement, it's a work that transforms private grief into an astonishing public statement. An international team of soloists includes the exciting young Norwegian soprano Lise Davidsen and renowned Scottish mezzo-soprano Karen Cargill. *See 'Musical Memorials', pages 60–65.*

BBC MUSIC INTRODUCING SHOWCASE
5.15pm–6.25pm • Imperial College Union A special showcase of live music from BBC Music Introducing artists.
Recorded for future broadcast on BBC Radio 3's 'In Tune'.

FRIDAY 31 AUGUST

PROM 65
7.30pm–c9.30pm • Royal Albert Hall

PRICE BAND **A**
WEEKEND PROMMING PASS *see page 170*

SEMYON BYCHKOV

Ravel La valse   13'
Berio Sinfonia   34'
INTERVAL
Stravinsky The Rite of Spring   34'

London Voices
BBC Symphony Orchestra
Semyon Bychkov *conductor*

Three 20th-century classics explore the fantastical beginnings of modern music. Semyon Bychkov leads the BBC Symphony Orchestra in a journey that contrasts the pre-war, avant-garde provocations of Stravinsky's infamous ballet *The Rite of Spring* with the darker post-war reflections of Ravel's *La valse*, also commissioned by Diaghilev for his Ballets Russes. At the centre of the programme is Berio's extraordinary *Sinfonia*. Dedicated to Leonard Bernstein, it is a technical tour de force for orchestra and eight solo voices that gathers together familiar fragments of classical music (including nods to both the Ravel and Stravinsky works) to create something bewilderingly brilliant and utterly, joyously original. *See 'Impressions in Colour', pages 8–15.*

PROMS PLUS TALK
5.45pm–6.25pm • Imperial College Union Writer and broadcaster Ivan Hewett introduces Berio's *Sinfonia*.
Edited version broadcast on BBC Radio 3 during tonight's interval

SATURDAY 1 SEPTEMBER

PROMS AT … ALEXANDRA PALACE
3.00pm–c5.00pm

For ticket prices, see page 162

MARY BEVAN

Music by contemporaries of Sullivan, including Parry, Coleridge-Taylor and Stanford   45'
INTERVAL
Sullivan Trial by Jury   45'

Cast to include:

Neal Davies *The Learned Judge*
Mary Bevan *The Plaintiff*
Sam Furness *The Defendant*
Ross Ramgobin *Counsel for the Plaintiff*

BBC Singers
BBC Concert Orchestra
Jane Glover *conductor*

The magnificent theatre at Alexandra Palace originally opened in 1875 – the same year that Gilbert and Sullivan's one-act operetta *Trial by Jury* was premiered. In this special 'Proms at …' event, Jane Glover conducts a concert performance of this Victorian comic masterpiece in the Palace's theatre as its ambitious new refurbishment reaches completion. A first half of music by Sullivan's contemporaries explores that favourite G&S theme of love and marriage. *See 'Restoration Drama', pages 70–73.*

PROMS FAMILY ORCHESTRA & CHORUS
11.00am–1.00pm • Alexandra Palace Join professional musicians for a family-friendly introduction to this afternoon's Prom. Bring your instrument and join in!
Suitable for all the family (ages 7-plus). See pages 78–79.

SATURDAY 1 SEPTEMBER

PROM 66

7.30pm–c9.55pm • Royal Albert Hall

PRICE BAND **C**
WEEKEND PROMMING PASS *see page 170*

YUJA WANG

Dukas La péri – Fanfare and
Poème dansé   21'

Prokofiev Piano Concerto No. 3
in C major   29'

INTERVAL

Schmidt Symphony No. 4 in C major 44'

Yuja Wang *piano*

Berliner Philharmoniker
Kirill Petrenko *conductor*

A landmark concert sees the Berliner Philharmoniker
perform for the first time in London under its new
Chief Conductor Designate, Kirill Petrenko. 'In this
work Mahler's spirit is resurrected,' said a colleague
of Franz Schmidt's Fourth Symphony, a piece whose
Romantic character is charged with the grief of
personal loss. Dynamic pianist Yuja Wang is the
soloist in Prokofiev's Third Piano Concerto, with
its explosive closing battle of wills between soloist
and orchestra. The concert opens with Dukas's
exotic, Impressionistic ballet score *La péri*, prefaced
by the a rresting curtain-raising fanfare the composer
later added. See *'Impressions in Colour'*, pages 8–15.

PROMS PLUS TALK
5.45pm–6.25pm • Imperial College Union Musicologist and
broadcaster Erik Levi introduces Schmidt's Symphony No. 4.
Edited version broadcast on BBC Radio 3 during tonight's interval

---

Allan Clayton • Prom 72
BBC Radio 3 New Generation Artist, 2007–9

'It's a completely heartbreaking part, and utterly
rooted in Britten's natural sense of theatre.' So
British tenor Allan Clayton describes his role in
Britten's hugely powerful *War Requiem*, whose
Proms performance in Prom 72 is all the more
poignant in the centenary year of the First World
War armistice. It's a role, he feels, that falls
somewhere between that of traditional concert
soloist and an operatic portrayal, matching
Britten's own blending of texts from the Mass for
the Dead with the poetry of Wilfred Owen, who
was himself killed in action just a week before
the armistice. 'It's Britten's setting of the Owen
texts that makes this piece connect so instantly
with listeners. I'm kind of a not-uninvolved
narrator, with my own painful sense of despair.'

'Britten's never afraid to pare his enormous
forces down to the bare bones – to expose the
pity, the tragedy and the hopelessness of war,'
continues Clayton. 'It's easy to admire his
orchestration: the shrieking and wailing of
bombs in the woodwind; the flashes of fire in
the brass; the ingenious use of such a large
chorus in the traditional Requiem Mass texts.
In a space like the Royal Albert Hall, the
contrast between the loudest passages in the
Dies irae and the quiet conversation between
a soldier and his dead enemy should be
spine-tingling. For me, my final "It seemed
that out of battle" monologue is one of the
most powerful things in all music to sing.'

Benjamin Grosvenor
Proms 46 & 56
BBC Radio 3 New Generation Artist, 2010–12

It's probably Mozart's best-known and best-
loved piano concerto that young British pianist
Benjamin Grosvenor performs in Prom 56:
No. 21 in C major, K467. 'I'm not sure the fact
that a piece is well known necessarily affects
your interpretation of it,' he explains. 'The
process remains the same, beginning with a
careful reading of the score. Trying to be as
diligent and as honest as possible in preparation
means that it's possible to produce an individual
interpretation where the desire to be individual
per se hasn't been a governing aim.'

It's a piece that Grosvenor has known for a long
time. 'It's actually the first concerto I performed,
with my secondary school orchestra, when I was
11.' What keeps bringing him back to the piece?
'It's certainly a concerto in which Mozart
delights in virtuosic display, while producing
the most beautiful music. It's doubtless the
most famous part of the concerto, but I enjoy
most of all the sublime second movement.'

He's also performing Gershwin's *Rhapsody in
Blue* a few days earlier (Prom 46). By the time his
two Proms come round he'll be just 26 but he's
already appeared at the festival six times, and
played at the Last Night in 2015. What does he
most enjoy about it? 'It's surprising how such a
cavernous space as the Royal Albert Hall can
take on such a feeling of intimacy,' he explains.

SUNDAY 2 SEPTEMBER

PROM 67
2.00pm–c3.50pm • Royal Albert Hall

PRICE BAND D
WEEKEND PROMMING PASS *see page 170*

SUSAN GRAHAM

Mahler Symphony No. 3 in D minor *102'*

Susan Graham *mezzo-soprano*

CBSO Chorus (female voices)
CBSO Youth Chorus
Boston Symphony Orchestra
Andris Nelsons *conductor*

There will be no interval

A weekend of starry international orchestras continues with the Boston Symphony Orchestra and its Music Director Andris Nelsons. They bring with them another American star, mezzo-soprano Susan Graham, as soloist in Mahler's Third Symphony. The sunniest and most joyful of all the composer's symphonies, this musical world teems with life, recreating the 'tumult' of human existence – from bird calls to marches, dances and songs – in its broad scope. The Boston Symphony Orchestra is joined by the CBSO Chorus and CBSO Youth Chorus.

> **Every Prom broadcast**
> **live on BBC Radio 3**

SUNDAY 2 SEPTEMBER

PROM 68
8.00pm–c10.05pm • Royal Albert Hall

PRICE BAND D
WEEKEND PROMMING PASS *see page 170*

KIRILL PETRENKO

R. Strauss
Don Juan *18'*
Death and Transfiguration *26'*

INTERVAL

Beethoven Symphony No. 7
in A major *38'*

Berliner Philharmoniker
Kirill Petrenko *conductor*

For their second concert, the Berliner Philharmoniker and its Music Director Designate Kirill Petrenko pair two of the 19th century's greatest symphonic poems with Beethoven's much-loved Seventh Symphony. If *Don Juan* celebrates the life of the body – energetic passions, desires and cynical ambitions – then the composer's *Death and Transfiguration*, a vivid portrait of the last hours of a dying artist, explores ideas of the mind and spirit. These two colourful musical narratives are set against the dance-driven energy of Beethoven's symphony. See 'All Types of Beethoven', pages 88–91.

PROMS PLUS TALK
6.15pm–6.55pm • Imperial College Union Novelists Belinda Bauer and Patricia Duncker consider sex and death in literature.
Edited version broadcast on BBC Radio 3 during tonight's interval

MONDAY 3 SEPTEMBER

PROMS AT … CADOGAN HALL 8
1.00pm–c2.00pm • Cadogan Hall

For ticket prices, see page 162

DAISHIN KASHIMOTO

L. Boulanger Nocturne for violin
and piano *3'*
Debussy Sonata for Flute, Viola
and Harp *18'*
Nina Šenk Baca *c8'*
BBC commission: world premiere

L. Boulanger Trois morceaux
for piano *7'*
Ravel Introduction and Allegro *11'*

Soloists of the Berliner Philharmoniker
Maja Avramović *violin*
Daishin Kashimoto *violin*
Amihai Grosz *viola*
Bruno Delepelaire *cello*
Emmanuel Pahud *flute*
Andreas Ottensamer *clarinet*
Marie-Pierre Langlamet *harp*

Alasdair Beatson *piano*

There will be no interval

Hear some of the Berliner Philharmoniker's finest players perform as soloists in a concert of 20th-century French chamber music. Marking the 100th anniversaries of both Debussy and Lili Boulanger, the programme includes the latter's evocative sequence of miniatures, *Trois morceaux*, alongside the neo-Classical melancholy of the former's Sonata for Flute, Viola and Harp. The concert also includes a world premiere by Slovenian composer Nina Šenk, using the same instrumental forces as Ravel's vivacious *Introduction and Allegro*. See 'Impressions in Colour', pages 8–15; 'The Other Boulanger Girl', pages 16–17; 'New Music', pages 96–101.

MONDAY 3 SEPTEMBER

PROM 69
7.30pm–c9.50pm • Royal Albert Hall

PRICE BAND **B**

BAIBA SKRIDE

Bernstein Serenade (after Plato's 'Symposium') *31'*

INTERVAL

Shostakovich Symphony No. 4 in C minor *64'*

Baiba Skride *violin*

Boston Symphony Orchestra
Andris Nelsons *conductor*

This second concert by Andris Nelsons and the Boston Symphony Orchestra sets Bernstein's intensely lyrical *Serenade (after Plato's 'Symposium')* for solo violin and orchestra – a work composed for Isaac Stern and performed here by the prize-winning Latvian violinist Baiba Skride – alongside Shostakovich's uncompromising Fourth Symphony. This dazzling musical manifesto of the composer's modernist beliefs was withdrawn under duress before its scheduled 1936 premiere and wasn't heard publicly until 25 years later. See 'An Embarrassment of Gifts', pages 30–33.

PROMS POETRY COMPETITION
5.25pm–6.25pm • Imperial College Union
Poet Ian McMillan, presenter of BBC Radio 3's *The Verb*, and Judith Palmer, Director of the Poetry Society, are joined by poet Helen Mort to announce the winners of the 2018 Proms Poetry Competition.
For further information, visit www.bbc.co.uk/proms.
Edited version broadcast on BBC Radio 3 after tonight's Prom

TUESDAY 4 SEPTEMBER

PROM 70
7.30pm–c9.45pm • Royal Albert Hall

PRICE BAND **B**

PABLO ZIEGLER

Tango Prom

Pablo Ziegler *piano*
Héctor Del Curto *bandoneon*
Claudio Ragazzi *guitar*
Pedro Giraudo *double bass*
Franco Pinna *drums*

Britten Sinfonia
Clark Rundell *conductor*

There will be one interval

A celebration of the heady, sexually charged Latin American tango, from its origins in the bars of 1880s Buenos Aires, through to Ástor Piazzolla's Nuevo Tango that emerged in the 1950s. The story also embraces the Finnish tango tradition of the early 20th century – steeped in the themes of love, sorrow and nature – and comes bang up to date with some of the latest tango music. Showcasing Grammy Award-winning pianist Pablo Ziegler along with leading singers, dancers and instrumentalists from Europe, the USA and Argentina, the raw and earthy vitality of the tango is explored, from the sultry intimacy of the bandoneon to the big-band orchestral forces of the Britten Sinfonia.

Broadcast on BBC Four on Friday 7 September

COUNTERPOINT – THE 2018 FINAL
5.25pm–6.25pm • Imperial College Union Paul Gambaccini chairs the Grand Final of the much-loved BBC Radio 4 music quiz, with amateur music-lovers from around the UK answering questions on a wide variety of music.
Tickets available from BBC Studio Audiences: bbc.co.uk/showsandtours/shows.
Edited version broadcast on BBC Radio 4 at a later date

SPOTLIGHT
BBC RADIO 3 NGA

Francesco Piemontesi • Prom 2
BBC Radio 3 New Generation Artist, 2009–11

'This is one of my favourite piano concertos by Mozart,' says Francesco Piemontesi. He's talking about No. 27 in B flat major, the concerto he plays with the Royal Philharmonic Orchestra in Prom 2. 'It has a very peculiar, elusive mood in the first and second movements. It's a mood of saying goodbye, even goodbye to the world. I have this image of Mozart taking his luggage, packing it and then taking you by the hand and saying, "Come with me."'

This was indeed to be the composer's final piano concerto and was first performed in 1791, the year of his death. 'It's the kind of work he couldn't have written when he was younger,' says the Swiss pianist. 'Of course, he died very young, but he had done an incredible amount of work and reached this distilled simplicity. The melodies seem so simple that every child could sing them, but they are actually incredibly harmonically daring.'

Piemontesi believes this is the Mozart concerto he's played most often through his career. Over the past decade, he has performed it with both modern and period-instrument orchestras. 'What interests me is not to recreate a museum atmosphere but to know what possibilities the composer had,' Piemontesi reflects. 'At the same time we need to reach an audience in the Royal Albert Hall. I say, let's profit from what we know about older music but translate it for today.'

Mark Simpson • Prom 4
BBC Radio 3 New Generation Artist, 2012–14

'That piece really packs a punch!' Clarinettist and composer Mark Simpson is talking about the 2002 Clarinet Concerto by Finnish composer Magnus Lindberg, which he performs with the BBC Philharmonic in Prom 4. 'It's one of the best contemporary clarinet concertos around, if not *the* best.'

What's so great about it? Simpson doesn't know where to start. 'It has a real lyrical quality and very rich harmonies. It's always vibrant, full of life, energetic, moving forward.' And fearsomely demanding on its soloist, too. 'I've played it three or four times over the past decade. It's fiendishly difficult, but I feel very comfortable playing it now.' Part of the work's difficulty lies in the unusual demands Lindberg places on his soloist, including multiphonics – playing whole chords rather than single notes. 'It almost sounds like a distorted guitar. It's a crunchy, dirty sound with a dark, metallic colour – not the kind of thing you'd expect from a clarinet.'

In 2006 Simpson earned the unique distinction of winning both the BBC's Young Musician competition as a clarinettist and the BBC Proms/ *Guardian* Young Composers Competition. How have those awards helped his career? 'They gave me enormous exposure,' he says. 'I was so grateful but I also felt a sense of naivety, so I stepped back from the limelight and went to university. I never really let it define me.'

Antoine Tamestit • Prom 71
BBC Radio 3 New Generation Artist, 2004–6

Antoine Tamestit has a confession to make. When he first started to play Berlioz's *Harold in Italy*, one of the landmarks of the viola repertoire, he didn't really like it. 'I found it so heavy,' he explains. The French viola player is in fine company. When the legendary Niccolò Paganini first saw the score he had commissioned, he was so disappointed at the lack of virtuoso fireworks that he refused to give the premiere. Happily, though, he later realised he was wrong. As did Tamestit.

'I think I was approaching it as if it was a German Romantic work,' he explains. 'When I started playing it with different conductors, such as Marc Minkowski, François-Xavier Roth and now Sir John Eliot Gardiner, and with period-instrument orchestras, I discovered a different world of colours.' Those transparent sounds, gut strings and original wind instruments transformed Tamestit's idea of this remarkable piece, a four-part symphony with solo viola based on Byron's *Childe Harold* and Berlioz's own visits to Italy. 'It's very interesting narratively as it's both a written story and based on personal experience,' says Tamestit. 'Gardiner made me realise that the viola player is an actor and has different roles. Sometimes he's part of the orchestra, sometimes a commentator, sometimes he's really the solo viola, and sometimes there's a dialogue, a bit like in Strauss's *Don Quixote*. I love the part.'

PRICE BAND **B**

JOYCE DiDONATO

Berlioz
Overture 'Le corsaire'	8'
La mort de Cléopâtre	21'
The Trojans – Royal Hunt and Storm	10'
The Trojans – Dido's death scene	7'

INTERVAL

Harold in Italy	42'

Antoine Tamestit *viola*
Joyce DiDonato *mezzo-soprano*

Orchestre Révolutionnaire et Romantique
Sir John Eliot Gardiner *conductor*

Sir John Eliot Gardiner and his Orchestre Révolutionnaire et Romantique continue their cycle of Berlioz performances, which will reach its climax next season in the 150th-anniversary year of the composer's death. Some of Berlioz's most colourful and dramatic works come together here in a programme that draws not only from concert works including the filmic overture *Le corsaire* and the magnificent symphony with solo viola *Harold in Italy*, but also from Berlioz's great opera *The Trojans*. Star mezzo-soprano Joyce DiDonato joins the orchestra to sing Dido's heartbreaking final scene. *See 'Impressions in Colour', pages 8–15.*

PROMS READING
5.45pm–6.25pm • Imperial College Union
Journalist Alex Clark and a celebrated classicist discuss the epic tales behind Berlioz's grand opera *The Trojans* and introduce readings from Virgil and others.
Edited version broadcast on BBC Radio 3 during tonight's interval

THURSDAY 6 SEPTEMBER

PROM 72
7.00pm–c8.35pm • Royal Albert Hall

PRICE BAND B

ERIN WALL

Britten War Requiem   80'

Erin Wall *soprano*
Allan Clayton *tenor*
Russell Braun *baritone*

Huddersfield Choral Society
RSNO Junior Chorus
RSNO Chorus
Royal Scottish National Orchestra
Peter Oundjian *conductor*

There will be no interval

A powerful statement of the composer's pacifist beliefs – composed in the shadow of the Second World War, but harking back to the carnage of the First via the war poetry of Wilfred Owen – Britten's *War Requiem* today remains one of the most devastating artistic responses to conflict: a work that mourns but also rages against the senseless violence and destruction of war. The Huddersfield Choral Society, RSNO Chorus (175 this year) and RSNO Junior Chorus (40 this year) join the Royal Scottish National Orchestra and its outgoing Music Director Peter Oundjian for a performance marking 100 years since the end of the First World War. *See 'Musical Memorials', pages 60–65.*

See 'Musical Memorials', pages 60–65.

PROMS PLUS TALK
5.15pm–5.55pm • Imperial College Union Join Director of the BBC Proms David Pickard, Controller of Radio 3 Alan Davey and Craig Hassall, Chief Executive of the Royal Albert Hall, as they look back over the 2018 Proms season.

THURSDAY 6 SEPTEMBER

PROM 73 • LATE NIGHT ☾
10.15pm–c11.30pm • Royal Albert Hall

PRICE BAND E

TALLIS SCHOLARS

Before the Ending of the Day

Hildegard of Bingen
Ordo virtutum – In principio omnes   4'
Padilla Deus in adiutorium   3'
Gallus Pater noster   5'
Allegri Miserere   12'
Tallis Te lucis ante terminum I   3'
Arvo Pärt Nunc dimittis   8'
Browne O Maria salvatoris mater   15'

interspersed with plainchant

Tallis Scholars
Peter Phillips *director*

There will be no interval

Before the fanfares and celebrations of the Last Night of the Proms comes a late-night moment of contemplation led by Peter Phillips and the Tallis Scholars. Recreating the Christian office of Compline, the final service of the church day, they weave together a sung meditation spanning over 1,000 years of sacred music. The delicate tracery of Renaissance polyphony by Padilla and Gallus gives way to the 21st-century 'Spiritual' Minimalism of Arvo Pärt, and at the centre of it all sits Allegri's exquisite *Miserere*.

Every Prom broadcast
live on BBC Radio 3

FRIDAY 7 SEPTEMBER

PROM 74
7.00pm–c10.05pm • Royal Albert Hall

PRICE BAND A

LOUISE ALDER

Handel Theodora   147'

Louise Alder *Theodora*
Iestyn Davies *Didymus*
Benjamin Hulett *Septimius*
Ann Hallenberg *Irene*
Tareq Nazmi *Valens*

Arcangelo Chorus
Arcangelo
Jonathan Cohen *conductor*

There will be one interval

In a battle between love and faith, which will triumph? Following the success of last year's *Israel in Egypt*, the Proms continues its journey through Handel's oratorios with the composer's own favourite and one of the most powerfully dramatic works he ever produced. An all-star cast is led by Louise Alder and Iestyn Davies as tragic lovers Theodora and Didymus. Jonathan Cohen directs his period ensemble Arcangelo. *See 'Love, Faith and Honour', pages 102–103.*

See 'Love, Faith and Honour', pages 102–103.

PROMS PLUS TALK
5.15pm–5.55pm • Imperial College Union
Musicologist Suzanne Aspden introduces Handel's *Theodora*.
Edited version broadcast on BBC Radio 3 during tonight's interval

PROM 75
7.15pm–c10.30pm • Royal Albert Hall

PRICE BAND G

GERALD FINLEY

Last Night of the Proms 2018

Programme to include:

Roxanna Panufnik Songs of
Darkness, Dreams of Light   c10'
BBC commission: world premiere

Stanford Songs of the Sea   18'

Parry Blest Pair of Sirens   11'

Milhaud Scaramouche   10'

Rodgers Carousel – 'Soliloquy'   8'

arr. Wood Fantasia on British
Sea-Songs   11'

Arne, arr. Sargent Rule, Britannia!   5'

Elgar Pomp and Circumstance March
No. 1 in D major ('Land of Hope and
Glory')   8'

Parry, orch. Elgar Jerusalem   3'

The National Anthem   3'

Auld Lang Syne   2'

Jess Gillam *saxophone*
Gerald Finley *baritone*

BBC Singers
BBC Symphony Chorus
BBC Symphony Orchestra
Sir Andrew Davis *conductor*

There will be one interval

Sir Andrew Davis, the much-loved former Chief Conductor of the BBC Symphony Orchestra and a veteran steersman of the Last Night, returns to direct the greatest annual party in classical music. The popular nautical theme of traditional favourites by Henry Wood and Thomas Arne is extended in Stanford's *Songs of the Sea,* featuring star Canadian baritone Gerald Finley. Another British choral classic, *Blest Pair of Sirens* – honouring the 'harmonious sisters, Voice and Verse' – joins *Jerusalem* in the centenary year of Hubert Parry's death. There's a

dash of Broadway in the touching 'Soliloquy' from Rodgers and Hammerstein's *Carousel,* in which the wife-battering Billy finds new eloquence while vowing to change his ways, and a more mischievous streak in Milhaud's delightful suite *Scaramouche.* Roxanna Panufnik's new commission rounds off a series of over 40 world, UK or London premieres this season, continuing the forward-looking vision of Proms founder-conductor Henry Wood. *See 'Impressions in Colour', pages 8–15; 'New Music', pages 96–101.*

First half live on BBC Two, second half live on BBC One

THE VERB
4.30pm–5.45 pm • Imperial College Union
Poet and presenter Ian McMillan hosts a special Last Night edition of his showcase of poetry and the spoken word, BBC Radio 3's *The Verb,* with guest writers and performers. *Tickets available from BBC Studio Audiences: bbc.co.uk/showsandtours/shows.*
Recorded for future broadcast on BBC Radio 3

SATURDAY 8 SEPTEMBER

PROMS IN THE PARK
Gates open 3.00pm • Entertainment from 5.00pm • Hyde Park, London

For ticket prices, see page 162

MICHAEL BALL

Michael Ball *presenter*

BBC Concert Orchestra
Richard Balcombe *conductor*

Join in the Last Night of the Proms celebrations
in Hyde Park, hosted by Michael Ball. The open-air
concert features a host of musical stars. In a new
addition for this year the traditional Last Night
anthems will be performed live on the Hyde Park
stage by Proms in the Park favourites, the BBC
Concert Orchestra, conducted by Richard Balcombe.
Forty thousand voices will join them for the mass
singalong as the evening brings to a close two months
of music-making with a spectacular finale.

Listen to BBC Radio 2 from Monday 23 April for
announcements of headline artists and special guests.

🎙 *Broadcast live on BBC Radio 2*

Booking tickets
Tickets available from 11.00am on Friday 27 April
from the Royal Albert Hall. Ticket requests may also
be included in the Proms Planner submitted from
9.00am on Saturday 12 May. See below for details
of how to book.

Online bbc.co.uk/promsinthepark

By phone from the Royal Albert Hall on
020 7070 4441 (a booking fee of 2% of the total
value – plus £2.00 per ticket up to a maximum
of £25.00 – applies for telephone bookings).

In person at the Royal Albert Hall Box Office
(no fees apply to tickets bought in person).

By post See page 169.

For details of how to order a picnic hamper for
collection on the day, or to find out about VIP
packages and corporate hospitality, visit
bbc.co.uk/promsinthepark.

**EXPERIENCE THE LAST NIGHT
MAGIC AROUND THE UK!**

—NORTHERN IRELAND
—SCOTLAND
—WALES

The BBC Proms in the Park events offer live
concerts featuring high-profile artists,
well-loved presenters and BBC Big Screen
link-ups to the Royal Albert Hall, when you
can join with audiences across the nations.
So gather your friends and your Last Night
spirit for an unforgettable evening.

Keep checking bbc.co.uk/promsinthepark
for announcements of artists, venues and
booking information.

Highlights of the Last Night celebrations
around the UK will feature as part of the
live television coverage of the Last Night
and you can watch more at bbc.co.uk/
proms. You can also access Proms in
the Park content via the red button.

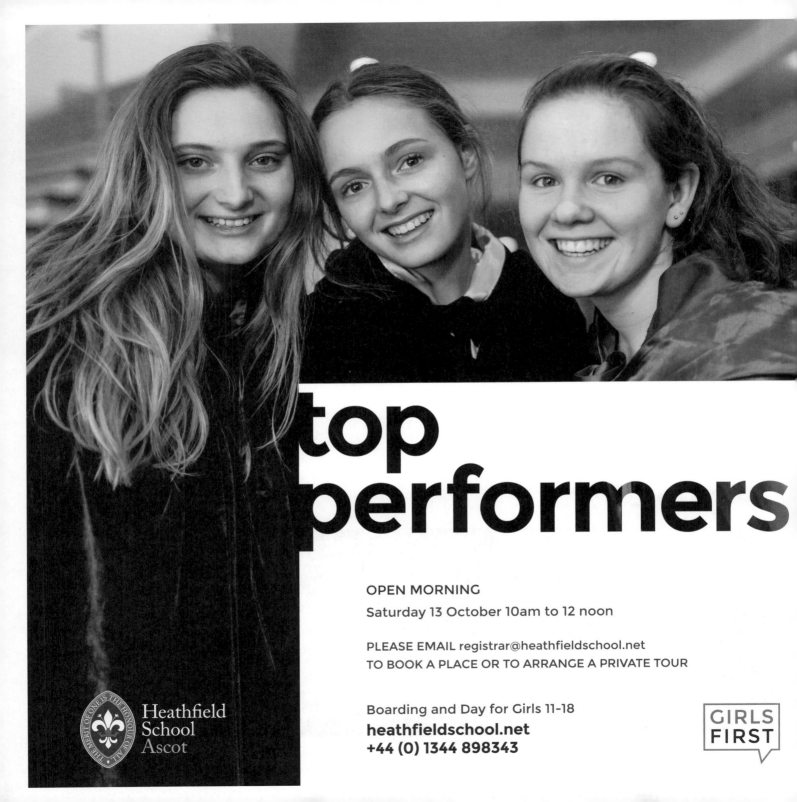

top performers

OPEN MORNING
Saturday 13 October 10am to 12 noon

PLEASE EMAIL registrar@heathfieldschool.net
TO BOOK A PLACE OR TO ARRANGE A PRIVATE TOUR

Boarding and Day for Girls 11-18
heathfieldschool.net
+44 (0) 1344 898343

Heathfield
School
Ascot

GIRLS
FIRST

Booking

WHEN

Thursday 19 April

CREATE YOUR PROMS PLAN ONLINE

From 2.00pm on Thursday 19 April, go to
bbc.co.uk/proms and create your personal Proms Plan

See page 169 for more details

Saturday 12 May

BOOK YOUR TICKETS

From 9.00am on Saturday 12 May, submit your Proms
Plan – or book online, by phone, in person or by post

See page 169 for more details

HOW

Online

bbc.co.uk/proms or
royalalberthall.com

By Phone

on 020 7070 4441[†]

In Person

at the Royal Albert Hall
Box Office

By Post

BBC Proms, Box Office,
Royal Albert Hall,
London SW7 2AP

[†]**CALL COSTS**
Standard geographic charges from landlines and mobiles will apply. All calls may be recorded and monitored for
training and quality-control purposes.

TICKET PRICES

Royal Albert Hall

Seated tickets for all BBC Proms concerts at the Royal Albert Hall fall into one of eight price bands, indicated beside each concert listing on pages 122–158. For Promming, see page opposite.

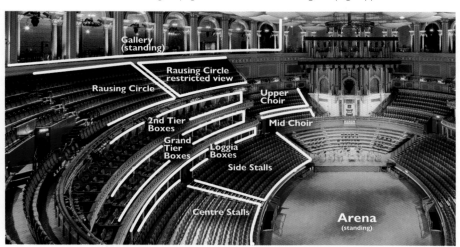

PRICE BANDS	A	B	C	D	E	F	G	H	
GRAND TIER BOXES 12 seats, price per seat*	£41.00	£50.00	£60.00	£72.00	£25.00	£35.00	£100.00	£20.00	
LOGGIA AND 2ND TIER BOXES Loggia: 8 seats, price per seat 2nd Tier: 5 seats, price per seat	£36.00	£45.00	£55.00	£67.00	£25.00	£35.00	£95.00	£20.00	
CENTRE STALLS	£32.00	£42.00	£52.00	£64.00	£20.00	£30.00	£90.00	£16.00	
SIDE STALLS	£29.00	£38.00	£48.00	£59.00	£20.00	£30.00	£87.00	£16.00	Relaxed Prom: all tickets £12.00/£6.00†
MID CHOIR	£26.00	£25.00	£34.00	£45.00	£20.00	£30.00	£65.00	£16.00	
UPPER CHOIR	£19.50	£22.00	£29.00	£38.00	£15.00	£20.00	£62.00	£12.00	
RAUSING CIRCLE FRONT	£19.50	£22.00	£29.00	£38.00	£15.00	£20.00	£62.00	£12.00	
RAUSING CIRCLE MID	£17.00	£20.00	£24.00	£30.00	£15.00	£20.00	£58.00	£12.00	
RAUSING CIRCLE REAR	£12.50	£15.50	£19.50	£25.00	£15.00	£20.00	£47.00	£12.00	
RAUSING CIRCLE RESTRICTED VIEW	£7.50	£9.50	£14.00	£18.00	£7.50	£10.00	£27.00	£7.50	

Please note: a booking fee of 2% of the total value – plus £2.00 per ticket (£1.00 per ticket for the Relaxed Prom) up to a maximum of £25.00 – applies to all bookings (including Season and Weekend Promming Passes), other than those made in person at the Royal Albert Hall. *As most Grand Tier Boxes are privately owned, availability is limited.

'Proms at …' concerts

Advance tickets can be bought from the Royal Albert Hall Box Office from Friday 8 June. A limited number of tickets will also be available from each venue. Promming tickets are limited to two per transaction.

Alexandra Palace
Seats (unreserved): £16.00
Promming tickets: £6.00
(booking fees apply)

As this event will take place prior to the full completion of the renovation works in the theatre, detailed booking information will be available when tickets go on sale on Friday 8 June.

Lincoln Drill Hall
Seats (reserved): £16.00, £13.00
Promming tickets: £6.00
(booking fees apply)

Roundhouse
Seats (reserved): £16.00, £13.00
Promming tickets: £6.00
(booking fees apply)

Proms at … Cadogan Hall
Stalls (reserved): £16.00
Centre Gallery (reserved): £13.00
(booking fees apply)
Promming tickets: £6.00, available on the day from Cadogan Hall

BBC Proms in the Park, Hyde Park, London, Saturday 8 September
Tickets (standard admission) £45.00
(booking fees apply)
See page 159 for details

†Relaxed Prom tickets cost £6.00 for 18s and under, wheelchair users and ambulant disabled

What is Promming?

Standing in the Arena or Gallery at the Royal Albert Hall is known as 'Promming' and is central to the unique and informal atmosphere of the BBC Proms. The Arena is the large space in the centre of the auditorium and gives you the opportunity to get up close to the performers. The Gallery runs around the top of the Hall; it offers a spectacular bird's-eye view of the stage.

Tickets not available for your favourite Prom? Don't give up!

Up to 1,350 standing tickets are available to buy on the day of each concert, for just £6.00. A limited number of these tickets are released online between 9.00am and 12 noon and the rest are sold in person when the doors open. If you arrive early enough on the day of the concert to collect a place number from a steward, you have a very good chance of getting in once the doors open (for details, see below).

Promming Passes

Book a Season or Weekend Promming Pass and benefit from guaranteed entry (until 30 minutes before each concert) as well as great savings. See page 170 for details.

Buying Promming tickets

Online

A limited number of Promming tickets are available to purchase online between 9.00am and 12 noon on the day of each concert, with the exception of Promming tickets for the Ten Pieces Proms, which will be available to purchase from 9.00am on the day before the concerts. Tickets are limited to one per person for Promming tickets, and four per person for Promming tickets for the Ten Pieces Proms.

A limited number of Promming tickets for the Relaxed Prom (Prom 59) are available to purchase online from 9.00am on Friday 11 May.

Promming tickets are not available to purchase online for the Last Night of the Proms.

In Person

All remaining Promming tickets are sold in person. Tickets are limited to one per person, and can be purchased with cash or contactless payment card as queues enter the Hall – approximately one hour before the start of each concert (30 minutes before Late Night Proms).

A numbering system will be in operation, so there is no need to stand in a queue all day. When you arrive at the Hall, ask a steward for your place number – these are handed out from 9.00am – and you can return later to take your numbered place in the queue.

Promming at the Last Night

A limited number of Promming tickets are available on the Last Night (priced £6.00, one per person). See page 164 for further details.

Seat Reservation Card – for wheelchair-users and ambulant disabled concert-goers

The Gallery can accommodate up to four wheelchair-users and a limited number of seats are available for reservation each day by ambulant disabled concert-goers (people with a wide range of disabilities who are not regular wheelchair-users) who wish to join the Promenaders. Just ask a steward when you arrive at the Hall. A Seat Reservation Card does not guarantee entry – you must also purchase a Promming ticket.

Proms at ... Cadogan Hall

Prom on the day – tickets can be purchased in person at Cadogan Hall from 10.00am.

Other 'Proms at ...' concerts

Promming tickets for the other 'Proms at ...' venues are available on the day from each venue. Check the Proms website for details.

ONLINE PROMMING TICKETS
All Promming tickets purchased online are subject to a booking fee of 2% of the total value plus £1.00 per ticket.

SEASON/WEEKEND PROMMING PASS-HOLDERS
Season and Weekend Promming Pass-holders arriving at the Royal Albert Hall less than 30 minutes before a concert are not guaranteed entry and should join the back of the relevant queue.

Booking and Venues

THE LAST NIGHT OF THE PROMS

Owing to high demand, the majority of tickets for the Last Night of the Proms are allocated by ballot.

The Five-Concert Ballot

Customers who purchase tickets for at least five concerts at the Royal Albert Hall are eligible to enter the Five-Concert Ballot.

You must do this before the Five-Concert Ballot closes on Thursday 31 May.

How to enter

When booking online, tick the Ballot opt-in box – or when booking by phone, in person or by post, inform the Box Office that you wish to enter this ballot.

If you require a wheelchair space for the Last Night of the Proms, you still need to book for five concerts but you must phone the Access Information Line on 020 7070 4410 (9.00am–9.00pm daily) by Thursday 31 May and ask to be entered into the separate ballot for wheelchair spaces. This ballot cannot be entered online.

Successful applicants will be informed by Friday 8 June.

Please note:

– If you are successful in the Five-Concert Ballot, you can apply to buy a maximum of two tickets for the Last Night; you will not be obliged to buy Last Night tickets should your preferred seating area not be available.

– If you are successful in the Ballot, your Last Night tickets will be issued from Friday 31 August.

– If you are unsuccessful in the Ballot, we regret that no refunds for other tickets purchased will be payable.

The Open Ballot

One hundred Centre Stalls seats (priced £90.00 each plus booking fee) and 100 Front Circle seats (priced £62.00 each plus booking fee) for the Last Night of the Proms at the Royal Albert Hall will be allocated by Open Ballot.

How to enter

Download and complete the official Open Ballot Form from bbc.co.uk/promstickets; or call 020 7765 2044 to receive a copy by post. The completed form should be sent by post only – to arrive no later than Thursday 28 June – to:

BBC Proms Open Ballot, Box Office Royal Albert Hall, London SW7 2AP

Please note:

– No other ticket purchases are necessary to enter the Open Ballot.

– Only one application (for a maximum of two tickets) may be made per household.

– The Open Ballot application envelopes should contain only the official 2018 Form.

– The Open Ballot takes place on Friday 29 June and successful applicants will be contacted by Thursday 5 July.

– If you are successful in the Five-Concert Ballot, you will not be eligible to enter the Open Ballot.

General availability

Any remaining Last Night tickets will go on sale on Friday 6 July at 9.00am, by phone and online only. There is very high demand for Last Night tickets, but returns occasionally become available.

Please note:

– Only one application (for a maximum of two tickets) can be made per household.

ROYAL ALBERT HALL

Kensington Gore, London SW7 2AP
www.royalalberthall.com • 020 7070 4441

Your Visit

Latecomers

Latecomers will only be admitted if and when there is a suitable break in the performance.

Security

Please do not bring large bags to the Royal Albert Hall. All bags and visitors may be subject to security checks as a condition of entry.

Cloakroom

A cloakroom is available for coats and small essential items. A charge of £1.00 per item applies. (Cloakroom season tickets, priced £20.40, are also available: conditions apply – see royalalberthall.com.) For reasons of safety and comfort, only one small bag per person is permitted in the Arena; please follow the guidance of the stewards if asked to deposit your bag in the cloakroom.

Children under 5

Out of consideration for audience and artists, it is not recommended that children under 5 years old be brought into the auditorium, with the exception of the Ten Pieces Proms (Proms 19 and 20) and the Relaxed Prom (Prom 59).

Tours of the Royal Albert Hall

Classical music tours of the Royal Albert Hall last approximately one hour during the Proms season. Other tours of the building also run regularly. For bookings and further information, call 0845 401 5045 or visit royalalberthall.com. For group bookings of 15 people or more, call 020 7959 0558. Special group rates apply.

QUEUING
Please note that queuing arrangements for the Last Night of the Proms differ from other Proms, but stewards will be on hand to assist Prommers from 9.00am. Visit royalalberthall.com/promsqueue from Thursday 23 August for details.

BOOKING FEES
A booking fee of 2% of the total value – plus £2.00 per ticket – applies to all bookings for Last Night tickets.

Dress code

Come as you are: there is no dress code at the Proms.

Proms programmes, gifts and merchandise

These are available inside the porches at Doors 6 and 12 and on the Rausing Circle level at Doors 4 and 8. Programmes are on sale throughout the building. Large-print programmes can be collected from the Merchandise Desk at Door 6.

Food and Drink

With a number of restaurants and bars, as well as box catering, there is a wide range of food and drink to enjoy at the Royal Albert Hall, from two and a half hours before each concert. Booking in advance is recommended. Visit royalalberthall.com/food or call the Box Office on 020 7070 4441[†] to make your reservation.

Bars

These are located throughout the building and open two hours before each concert. Interval drinks are available from any bar; to beat the queues, you can order before the concert. Visit royalalberthall.com/bars.

Restaurants

Verdi – Italian Kitchen (Grand Tier, Door 12)
Laurent Perrier Champagne Bar (Grand Tier, Door 3)
Elgar Bar & Grill (Rausing Circle level, Door 9)
Coda by Éric Chavot (Rausing Circle level, Door 1)
Wine Bar (Second Tier level, Door 3)
Arena Bars (basement level, Doors 1 and 6)
Café Bar (ground floor, Door 12)

Grand Tier, Second Tier and Loggia Box seats

If you have seats in one of the Royal Albert Hall's boxes, you can pre-order food and drinks to be served upon arrival or at the interval. Visit boxcatering.royalalberthall.com and please order at least 36 hours before the concert that you are attending. Please note that the consumption of your own food and drink in the Hall is not permitted. Glasses and bottles are permitted in boxes only, as part of box catering ordered through the Royal Albert Hall.

Access

Full information on the facilities offered to disabled concert-goers at the Royal Albert Hall is available online at royalalberthall.com or by calling the Access Information Line on 020 7070 4410 (9.00am–9.00pm daily). The Royal Albert Hall has a Silver award from the Attitude is Everything Charter of Best Practice.

Facilities, services and ticketing arrangements

Twenty spaces are bookable for wheelchair-users with adjacent companion seats for the majority of concerts. To book, please call the Access Information Line or visit the Royal Albert Hall Box Office in person.

Six additional Side Stalls wheelchair spaces are available for Proms 56–75 from Friday 24 August. For information on wheelchair spaces available for the Last Night of the Proms via the Five-Concert Ballot, see page opposite.

Seats are available in the Arena and Gallery for reservation each day by ambulant disabled Prommers (see page 163 for details).

A limited number of car parking spaces for disabled concert-goers can be reserved close to the Hall; please contact the Access Information Line to book.

Ramped venue access is available at Doors 1, 3, 8, 9 and 12. The most convenient set-down points for vehicle arrival are near Doors 3 and 9.

Public lifts are located at Doors 1 and 8.

All bars and restaurants are wheelchair-accessible.

To request the specific services below, please call the Access Information Line or complete an accessibility request form online at royalalberthall.com 48 hours before you attend. Alternatively, you can ask for assistance at the Information Desk at Door 6 on the ground floor, subject to availability.

The Royal Albert Hall auditorium has an infra-red system with a number of personal headsets for use with or without hearing aids. Headsets can be collected from the Information Desk at Door 6.

Assistance dogs are very welcome and can be easily accommodated in the boxes. If you prefer to sit elsewhere, please call the Access Information Line for advice. The Royal Albert Hall stewards will be happy to look after your dog while you enjoy the concert.

Transfer wheelchairs are available for customer use. The Royal Albert Hall has busy corridors and therefore visitors using mobility scooters are asked to enter via Door 3 or Door 8 and to transfer to a wheelchair on arrival. Scooters can be stored in designated places. We are unable to offer charging facilities for scooters.

A Royal Albert Hall steward will be happy to read excerpts of your concert programme to visually impaired visitors.

Assisted Proms

The Ten Pieces Proms (Proms 19 and 20) and the Relaxed Prom (Prom 59) will be British Sign Language-interpreted. Please book your tickets online in the usual way. If you require good visibility of the signer, please choose the Stalls Signer Area online when selecting your tickets, or call the Access Information Line and request this area.

For information about the Relaxed Prom on Monday 27 August, please see page 149. Information about Audio Description services provided for the Relaxed Prom is available on the Proms website.

Getting There

The nearest Tube stations are South Kensington (Piccadilly, Circle & District Lines), Gloucester Road (Piccadilly, Circle & District Lines) and High Street Kensington (Circle & District Lines). They are all a 10- to 15-minute walk from the Hall.

The following buses serve the Royal Albert Hall and Imperial College Union: 9, 10 (24-hour service), 49, 52, 70, 360 & 452. Coaches 701 and 702 also serve this area.

CALL COSTS
[†]Standard geographic charges from landlines and mobiles will apply. All calls may be recorded and monitored for training and quality-control purposes.

BEIT VENUES, IMPERIAL COLLEGE UNION

Prince Consort Road, London SW7 2BB
www.beitvenues.org

CADOGAN HALL

5 Sloane Terrace, London SW1X 9DQ
www.cadoganhall.com • 020 7730 4500

Free Proms events

Pre-concert events are held in the Concert Hall at Beit Venues, Imperial College Union. Family Workshops are held in the Dining Hall. Entry for all events is through Beit Quad, Prince Consort Road.

Pre-concert events are free of charge and unticketed (seating is unreserved), with the exception of selected recordings of radio programmes as detailed in the concert listings, for which free tickets will be available from BBC Studio Audiences (bbc.co.uk/showsandtours/shows).

Places must be reserved in advance for all Proms Family Orchestra & Chorus events and most Proms Sing events (visit bbc.co.uk/proms or call 020 7765 0557).

Access

Beit Venues, Imperial College Union, has a range of services to assist disabled visitors, including:

– a limited number of spaces for wheelchair-users in the Concert Hall and Dining Hall

– an induction loop installed in the Concert Hall

– accessible lifts throughout the building

– provision for wheelchair access points into the building. This is available via Prince Consort Road and Kensington Gore, but please contact the venue prior to arrival for access via Kensington Gore.

– provision for assistance dogs. Please contact the venue prior to arrival, so that any special arrangements can be made if necessary.

Contact the Beit Venues team on 020 7594 8113 or email beitvenues@imperial.ac.uk.

First opened in 1907 as a New Christian Science Church, designed by Robert Fellowes Chisholm, the hall hosted congregations of 1,400 in its heyday. However, like most churches, there was a decline in attendance. In 1996 the congregation moved to a smaller venue and the property fell into disuse for several years.

Cadogan Estate purchased the Hall in 2000 and discovered that the Royal Philharmonic Orchestra was looking for a permanent London base. Cadogan Hall was an excellent opportunity for the orchestra to benefit from bringing the former church back into life in a manner befitting its character and civic presence. The Hall reopened as a concert venue in June 2004.

Cadogan Hall has since become one of London's leading concert halls. With 950 seats, an excellent acoustic and luxurious surroundings, it is the chosen venue for a wide range of contemporary, jazz, folk and world music and literary and conference events.

 Nearest Tube station: Sloane Square (Circle & District Lines)

 Bar on site

 Cloakroom available

 Wheelchair-accessible

PLEASE NOTE

Prommers who have joined the Royal Albert Hall queue and wish to attend a pre-Prom event should make sure they take a numbered slip from one of the Royal Albert Hall stewards to secure their place back in the queue in time for doors opening.

Seating at Beit Venues, Imperial College Union, is limited and all pre-Prom events are subject to capacity. We advise arriving early for the more popular events. Latecomers will be admitted where possible but, as many of these events are recorded for broadcast, you may have to wait until a suitable break. The event stewards will guide you.

ALEXANDRA PALACE

Alexandra Palace Way, London N22 7AY
www.alexandrapalace.com • 020 8365 2121

Opened in 1873 as an entertainments venue for Victorian London, Alexandra Palace has been the centre of events for over 140 years, including the first regular television broadcasts in 1936 by the BBC.

The Theatre at Alexandra Palace opened in 1875 with Offenbach's *Breaking the Spell*. It was a place of spectacle and delight, where audiences of up to 2,500 were entertained by pantomime, opera, drama, ballet, music hall and cinema. The impressive stage machinery was designed so that performers could appear, fly into the air and disappear through the stage. However, it has not hosted regular performances for over 80 years.

The theatre (pictured above before refurbishment) has undergone sensitive restoration work by heritage specialists that will see many of its original features retained. The Proms performance will be the first public event in the theatre and will take place prior to the full completion of the renovation works; the full opening is scheduled for December 2018.

 Nearest train station: Alexandra Palace (National Rail)

Nearest Tube station: Wood Green (Piccadilly Line)

Bar on site

Wheelchair-accessible

LINCOLN DRILL HALL

Free School Lane, Lincoln LN2 1EY
www.lincolndrillhall.com • 01522 873894

Lincoln Drill Hall was gifted to the city by the industrialist Joseph Ruston and opened in 1890 by Edward Stanhope, the Secretary of State for War. Primarily used as a headquarters of the Lincolnshire Regiment, the building was often given over to public use, most notably as a hospital during a typhoid epidemic in 1905. During the Second World War it hosted dances for the county's RAF and US Air Force personnel and after the war staged wrestling, roller-skating, exhibitions and live bands. The Rolling Stones played at the venue on New Year's Eve in 1963, prior to their appearance on the very first *Top of the Pops* the next day.

By the late 1990s the building had fallen into a state of disrepair and it was closed in 1999. Four years later, following a £2.6m refurbishment, the building re-opened as an arts and community venue.

Nearest train station: Lincoln (National Rail)

Bar/café on site

Wheelchair-accessible

ROUNDHOUSE

Chalk Farm Road, London NW1 8EH
www.roundhouse.org.uk • 0300 678 9222

The Roundhouse was launched in 1966 with an event that featured Yoko Ono's 'happening' and a little-known band called Pink Floyd. The venue's key role in the youth and counter-culture movements in music and theatre continued in the 1960s and 1970s, with Allen Ginsberg and Stokely Carmichael's 'Dialectics of Liberation' congress, Kenneth Tynan's 'tasteful pornography', *Oh! Calcutta!* and Andy Warhol's play *Pork*. During the early 1970s the Roundhouse hosted a number of BBC Proms concerts conducted by Pierre Boulez.

In the 1980s the venue closed and faced dereliction and uncertainty. In 2006 the Roundhouse was reborn with a charitable purpose, since when over 30,000 young people have benefited from its performing arts, circus and digital projects. The venue continues to be a popular live performance space where the biggest names in music, theatre, circus and the spoken word take to the stage every day.

Nearest train station: Kentish Town West (Overground)

Nearest Tube stations: Camden Town and Chalk Farm (Northern Line)

Bar/café on site

Cloakroom available

Wheelchair-accessible

BBC Proms Festival Guide – audio, Braille and large-print formats

Audio CD and Braille versions of the guide are available in two parts, 'Articles' and 'Concert Listings/Booking Information', priced £3.50 each. To order, call the RNIB Helpline on 0303 123 9999.

A text-only large-print guide is available, priced £7.00.

BBC Proms concert programmes – large-print format

These can be purchased on the night, priced £7.00. Large-print sung texts and opera librettos are available free of charge, with purchase of a standard programme.

All large-print formats must be ordered in advance. For details of how and when to order and pay, visit the BBC Proms website, call Deborah Fether on 020 7765 3246 or email PromsPublications@bbc.co.uk.

Booking and Venues

SEASON TICKETS AND DISCOUNTS

Royal Albert Hall Season and Weekend Promming Passes

Frequent Prommers can save money on Royal Albert Hall concerts by purchasing a Season Pass for either the Arena or the Gallery. Passes are available for either the whole Proms season (including the Last Night), the first or second halves, or any of the eight weekends (exclusions apply, see box on page 170).

Weekend Promming Passes must be purchased a minimum of two hours before the start of the first concert covered. Prices vary for each weekend depending on the number of concerts included (see page 170).

Proms at ... Cadogan Hall Pass

Hear all eight Monday-lunchtime Proms concerts at Cadogan Hall for just £40.00 (booking fees apply).

18s and under go half-price

Tickets for persons aged 18 and under can be purchased at half-price in any seating area for all Proms except the Last Night (Prom 75) and in any price band except for £6.00 tickets at any venue. This discount is available through all booking methods.

Great savings for groups

Groups of 10 or more attending concerts at the Royal Albert Hall can claim a 5% discount on the price of Stalls (Centre or Side) or Rausing Circle (Front, Mid or Rear) tickets, excluding the Last Night, subject to availability. To make a group booking, or for more information, call the Group Booking Information Line on 020 7070 4408.

Tickets and discounts for disabled concert-goers

All disabled concert-goers (and one companion) receive a 50% discount on all ticket prices (except Arena and Gallery areas) for concerts at the Royal Albert Hall and Cadogan Hall.

To book, call the Access Information Line on 020 7070 4410 or purchase in person at the Royal Albert Hall.

Please note that wheelchair spaces cannot be booked online or via the Proms Planner.

Discounts for disabled concert-goers cannot be combined with other ticket offers.

Ticket exchange

Unwanted tickets for all Proms that have been purchased through the Royal Albert Hall Box Office may be exchanged for tickets to other Proms concerts (subject to availability). A fee of £1.00 per ticket will be charged for this service. Call the Royal Albert Hall Box Office (020 7070 4441†) for further details.

†CALL COSTS
Standard geographic charges from landlines and mobiles will apply. All calls may be recorded and monitored for training and quality-control purposes.

HOW AND WHEN TO BOOK – FURTHER DETAILS

Online
Between Thursday 19 April (2.00pm) and Friday 11 May (11.59pm) use the Proms Planner, accessible via bbc.co.uk/proms, to create your personal Proms Plan.

From 9.00am on Saturday 12 May you can redeem your Proms Plan and submit your booking. If you do not have a Proms Plan, you can just book online at royalalberthall.com.

The 'Select Your Own Seat' option is not available via the Proms Planner or during the first few days that Proms tickets are on sale. You will be allocated the best available places within your chosen seating area.

It is not possible to book entire boxes online. If you would like to book a full box, call the Box Office on 020 7070 4441[†].

By phone
From 9.00am on Saturday 12 May, call the Royal Albert Hall Box Office on 020 7070 4441[†] (open 9.00am–9.00pm daily).

In person
From 9.00am on Saturday 12 May, visit the Royal Albert Hall Box Office at Door 12 (open 9.00am–9.00pm daily).

By post
Please write to BBC Proms, Box Office, Royal Albert Hall, London SW7 2AP with the following details:

- your name, address, phone number(s) and email address (if applicable)
- the concerts you wish to attend
- number of tickets required
- preferred seating area, ideally with alternatives (see ticket prices and seating plan on page 162).
- applicable discounts (see page opposite)

- a cheque, payable to 'Royal Albert Hall' and made out for the maximum amount (including booking fees); or your credit card details, including type of card, name on the card, card number, issue number (Maestro only), start date, expiry date and security code (last three digits on back of Visa/Mastercard or last four digits on front of American Express). Your details will be held securely.

General postal bookings will start to be processed from 9.00am on Saturday 12 May.

Postal bookings for Season and Weekend Promming Passes and for Proms at … Cadogan Hall Passes must be made separately to other booking requests. Mark your envelope 'Proms Season Pass', 'Weekend Promming Pass' or 'Proms at … Cadogan Hall Pass' as appropriate. These bookings will be processed from 9.00am on Thursday 10 May.

Following the start of booking, all postal applications are processed in random order, not the order in which they are received.

When booking opens

Season and Weekend Promming Passes
THURSDAY 10 MAY, 9.00AM

Proms at … Cadogan Hall Passes
THURSDAY 10 MAY, 9.00AM

Ten Pieces Proms (Proms 19 and 20)
FRIDAY 11 MAY, 9.00AM

Relaxed Prom (Prom 59), including a limited number of Promming tickets
FRIDAY 11 MAY, 9.00AM

General booking
SATURDAY 12 MAY, 9.00AM

Proms at … concerts, excluding Proms at … Cadogan Hall Passes (see above)
FRIDAY 8 JUNE, 9.00AM

▶ FOR LAST NIGHT OF THE PROMS TICKETS, SEE PAGE 164

▶ FOR PROMMING TICKETS, SEE PAGE 163

▶ FOR PROMS IN THE PARK TICKETS, SEE PAGE 162

[†]**CALL COSTS**
Standard geographic charges from landlines and mobiles will apply. All calls may be recorded and monitored for training and quality-control purposes.

PLEASE NOTE
The Proms Planner cannot be used to book Season, Weekend or Proms at … Cadogan Hall Passes or tickets for the Ten Pieces Proms (Proms 19 and 20), the Relaxed Prom (Prom 59) or any of the Proms at … concerts.

PROMMING PASSES – FURTHER DETAILS

Season and Weekend Promming Passes are available to purchase online, by phone, in person or by post from 9.00am on Thursday 10 May, and are subject to availability.

Postal bookings for Season and Weekend Promming Passes (see 'By post' on page 169) will be processed in random order from 9.00am on Thursday 10 May.

Please note:

– Season Passes are non-transferable and two passport-sized photographs must be provided before passes can be issued. ID may be requested upon entry.

– You may purchase a maximum of four Weekend Promming Passes per weekend.

– There is no Weekend Promming Pass covering Proms 74 and 75.

– Season and Weekend Promming Passes are only valid for concerts at the Royal Albert Hall.

Proms at … Cadogan Hall Passes are available to purchase from 9.00am on Thursday 10 May. Two passport-sized photographs must be provided before passes can be issued.

Please note:

– Proms at … Cadogan Hall Passes can only be purchased from the Royal Albert Hall and are subject to availability.

Promming at the Last Night

Whole Season Promming Passes include admission to the Last Night.

A limited allocation of Last Night tickets (priced £6.00) is also reserved for Prommers who have attended five or more concerts (in either the Arena or the Gallery). They are eligible to purchase one ticket each for the Last Night (priced £6.00) on presentation of their used tickets (which will be retained) at the Box Office. Tickets will be available to buy from the Box Office from the following dates:

– Wednesday 18 July for First Half Season Pass-holders, Weekend Promming Pass-holders and Day Prommers with five used tickets

– Wednesday 15 August for Second Half Season Pass-holders, Weekend Promming Pass-holders and Day Prommers with five used tickets

– Monday 3 September for both First and Second Half Season Pass-holders, Weekend Promming Pass-holders and Day Prommers with five used tickets.

PROMMING PASSES (ROYAL ALBERT HALL)

Passes	Concerts	Price
Whole Season (13 July – 8 September)	Proms 1–75 (excluding 19, 20, 38 and 59)	£240.00
First Half (13 July – 11 August)	Proms 1–38 (excluding 19, 20)	£144.00
Second Half (11 August – 7 September)	Proms 39–74 (excluding 59)	£152.00
Weekend 1 (13–15 July)	Proms 1, 2, 3	£16.50
Weekend 2 (20–22 July)	Proms 8, 9, 10, 11	£22.00
Weekend 3 (27–28 July)	Proms 17 and 18	£11.00
Weekend 4 (3–5 August)	Proms 27, 28, 29, 30	£22.00
Weekend 5 (10–12 August)	Proms 37, 39, 40, 41	£22.00
Weekend 6 (17–19 August)	Proms 47, 48, 49, 50	£22.00
Weekend 7 (24–27 August)	Proms 56, 57, 58, 60	£22.00
Weekend 8 (31 August – 2 September)	Proms 65, 66, 67, 68	£22.00

BOOKING FEES

All Promming tickets purchased online are subject to a booking fee of 2% of the total value plus £1.00 per ticket.

FOR TICKET PRICES, SEE PAGE 162

EVERY PROM LIVE ON BBC RADIO 3

The spirit of the Proms continues after the Last Night with concerts from around the UK, weeknights at 7.30pm.

BBC RADIO 3

Listen anytime at
bbc.co.uk/radio3

"Bedales arts feels a thoroughly professional affair."

Good Schools Guide 2016

Bedales Schools

3–18 | Boarding & Day | 1 hour from London

To book a place on an open morning or to arrange an individual visit, please contact Janie Jarman, Registrar.

T 01730 711733 **E** jjarman@bedales.org.uk
Petersfield, Hampshire GU32 2DG

www.bedales.org.uk

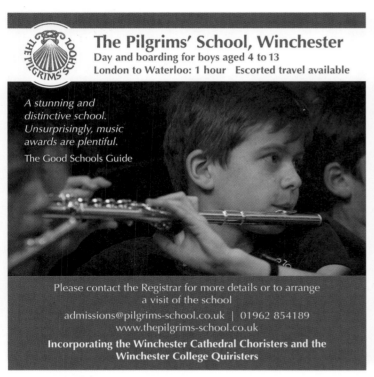

INDEX OF ARTISTS

Bold italic figures refer to Prom numbers
P@CH indicates 'Proms at … Cadogan Hall' chamber music concerts
P@R 'Proms at … Roundhouse', Saturday 21 July
P@LDH 'Proms at … Lincoln Drill Hall', Saturday 4 August
P@AP 'Proms at … Alexandra Palace', Saturday 1 September
*first appearance at a BBC Henry Wood Promenade Concert
†current / ‡former member of BBC Radio 3's New Generation Artists scheme

Index of Artists

INDEX OF WORKS

Bold italic figures refer to Prom numbers
P@CH indicates 'Proms at … Cadogan Hall' chamber music concerts
P@R 'Proms at … Roundhouse', Saturday 21 July
P@LDH 'Proms at … Lincoln Drill Hall', Saturday 4 August
P@AP 'Proms at … Alexandra Palace', Saturday 1 September
*first performance at a BBC Henry Wood Promenade Concert

BBC Proms 2018

Director, BBC Proms David Pickard
Controller, BBC Radio 3 Alan Davey
Personal Assistant Yvette Pusey

Editor, BBC Radio 3 Emma Bloxham

Head of Marketing, Publications and Learning Kate Finch

Concerts and Planning Helen Heslop (Manager), Hannah Donat (Artistic Producer), Alys Jones, Helen White (Event Producers), Alison Dancer, Victoria Gunn (Event Co-ordinators)

Press and Communications Camilla Dervan (Communications Manager), Anna Hughes (Publicist), Roni Newman (Assistant Publicist)

Marketing Emily Caket (Manager), Sanjeet Riat (Co-ordinator)

Learning Ellara Wakely (Senior Learning Manager), Lauren Creed, Chloe Shrimpton, Melanie Fryer (Managers), Rebecca Burns, Catherine Humphrey, Naomi Selwyn (Co-ordinators), Malia Choudhury (Administrator)

Business Co-ordinator Tricia Twigg

Music Television Jan Younghusband (Head of Commissioning, BBC Music TV), Mark Cooper (Head of Music Television, BBC Studios), Francesca Kemp (Executive Producer, BBC Studios), Michael Ledger (Series Production Manager, BBC Studios)

Digital Rory Connolly (Digital Editor, BBC Music), Andrew Downs (BBC Proms Digital Editorial Lead), Rhian Roberts (Digital Editor, BBC Radio 3)

BBC Music Library Natalie Dewar (Archive Collections Manager), Joe Schultz (Proms Co-ordinator), Michael Jones (Hire Co-ordinator), Tim Auvache, Anne Butcher, Raymond Howden, Richard Malton, Steven Nunes, David Vivian Russell, Chris Williams (Music Librarians), Alison John, Claire Martin (Archive Assistants)

Commercial Rights and Business Affairs Emily Antoniades, Sarah Bredl-Jones, Sue Dickson, Hilary Dodds, Kate Foreman, Catherine Grimes, Emma Trevelyan, Mark Waring, Pamela Wise

---

Publications Editor Christine Webb
Editorial Manager Edward Bhesania
Sub-Editor Daniel Meldrum
Publications Designer Reenie Basova
Junior Publications Designer Jack Shaw
Publications Assistant Deborah Fether

Advertising John Good Ltd
Cover illustration BBC Creative/BBC
Published by BBC Proms Publications, Room 3015, Broadcasting House, London W1A 1AA
Distributed by Bloomsbury Publishing, 50 Bedford Square, London WC1B 3DP

Printed by APS Group

ISBN 978-1-912114-01-6   © BBC 2018. All details correct at time of going to press.